Law and Order in Ancient Athens

The classical Athenian "state" had almost no formal coercive apparatus to ensure order or compliance with law: there was no professional police force or public prosecutor, and nearly every step in the legal process depended on private initiative. And yet Athens was a remarkably peaceful and well-ordered society by both ancient and contemporary standards. Why? *Law and Order in Ancient Athens* draws on contemporary legal scholarship to explore how order was maintained in Athens. Lanni argues that law and formal legal institutions played a greater role in maintaining order than is generally acknowledged. The legal system *did* encourage compliance with law, but not through the familiar deterrence mechanism of imposing sanctions for violating statutes. Lanni shows how formal institutions facilitated the operation of informal social control in a society that was too large and diverse to be characterized as a "face-to-face community" or "close-knit group."

Adriaan Lanni is Professor of Law, Harvard Law School. She is trained as both a lawyer and an ancient historian (J.D. Yale Law School; MPhil (Classics), Cambridge University; Ph.D. History, University of Michigan) and teaches courses in ancient law and modern American criminal law and procedure at Harvard Law School. Her previous book is *Law and Justice in the Courts of Classical Athens* (Cambridge University Press 2006).

Law and Order
in Ancient Athens

ADRIAAN LANNI

Harvard Law School

CAMBRIDGE
UNIVERSITY PRESS

University Printing House, Cambridge CB2 8BS, United Kingdom

One Liberty Plaza, 20th Floor, New York, NY 10006, USA

477 Williamstown Road, Port Melbourne, VIC 3207, Australia

314-321, 3rd Floor, Plot 3, Splendor Forum, Jasola District Centre, New Delhi - 110025, India

79 Anson Road, #06-04/06, Singapore 079906

Cambridge University Press is part of the University of Cambridge.

It furthers the University's mission by disseminating knowledge in the pursuit of
education, learning and research at the highest international levels of excellence.

www.cambridge.org
Information on this title: www.cambridge.org/9781108469081

© Cambridge University Press 2016

First published 2016
First paperback edition 2018

A catalogue record for this publication is available from the British Library

Library of Congress Cataloging in Publication data
Names: Lanni, Adriaan, 1972– author.
Title: Law and order in ancient Athens / Adriaan Lanni.
Description: New York: Cambridge University Press, 2016. |
Includes bibliographical references and index.
Identifiers: LCCN 2016010903 | ISBN 9780521198806 (hardback)
Subjects: LCSH: Justice, Administration of (Greek law). | Judicial process –
Greece – Athens – History. | Courts – Greece – Athens – History.
Classification: LCC KL4345.L37 2016 | DDC 349.38/5–dc23
LC record available at http://lccn.loc.gov/2016010903

ISBN 978-0-521-19880-6 Hardback
ISBN 978-1-108-46908-1 Paperback

For Susanna and Theo

Contents

Acknowledgments

Many of the ideas in this book stem from daily exposure to legal scholarship and conversations with law professors at Harvard Law School and elsewhere. Two former colleagues in particular – Daryl Levinson and the late Bill Stuntz – were instrumental in helping me frame the project at the outset. Over the years, numerous law professors have been generous enough to offer helpful comments on chapter drafts: Oren Bar-Gill, Gabriella Blum, Glenn Cohen, Bob Ellickson, Amalia Kessler, Mike Klarman, Duncan Kennedy, Bruce Mann, Martha Minow, Bill Nelson, Gerry Neuman, Dan Richman, Jed Shugerman, Matthew Stephenson, Adrian Vermeule, Jim Whitman, and Lloyd Weinreb. Tom Green's characteristically incisive comments on a complete draft improved the manuscript immeasurably. I am also indebted to participants in the Harvard Law School "juniors" workshop, the Harvard Law School faculty workshop, the Boston College legal history workshop, the Iowa Law School faculty workshop, the University of Michigan legal history workshop, the University of Minnesota legal history colloquium, the NYU law, economics, and politics colloquium, the Stanford Law School faculty workshop, the Stanford legal history colloquium, the Stanford political theory workshop, the UCLA legal history workshop, the University of Virginia Law School faculty workshop, and the Yale legal history colloquium.

The ancient Greek law community is an uncommonly generous one, and several classicists read some or all of the manuscript with great care, pointing me to recent literature and noting problems great and small: Ed Cohen, Sara Forsdyke, Bruce Frier, Michael Gagarin, Steven Johnstone, Tom

McGinn, Josh Ober, Lene Rubinstein, Adele Scafuro, and Mike Zimm. As usual, Victor Bers endured multiple drafts of every chapter and countless conversations. I have also benefitted from conversations with the participants of the Symposion conferences in Salerno, Paris, and Cambridge; the University College, London Use and Abuse of Law in Athenian courts conference, particularly Chris Carey, Nick Fisher, and Robin Osborne; the Classical Association of the Pacific Northwest's Vancouver conference, particularly Ed Carawan and David Mirhady; the Columbia University classics colloquium, and the University of Texas at Austin classics colloquium. I am also grateful to the anonymous reviewers for Cambridge University Press and to my patient editors, Beatrice Rehl, Asya Graff, and Isabella Vitti. Rita Lomio provided excellent research assistance early in the project. Translations from the Attic orators come from the University of Texas Press's *The Oratory of Classical Greece* series, with some modifications. The most relevant secondary sources are placed first in the notes; sources of equal relevance are listed by publication date, beginning with the most recent.

My greatest debt is to my husband Wes Kelman, a superb sounding board and editor who made this book much better, and a true super-dad who made this book possible.

Abbreviations

Aesch.	Aeschines
Anac.	Anacreon
And.	Andocides
Ant.	Antiphon
Ar.	Aristophanes
Arist.	Aristotle
Ath. Pol.	[Ar.] *Athenaion Politeia* (*"The Athenian Constitution"*)
Callim.	Callimachus
D.-K.	Diels-Kranz, *Die Fragmente der Vorsokratiker*
D.L.	Diogenes Laertius
Dem.	Demosthenes
Din.	Dinarchus
Dio. Chyrs.	Dio Chyrsostomus
Diod.	Diodorus Siculus
Eur.	Euripides
Harp.	Harpokration
Hdt.	Herodotus
Hyp.	Hyperides
Ibyc.	Ibycus
IG	*Inscriptiones Graecae*
Is.	Isaeus
Isoc.	Isocrates
Lyc.	Lycurgus
Lys.	Lysias

Men.	Menander
Plaut.	Plautus
Plut.	Plutarch
Poll.	Pollux
SEG	*Supplementum epigraphicum Graecum*
Sol.	Solon
Soph.	Sophocles
Theog.	Theognis
Theophr.	Theophrastus
Thuc.	Thucydides
Xen.	Xenophon
[Xen.]	Pseudo-Xenophon

Introduction

The Puzzle of Athenian Order

This book is motivated by a puzzle. Classical Athens had only a limited formal coercive apparatus to ensure order or compliance with law. There was no professional police force or public prosecutor, and nearly every step in the legal process depended on private initiative. Moreover, Athens did not have a "rule of law" in the sense that the courts did not enforce norms expressed in statutes in a predictable and consistent manner. And yet Athens was a remarkably peaceful and well-ordered society by both ancient and contemporary standards. Why? This book draws on contemporary legal scholarship that understands "law" as the product of the complex interaction between formal and informal norms and institutions to explore how order was maintained in Athens.

Before turning to solutions, it may be helpful to examine each piece of the puzzle. First, what does it mean to say that Athens was a peaceful, well-ordered society? At the most basic level, Athens enjoyed remarkable political stability, particularly by comparison to other Greek city-states and the Roman Republic.[1] Aside from two short-lived oligarchic revolutions near the end of the fifth century, both of which were precipitated by major military defeats, the democracy largely avoided serious civil and political violence and unrest throughout the classical period.[2]

---

[1] Ober 2008a:39–48; Fisher 1999:70; D. Cohen 1995:6; Herman 2006:76.
[2] External violence, of course, was another matter. Athens' ability to maintain political stability and social order is all the more impressive given the relentless stress of frequent military conflict during our period.

The level of ordinary crime and violence is harder to assess and impossible to quantify, but our evidence suggests that Athens enjoyed "relatively low rates of criminality."[3] Literary sources indicate that it was not unusual to walk alone or at night in both the city and the countryside without excessive fear of crime.[4] Athenians did not ordinarily carry weapons,[5] and the fights and violence that did occur were generally limited to the use of fists, stones, sticks, and potsherds.[6] Despite the existence of banks for safekeeping, we hear of Athenians keeping significant amounts of money and valuables in their homes.[7] To be sure, there is also evidence of theft, banditry, drunken brawls, and enmity erupting into violence.[8] But the overall picture that emerges is one in which fear of crime and violence did not disrupt everyday activities.

Athens also exhibited a high level of social order. Most Athenians appear to have fulfilled their public duties with remarkable regularity. Ordinary Athenians presented themselves for military service despite a near-constant state of war. Hundreds of citizens chosen by lot served as unpaid government officials each year. Despite some shirking,[9] the wealthy and powerful contributed enough in taxes and liturgies – for much of our period several hundred trierarchs were needed each year to outfit the navy[10] – to support a highly successful military, economic, and cultural power.[11] Athens' economic success would not have been possible unless Athenians could normally rely on compliance with the requirements of fair dealing and other business norms in ordinary commercial transactions.

And here is the paradox: order was maintained despite relatively weak mechanisms of formal coercion. Indeed, some scholars have gone so far as to challenge whether Athens should be categorized as a "state" and whether Athenian officials can be said to have exercised a monopoly of legitimate

3 Fisher 1999:83; 1998:86–92; Ober 2008a:256; Herman 1994; 2006:206–215; cf. Riess 2012:33–49.
4 Pl. *Republic* 1.327a1–328b8; Andoc. 1.38–39; Dem. 54.7; for discussion, see Fisher 1999:73–74.
5 Thuc. 1.5–8; Ar. *Politics*1268b40. For discussion, see Fisher 1999:74–75; Herman 2006:206–215.
6 E.g., Lys. 3 and 4; Dem. 53.17; Ar. *Birds* 493–498; Fisher 1999:74–75; Herman 2006:206–215.
7 E.g., Lys. 12.10; 19.22; Dem. 27.53–57; 29.46–49; Is. 11.43; Herman 2006:208; Hunter 1994:150. Many rural farms included a stone tower, but these seem most likely to have served primarily as a means of preventing slave laborers from escaping rather than as a protection of person or property from theft. For discussion of the evidence for these towers and the various theories attempting to explain their function, see Morris and Papadopoulos 2005.
8 For examples, see Fisher 1999:59–60; Riess 2012:33–49.
9 On which generally, see Christ 2006.
10 Christ 2006:146–147.
11 On Athens' success, see Ober 2008a:39–79.

violence.[12] What is most important for our purposes is that with limited exceptions (which we will discuss in due course), Athens was dependent on private initiative to enforce the law.[13] There was no police force charged with investigating crimes or arresting wrongdoers.[14] In most circumstances, public offenses went unprosecuted unless a private individual volunteered to initiate a suit. Even a court judgment could mean little if a victorious private litigant was unable to force his opponent to pay up. This reliance on private initiative resulted in spotty enforcement and reduced deterrence.

The deterrent effect of statutes was further limited because Athenian juries did not enforce clearly defined statutory norms in a consistent and predictable manner. The question of whether Athens had a "rule of law"[15] has been intensely debated by classicists in recent decades. Some scholars, primarily those of an anthropological bent, contend that courts served primarily a social, political, or ritual role, and did not attempt to resolve disputes according to established rules or principles equally and impartially applied.[16] At the other extreme, some historians have argued that Athenian juries did strictly and predictably enforce the law.[17] Still others, myself included, have argued that while Athenian juries sought to reach a just outcome to the legal dispute before them, in doing so they had the discretion not only to apply the relevant statute, but also to consider, if they wished, a variety of other legal, equitable, and contextual considerations.[18]

---

[12] Berent 2000; Osborne 1985b:7; cf. Hansen 2002; Hunter 1994:188.

[13] See Chapter 2 for further discussion.

[14] Hunter 1994:120–153.

[15] While the "rule of law" can have many different meanings, the feature most relevant for debates about the Athenian legal system is the consistent and predictable application of clear rules. Most classicists agree that the Athenian system satisfied narrow definitions of "rule of law" that focus on formal equality before the law or protection from arbitrary exercise of power by officials. For a sophisticated discussion of the debate, see Forsdyke Forthcoming a. For a discussion of the rule of law in Athenian sources, see Forsdyke Forthcoming c.

[16] D. Cohen (1995:87–88) portrays Athenian litigation as a form of feuding behavior; Osborne (1985a:52) sees Athenian litigation as status competition; Riess (2012:143–145) views Athenian litigation as ritual performances that were "always unpredictable" and did not necessarily "operate rationally."

[17] E. Harris 2013; Meyer-Laurin 1965; Meineke 1971. Others (Hansen 1999:161–177; Ostwald 1986:497–524; Sealey 1987:146–148) have emphasized that the institutional reforms at the end of the fifth century signaled a shift from the sovereignty of the people to the sovereignty of law, without specifically arguing that Athenian juries faithfully and predictably applied statutes. Gowder (2014:10–18) argues that Athens had a rule of law based primarily on a narrow definition of "rule of law" that emphasizes the limits on officials' use of coercion against citizens.

[18] Lanni 2006:2–3, 41–75, 115–148; Christ 1998a:195–196; Scafuro 1997:50–66; Humphreys 1983:248; Forsdyke Forthcoming a; see also Gagarin 2012:312 (noting that the Athenian concept of law

For example, litigants regularly argue that jurors should consider excuses or defenses not expressed in the statute, the relationship and long-term inter-actions between the parties, the effect a conviction might have on the defen-dant and his family, and the character of the parties, including unrelated crimes and a record of military or public service.[19] As discussed in detail in Chapter 2, this ad hoc, discretionary form of jury decision-making, together with the vagueness of many statutes, made it difficult to predict ex ante when a jury would find a violation, thereby reducing incentives to comply with the statute nominally at issue. If crime did not pay in Athens, it was not because the punishment for breaking a law was sure and certain.

To a modern, a natural place to begin to explain social order and compliance with norms would be the straightforward mechanism of law enforcement articulated most clearly by Austin: rules backed by sanctions.[20] But in Athens, the direct deterrent effect of statutes was reduced by the uncertainty surrounding jury verdicts and the lowered probability of prosecution and enforcement of judgments caused by the reliance on private initiative. So it is not surprising that scholars who have attempted to explain how order was maintained in Athens tend to empha-size informal enforcement mechanisms and internalized norms growing out of a small, relatively homogenous community.[21] In *Policing Athens*,[22] for example, Virginia Hunter focuses on informal social sanctions such as gossip and private dispute-resolution mechanisms such as self-help and private arbitration. Central to Gabriel Herman's explanation for Athens' success in *Morality and Behaviour in Democratic Athens*[23] is an internalized code of behavior requiring self-restraint and cooperation that fostered order and compliance with law.

In this book I will argue that Athenian legal institutions, though very different from the straightforward deterrence mechanisms that dominate

---

"was broader than our own" and included "the broad set of customs or traditional rules that Athenians generally accepted whether or not they were enshrined in statute").

19 See Lanni 2006:41–75; Chapter 2 in this book.

20 Austin 1995:13–15.

21 E.g., Hunter 1994; Herman 2006; Allen 2000a:142–145; Finley 1985a:29–30. D. Cohen (1995:24) is an exception: he describes the role of courts as an arena for feuding and pursuing conflict that paradoxically both "contributed to the maintenance of social order as well as help[ed] to threaten it."

22 Hunter 1994.

23 Herman 2006:23, 352–354, 392–393. It is important to note that Herman does, however, con-tend that the demos also had the potential to exercise significant coercive force (Herman 2006:221).

modern legal systems, played an indirect but important role in maintaining order. I want to show that the Athenian legal system *did* encourage compliance with law, but not through the familiar Austinian mechanism of imposing sanctions for violating statutes.[24] I use contemporary research on the interaction between law, social norms, and behavior to explore the various ways in which formal legal institutions promoted order in Athens.[25] For example, the Athenian procedures for enacting and publicizing laws meant that even statutes that were rarely enforced may have altered behavior, as part of what modern legal scholars call the expressive function of law. The use of character arguments in court and the frequency of legal procedures provided powerful incentives for Athenians to abide by social norms: prior misconduct could be brought up in a later unrelated court case, which not only might influence the verdict, but would also facilitate social sanctions by publicizing the prior norm violation. Court arguments were a form of moral persuasion performed before a large number of Athenian citizens on a daily basis, providing an arena for debating, shaping, and reinforcing internalized norms. Through these examples and others, I show how formal institutions facilitated the operation of informal social control in a society that was too large and diverse to be characterized as a "face-to-face community" or "close-knit group." In this way, Athens provides a provocative example of how recent theories about how law can create order may have worked in a time and place far from our own.

Although I focus on formal legal institutions that were dominated by adult male citizens, my account also addresses how order was maintained among the less privileged members of society. Women and slaves were almost always disciplined privately, within the household.[26] Metics (resident aliens) could be disciplined through the court system, though their participation in trade and commercial matters may have made them more likely to experience the special, and more straightforward and predictable,

---

24 Riess (2012) and D. Cohen (1995) also contend that Athenian litigation fostered order through non-Austinian means, though their proposed mechanisms (respectively, ritual performance and feuding arena) are quite different from mine.

25 I agree with Forsdyke's (2012:176–177; Forthcoming a) observation that informal and formal modes of justice were inextricably intertwined in Athens throughout the classical period. I focus here on exploring the role played by formal legal institutions because they fostered order through mechanisms other than a familiar deterrence regime. Throughout, we will see that formal legal institutions worked in conjunction with informal mechanisms of social control.

26 For discussion, see Chapter 1.

procedures and regulations that applied to selected market transactions.[27] Perhaps most interesting, we will see that noncitizens, including slaves, were protected to some extent from violence and mistreatment by the formal legal system, though not primarily through the straightforward mechanism of lawsuits charging individuals with committing offenses against noncitizens. Rather, the protection of noncitizens in well-publicized statutes may have influenced behavior even in the absence of enforcement through the expressive function of law,[28] and litigants may have been indirectly punished for offenses against noncitizens when they were raised as character evidence in unrelated cases.[29]

It may be helpful to clarify the aims and limits of my argument. We cannot quantify the relative contribution of the various elements that helped foster order in Athens. And while I attempt to demonstrate that neither a traditional deterrence regime nor informal mechanisms like self-help or social sanctions can entirely explain the puzzle of Athenian orderliness, I do not deny that all these mechanisms played a role in maintaining order. The chapters that follow explore how formal legal institutions, often working in conjunction with informal means of social control, helped foster order through mechanisms quite different from the straightforward operation of deterrence created by punishment for violations of law. My analysis applies insights drawn from modern legal sociology, particularly the academic literature on social norms and the expressive function of law, to classical Athens. We will see that the high level of publicity surrounding Assembly and court activity and the Athenians' contextualized approach to adjudication made these mechanisms much more powerful in the Athenian context than they are in modern legal systems.

It is important to emphasize that I am not providing a functionalist analysis. That is, I am not arguing that the features of the legal system I describe developed as they did because they fostered order and compliance with norms. Nor do I contend that the Athenians consciously created their legal system with these benefits in mind. We will see that widespread citizen participation in the assembly and courts, together with the loose approach to relevance and legal argument in Athenian adjudication, were central to the mechanisms that helped foster order in Athens. As

27 For discussion, see Chapter 2.
28 For discussion, see Chapter 3.
29 For discussion, see Chapter 4.

I have argued elsewhere, these features arose from two ingrained cultural values: (1) a normative belief in contextualized and individualized justice and (2) a democratic commitment to popular participation and wide jury discretion.[30] I focus here not on the origins of Athenian legal institutions and practices, but on their operation and effects.[31] To borrow the terms used by Ian Morris to distinguish between "humanistic" and "social scientific" approaches, this book aims to help us "understand" how Athenian legal culture worked rather than to "explain" how it came to take the form it took or to quantify the precise degree to which social order can be attributed to the operation of formal legal institutions.[32]

A Brief Introduction to Athens and Its Legal System

Some background information may be helpful for readers unfamiliar with Athens and its legal system.[33] Athens' territory of approximately 900 square miles included rural farming villages, small towns, a cosmopolitan port known as the Piraeus, and the teeming city that served as the political, commercial, social, and religious center of the polis. Athens was a direct democracy, but an extremely limited one: most legal and political rights were limited to male citizens. And citizens accounted for only a small portion of the total population. Metics were either manumitted slaves or freeborn foreigners living in Athens,[34] generally as craftsmen, traders, or businessmen. Slaves occupied the bottom rung of Athenian society, though slaves' lifestyles could vary considerably. The majority worked the land (either on small plots owned by a modest farmer, or on a larger holding supervised by an overseer) or in their masters' house or workshop. The least fortunate toiled in the silver mines and the most fortunate

---

[30] Lanni 2006.

[31] This is not to deny the possibility that the effectiveness of Athenian legal practices in maintaining order contributed to the persistence of Athenian legal institutions. But we have no direct evidence that this is the case, and process-oriented anthropological studies have demonstrated that societies can reach a successful equilibrium in the absence of social order (e.g., Roberts 1976; Comaroff and Roberts 1981; Bourdieu 1977; for an excellent discussion of trends in legal anthropology as they relate to classical Athens, see D. Cohen 1995:1–24).

[32] Morris 2002:8.

[33] For a more detailed description of the legal system as well as Athenian society, see Lanni 2006:15–40.

[34] It seems likely that a foreigner was obliged to register as a metic (and pay the metic tax) once he had spent a short time – perhaps one month – living in Athens. For discussion of the evidence, see Whitehead 1977:7–10.

worked as skilled craftsmen, bankers, or shopkeepers and enjoyed de facto independence.

The number of citizens, metics, and slaves in classical Athens can only be guessed at from a census taken in 317 BCE, after the fall of the democracy, and from sporadic statements in our earlier sources providing estimates of troop strengths or the adult male citizen population. In the fourth century, the adult male citizen population was perhaps 30,000, the total citizen population approximately 100,000.[35] The numbers of metics and slaves are much less certain and are likely to have fluctuated at different times depending on the economic and political circumstances. Hansen's estimate of 40,000 metics, somewhere in the range of 150,000 slaves, and a total population of close to 300,000 seems reasonable.[36]

Within the citizenship group, Classical Athens was a highly participatory democracy run primarily by amateurs: with the exception of military generalships and a few other posts, state officials were selected by lot to serve one-year terms.[37] The Council (Boulé), or executive body of the Assembly, was composed of 500 men chosen by lot, and a new *epistates* ("president") of the Council was chosen by lot for each day's session. Adult male citizens voted in the Assembly on nearly every decision of the Athenian state, from the making of war and peace to honoring individuals with a free dinner. At the end of the fifth century a distinction was made between laws (*nomoi*) which specified rules of general application, and decrees (*psephismata*) which were specific, short-term measures. In the fourth century, laws, unlike decrees, required not just the vote of the Assembly, but also the approval of a board chosen from the jury pool following a trial-like hearing on the merits of the law.[38]

The Athenian law courts are remarkably well-attested, at least by the standards of ancient history: roughly one hundred forensic speeches survive from the period between 420 and 323 BCE.[39] These speeches represent not an official record of the trial proceedings, but the speech written by a speechwriter (*logographos*) for his client (or, in a few cases, for himself) and later published, possibly with minor revisions in some cases, with a view to attracting future clients or promoting a political position in political trials.

35 Hansen 1999:90–93.
36 Hansen 1999:90–94.
37 Hansen 1999:233–237.
38 Hansen 1999:161–175.
39 Ober 1989:341–348 provides a catalog.

Only speeches that were attributed to one of the ten Attic orators subsequently deemed canonical have been preserved. As a result, the speeches in our corpus are atypical in the sense that they represent cases in which one of the litigants could secure the services of one of the best speechwriters in the city. We do not know for certain whether and how the speeches of poor litigants might have differed from our surviving speeches.[40] But it is important to note that the social class of the parties involved in the surviving cases are quite varied: we have, for example, cases involving a wealthy banker who was formerly a slave (Demosthenes 36), a man who admits that his family was so poorly off that his mother was reduced to selling ribbons in the agora (Demosthenes 57), an accusation against an admitted prostitute for impersonating a citizen (Demosthenes 59), and, if the case is authentic, even a disabled man receiving the Athenian equivalent of social security payments (Lysias 24). The speeches in the corpus run the gamut from politically charged treason trials and violent crimes to inheritance cases and property disputes between neighbors.

Despite their copiousness, these sources are not without their problems. The Attic orations were preserved not as legal documents but as tools for teaching boys and young men the art of rhetoric in the Hellenistic and Roman periods. As a result, the information a legal historian would most like to know about any particular case is generally lost. We almost never have speeches from both sides of a legal contest;[41] we rarely know the outcome of the case. Citations of laws and witness testimony are often omitted or regarded as inauthentic later additions. Most important, any statement we meet in the speeches regarding the law or legal procedures may be a misleading characterization designed to help the litigant's case.[42] As is often pointed out, however, a litigant who wished to be successful would presumably limit himself to statements and arguments that were likely to be accepted by a jury. Speakers may at times give us a self-serving account of the law, but their arguments generally remain within the realm of plausible interpretations of the legal situation in question.[43]

---

[40] On amateur speech, see Bers 2009.
[41] Only two pairs of speeches survive (Demosthenes 19 and Aeschines 2; Aeschines 3 and Demosthenes 18); in two other instances (Lysias 6 and Andocides 1; Demosthenes 43 and Isaeus 11) we have imperfectly matched speeches on both sides of a particular issue.
[42] On how to deal with apparent outliers in our sources, see Bers 2002.
[43] Dover 1994:8–14.

In what the Athenians called "private cases" (*dikai*), the victim (or his family in the case of murder) brought suit. In "public cases" (*graphai*), any adult male citizen – literally *ho boulomenos* ("he who is willing") – was permitted to initiate an action. However, our surviving *graphai* suggest that volunteer prosecutors were rarely disinterested parties seeking to protect third-party victims; *graphai* are more often brought by the primary party in interest or enemies of the defendant.[44] Although no ancient source explains the distinction between *graphai* and *dikai*, most *graphai* seem to have been cases regarded as affecting the community at large.[45] This division is not quite the same as the modern criminal–civil distinction; murder, to take a spectacular example, was a *dike* because it was considered a crime against the family rather than the state.

Athenian courts were largely, but not entirely, the province of adult male citizens. Foreigners and resident aliens (metics) could be sued in Athenian courts, and could initiate private suits.[46] It is unclear to what extent metics were permitted to bring public suits.[47] With a few exceptions, slaves could serve neither as plaintiffs nor defendants.[48] When a slave was involved in a dispute or the victim or perpetrator of a crime, the case was generally brought by or against the slave's owner.[49] Similarly, women were forced to depend on their male legal guardians to act on their behalf in court.[50]

This book focuses primarily on the popular courts, the largest jurisdiction in the Athenian legal system.[51] Litigants were required to present their case to the jury, though they could share their time with a "co-speaker."[52] Each Athenian litigant was allotted a fixed amount of time to present his

44 Osborne 1985a; Christ 1998a:118–159.
45 Todd 1993:102–109. For discussion of whether the Athenians had a conception of crime, see D. Cohen 2005a; Hunter 2007.
46 MacDowell 1993:221–224; Patterson 2000; Todd 1993:196; Whitehead 1977:92–95.
47 A prominent theory is that metics could pursue *graphai* only in cases where they were the victim, and were not permitted to prosecute on behalf of a third party or the state (Whitehead 1977:94); for some skepticism on this point, see Hunter 2000a:17 and n.29.
48 Todd 1993:187.
49 MacDowell 1993:81. The suit could be brought directly against the slave if the slave was acting without his owner's permission (Dem. 55.31), but the owner was still responsible for defending the suit in court and for any damages awarded.
50 Todd 1993:208.
51 Homicide and maritime cases followed somewhat different procedures and, most importantly, may have had a more developed concept of relevance. Lanni 2006:75–114, 149–174.
52 In ordinary cases, "co-speakers" were relatives or friends and take pains not to act the part of an expert advocate. For an in-depth study of the use of supporting speakers in Athenian courts, see Rubinstein 2000.

case. Some private cases were completed in less than an hour, and no trial lasted longer than a day.[53] Although a magistrate chosen by lot presided over each popular court, he did not interrupt the speaker for any reason or permit anyone else to raise legal objections, and did not instruct the jury as to the relevant laws. Athenian laws were inscribed on stone *stelai* in various public areas of Athens. Litigants were responsible for finding and quoting any laws they thought helped their case, though there was no obligation to cite even the law under which the case was brought.

Cases in the popular courts were heard by juries[54] chosen by lot from adult male citizens and generally ranged from 201 to 501 in size, though in high-profile political cases multiple panels of 500 could be used.[55] A simple majority vote of the jury, taken without formal deliberation,[56] determined the outcome of the trial. No reasons for the verdict were given, and there was no provision for appeal.[57]

While the punishment for some offenses was set by statute, in many cases the jury was required to choose between the penalties suggested by each party in a second speech in a process known as *timesis*. Unlike modern American jurors, Athenian jurors were generally made aware at the guilt phase of the statutory penalty or the penalty the prosecutor intended to propose if he won the case. For this reason, the guilt decision often incorporated considerations typically limited to sentencing in modern American courts, including questions of the defendant's character and past convictions.[58]

---

53 A public suit was allotted an entire day (*Ath. Pol.* 53.3). Private cases varied according to the value of the suit and were timed by a water-clock. MacDowell (1993:249–250) estimates the length of various types of suit based on the one surviving water-clock.

54 I have been using the term "jurors" as a translation for the Greek *dikastai* to refer to the audience of these forensic speeches, but some scholars, notably E. Harris (1994a:136), prefer the translation "judges." Neither English word is entirely satisfactory, since these men performed functions similar to those both of a modern judge and a modern jury. I refer to *dikastai* as jurors to avoid the connotations of professionalism that the word "judges" conjures up in the modern mind.

55 Hansen 1999:187.

56 Audience clamor and conversation while approaching the voting urns may have provided the opportunity for informal deliberation.

57 A dissatisfied litigant might, however, indirectly attack the judgment by means of a suit for false witness or might bring a new case, ostensibly involving a different incident and/or using a different procedure. Some of our surviving speeches point explicitly to a protracted series of connected legal confrontations. For discussion, see Osborne 1985a.

58 Lanni 2006:53–59.

Imprisonment was rarely, if ever, used as a punishment;[59] the most common types of penalties in public suits were monetary fines, loss of citizen status (*atimia*), exile, and execution.[60] With some exceptions, the fine in a public suit was paid to the city.[61] In most private cases damages were paid to the prosecutor, though the penalties for some *dikai* included public fines in addition to compensation.[62]

Plan of the Book

Before proceeding to the positive claim in Part Two that formal legal institutions helped foster order (albeit in indirect ways), I try to show that the two most obvious explanations for Athenian orderliness cannot be the whole story. Specifically, Part One demonstrates that Athens' high level of social order cannot be fully explained by either informal social control or the traditional Austinian mechanism of law backed by sanctions. Chapter 1, *Informal Social Control and Its Limits*, surveys what we know about how informal social control operated in practice, including social sanctions, internalized norms, self-help, private discipline, and private dispute resolution. I argue that informal social control, though important, cannot on its own account for the high level of social order in Athens. Chapter 2, *Law Enforcement and Its Limits*, discusses the role played by straightforward deterrence arising from enforcement of statutes in maintaining order. The reliance on private initiative and the lack of legal certainty significantly reduced the deterrent effect of statutes. At the same time, more straightforward enforcement of laws was available in a few special instances: selected market and shipping transactions and offenses that threatened the public order, including threats to the state and certain theft-related offenses. In this way, Athens ensured a minimum level of public order and economic security, making it possible for a more limited formal coercive apparatus to operate effectively in the rest of the system.

Part Two turns to examine various non-Austinian mechanisms through which the legal system fostered order and compliance with norms. While my focus is on exploring the operation of formal legal institutions, I emphasize

---

59 Hunter 1997.

60 Todd 1993:139–144; 2000a; Allen 2000a:197–243; Debrunner Hall 1996.

61 As we will see in Chapter 2, in some special procedures, such as *phasis* and *apographe*, the prosecutor was entitled to a portion of the fine collected.

62 MacDowell 1993:257.

throughout how these institutions interacted with and complemented informal modes of discipline. Chapter 3, *The Expressive Effect of Statutes*, argues that Athenian statutes may have fostered compliance with law even though they were not directly enforced. A law may serve an "expressive" or "symbolic" function: it makes a statement about what the society considers acceptable and unacceptable behavior. Under some circumstances, legal scholars have shown that law can strengthen or weaken the social norms surrounding a practice, and thereby indirectly influence behavior. I argue that the expressive function of law may have served an even more important role in ancient Athens than it does today because Athenian laws were relatively direct, well-publicized expressions of community sentiment. This chapter also includes two detailed case studies of laws that were rarely enforced but appear to have had some effect on behavior: (1) the protection of slaves in the law forbidding *hubris*; and (2) the laws forbidding former male prostitutes from actively participating in politics.

Chapter 4, *Enforcing Norms in Court*, contends that the courts may have had a substantial impact on behavior despite the ad hoc nature and inherent unpredictability of individual verdicts. Because of the wide use of character evidence in court speeches and the frequency of ligation, the court system provided concrete incentives to conform to a host of relatively stable extrastatutory norms lest they be used against them in a later, unrelated case. This approach facilitated the use of informal social sanctions by giving litigants incentives to discover and publicize their opponents' past norm violations. I argue that this peculiar approach of enforcing extrastatutory norms through the formal court system mitigated the effects of underenforcement in a system dependent on private initiative.

Chapter 5, *Court Argument and the Shaping of Norms*, argues that Athenian court arguments, delivered before hundreds of jurors, helped maintain order by shaping and reinforcing norms. Paradoxically, the courts' ad hoc and incremental approach may have given them advantages over the Assembly as a better forum for collective norm elaboration, particularly where norms were controversial or in flux. I also offer case studies of how court arguments may have helped shape and shift norms on controversial topics including sexual behavior, interpersonal violence, self-help, and the relation between public and private spheres.

Chapter 6, *Transitional Justice in Athens: Laws, Courts, and Norms*, draws together the themes of the book through an examination of Athens' successful transition to democracy in 403 BCE following the bloody reign of the Thirty Tyrants. Athens' approach to reconciliation illustrates each of the mechanisms discussed in Chapters 3–5. I examine the symbolic function of the amnesty forbidding prosecutions based on actions taken during the coup, how the courts nevertheless rewarded and punished litigants for their actions during the revolution in unrelated cases, and how court arguments in this period helped persuade the Athenians to carry out a peaceful transition.

PART ONE

ONE

Informal Social Control and Its Limits

The most obvious explanation for Athens' orderliness in the absence of a strong state may be that informal controls such as social sanctions and internalized norms were much more important than the operation of the law courts. After all, recent research suggests that fear of punishment is not the primary reason contemporary Americans obey the law,[1] and no society could function if all citizens operated as Holmesian "bad men,"[2] restrained only by the likelihood of detection and punishment. It may be tempting to think that informal controls must have been even more potent in a small, relatively homogenous, city-state like Athens. But the power of informal mechanisms, standing alone, is easily overstated.

This chapter explores the four major categories of informal social control in Athens: social sanctions like ridicule and shunning; internalized norms (i.e., compliance based on belief in the norm rather than the fear of getting caught); self-help and private discipline such as revenge killings and private punishment of slaves; and alternative dispute resolution like settlement and arbitration.[3] I argue that these methods, though significant, were less pervasive and effective than one might think. Specifically, I contend that social sanctions may not have been as frequent or as powerful as is commonly supposed, that internalized norms were unlikely to have been

---

[1] Tyler 1990.
[2] Holmes 1997.
[3] In some cases, the lines between these four categories become blurred, as for example, cases where self-help carried out by a victim against an adulterer in public also includes elements of social sanction. For clarity, I treat these four categories distinctly and note the ambiguous cases in the course of the discussion.

the *primary* factor driving widespread compliance, that self-help and private discipline, though important, were primarily limited to matters involving the household, and that alternative dispute procedures applied only to private disputes and therefore could not promote compliance with public norms. Perhaps most important, I explain how the operation of each of these "informal" mechanisms was dependent in critical respects on the formal legal system.[4]

Throughout, I emphasize the limitations of informal means of social control in Athens not because I believe these mechanisms were unimportant – quite the contrary. Rather, my argument is simply that informal means of control alone cannot explain the enigma of Athens' orderliness. This book seeks to illuminate the role played by formal legal institutions, a role that has not been fully appreciated and explored. As we will see in Chapters 3–6, to understand how order was maintained in Athens, we will need to examine the various ways in which formal legal institutions interacted with informal mechanisms to foster compliance with norms.

1.1. Social Sanctions and the Economy of Reputation

Social Sanctions: Definitions

I begin with the most popular scholarly explanation for Athens' high level of order: social sanctions and the politics of reputation.[5] These forms of informal discipline were undoubtedly significant in classical Athens just as they are today. But the idea that gossip "over[saw] people's lives down to the smallest detail"[6] and had "a special power in classical Athens"[7] in comparison to other societies may be exaggerated. Because Athens was not a face-to-face society,[8] gossip and social sanctions were not as powerful

---

4 For a discussion of how formal and informal modes of justice existed side-by-side in the Athens, see Forsdyke 2012:144–172, 176–177; Forthcoming a. The Athenians may not have drawn as sharp a line between formal and informal forms of justice as moderns: for example, the law explicitly authorized purely private punishments in the case of some crimes, such as subverting the democracy. But there is no question that the Athenians did distinguish between formal and popular/private justice, and as we will see in Chapter 5, the former gradually and fitfully became accepted as the proper venue for resolving serious disputes.
5 E.g., Hunter 1994:116; D. Cohen 1991a:88–94; D. Allen 2000a:142–145; Forsdyke 2012:146–147.
6 Hunter 1994:116.
7 Hunter 1994:116.
8 For discussion, see the section on potential limits on the power of social sanctions below.

as sometimes assumed, and they often depended on formal legal institutions. Moreover, our surviving evidence suggests that gossip generally resulted in social sanctions only in cases of serious transgressions, perhaps in part because of an ideology that frowned on interfering with citizens' private lives.

The notion that concern for one's reputation and desire for prestige may have induced Athenians to comply with norms requires little elaboration. The importance of honor in the classical Athenian value system has been well documented,[9] and is commonly thought to have fostered participation in the liturgical system.[10] Court speakers sometimes claim that they care more about their reputation than the formal outcome of the case,[11] and one speaker suggests that his opponents' spreading false rumors about him in the agora was a "devastating ... [attempt] to destroy [the speaker] by any means...."[12] Gossip and reputation appear to have exerted a disciplinary force on women as well as men: court speeches are full of allegations about women's misbehavior.[13]

Because the use of social sanctions in Athens has not been studied in any detail,[14] it may be helpful to briefly discuss what we know about how

---

9 E.g., D. Cohen 1995:69–75; Dodds 1951:18; Dover 1994:228, 236–242; Lambert 2011.

10 See, e.g., Whitehead 1983; but see Christ 2006:45–52; 190–199 on attempts to avoid public services such as liturgies and military service.

11 E.g., Andoc. 1.56; Isoc. 17.1.

12 Dem. 21.104–105.

13 E.g., Is. 3.11, 15; 7.31–32; Dem. 21.158; 39.26; 45.27, 39. Examples of women's concern for reputation from tragedy: Eur. *Medea* 214–218; *Alcestis* 315–316. For discussion, see Hunter 1994:111–116; Lewis 1996:12. Conversely, women and even slaves could play a role in enhancing or injuring others' reputation through gossip. See, e.g., D. Cohen 1991a:15–154 (on women interacting outside the house, including transmitting gossip); Hunter 1994:70–90 (discussing the access of slaves to Athenians' private lives and their concomitant power to influence their masters' reputations).

14 There are two notable exceptions. In *Nachbarschaft und Dorfgemeinschaft im archaischen und klassichen Griechenland*, Schmitz (2004) argues that in the classical period we can see ritual remnants of quite formalized social sanctions in the archaic period in the form of house razing and public punishments. He argues that with the exception of some survivals in the form of shame punishments, such as the stocks, and various humiliations inflicted on adulterers, social sanctions were eliminated in the classical period as the state declared private violence to be *aikeia*. Forsdyke (2012:144–172) argues, by contrast, that public shaming continued to be an important component of social control in classical Greece. Forsdyke focuses on public shaming, particularly treatment of adulterers, the razing of houses, and stoning. The latter two are barely attested in classical Athens; the first I treat as an example of self-help in the following text because they are initiated by the victim. As will become clear in the discussion that follows, I see the treatment of adulterers as one of the exceptional areas where informal social control remained dominant in the classical period, rather than representative of how order was

social sanctions operated before attempting to weigh their effectiveness. "Social sanctions," sometimes called "informal sanctions" in modern legal sociology, is a term that refers to punishments beyond mere diminishment in reputation that are unilaterally imposed by third parties with no involvement of government institutions.[15] Classic modern examples are public ridicule and shunning by neighbors and fellow villagers, being expelled from a church or merchant organization, or having one's business boycotted. The sanction may be imposed by either an individual or a private group (e.g., a religious or economic association), but social sanctions are typically understood as being imposed by third parties only: self-help or retaliation by an injured party is generally not included.[16] Social sanctions may be meted out for violations of legal norms – that is, norms that are the subject of legal regulation – or for violations of purely informal social norms. What is distinctive about social sanctions is that they are private punishments: the state (or in this case polis) institutions play no role in determining the guilt or penalty for transgression of a norm.[17]

Social Sanctions in Action

In classical Athens, the most common form of attested social sanction is the refusal to eat with, share food with, or otherwise engage in reciprocal relations with the offender.[18] In some cases, this type of social sanction could be limited in scope and effect. For example, Aeschines reports that Demosthenes' fellow envoys refused to eat with him and tried to stay in different inns when traveling,[19] and the shunning in Isaeus 9 for homicide is imposed only by the immediate family members of the deceased.[20] But

maintained in most aspects of Athenian social life. Neither Schmitz nor Forsdyke discusses in any depth the kind of social sanctions from the classical period that I focus on here, such as shunning or withdrawal of lending or commercial interaction.

15 See Piddocke 1968 for a discussion of social sanctions from an anthropological perspective; for the economic approach, see Posner 2007.

16 The borders of these categories are necessarily blurry, particularly where "self-help" may take place in public and involve public humiliation, as, for example, in some punishments for adulterers (Forsdyke 2012:144–172). I focus here only on sanctions initiated by third parties, and subsequently discuss remedies for adultery as an example of "self-help."

17 For this reason I do not include what might be termed "legalized informal sanction": laws that explicitly permit a citizen to take it upon themselves to punish an offender, such as an exile who returns illegally.

18 E.g., Xen. *Hellenica* 1.7.35; Aesch. 2.97; Lys. 13.79–80; Dem. 25.60; Is. 9.16–20.

19 Aesch. 2.97.

20 Is. 9.16–20.

other offenders faced more widespread sanction. The speaker in Lysias 13
reports that when Agoratus, who had been an informer under the reign of
the Thirty Tyrants, tried to join the democratic resistance at Phyle, he was
shunned by everyone: "nobody shared his food or his tent with the defendant, and the Taxiarch did not assign him to his Tribe. Instead, no human
being spoke to him — it was as if he were polluted."[21] Xenophon tells us
of another case in which the complete withdrawal of mutual support by
fellow citizens resulted in death: when Callixenus, the instigator of the
infamous condemnation of the Arginusae generals, returned to Athens,
"he was hated by everybody and died of hunger."[22]

We have only one example in which social sanctions escalated into
physical violence: the remarkable case of the stoning of Lycidas.[23]
Lycurgus tells us that when Lycidas proposed an alliance with Persia in the
Council, the other Councilors decided to kill him and then stoned him to
death with their own hands. Lycurgus points out that the members of the
Council took off their wreaths first to emphasize that they were imposing
punishment as private citizens rather than city officials.[24] In Herodotus'
account of the incident,[25] other Athenians joined the Councilors in the
stoning of Lycidas. This incident also gives us our only attested example of
women imposing social sanctions: according to Herodotus, "the Athenian
women learned what happened, and acting on their own, one woman passing the word to another, went to Lycidas' house and stoned his wife and
his children."[26]

It appears that social sanctions were considered complements to legal
sanctions, rather than substitutes.[27] It is clear that there was no belief
that social sanctions should be limited to enforcing norms that were not

---

[21] Lys. 13. 78–79.
[22] Xen. *Hellenica* 1.7.35.
[23] Lyc. 1.122; Hdt. 9.4-5; cf. Dem. 18.204. For discussion of this incident, see Allen 2000a:143–146;
      Forsdyke 2012:152–153. The other example of stoning in Athens was not a social sanction
      but military discipline: a traitor was captured on an enemy ship and stoned at the order of
      the general (Xen. *Hellenica* 1.2.13; Forsdyke 2012:165). According to the speaker in Lysias 13,
      the democrats at Phyle were getting ready to kill Agoratus but were prevented from doing so
      by Anytus the general (Lys. 13.77–79). House razing is attested elsewhere in Greece, but not in
      classical Athens. On house razing, see Forsdyke 2012:158–162; Connor 1985.
[24] Lyc. 1.122.
[25] Hdt. 9.4–5.
[26] Hdt. 9.5 (tr. Selincourt).
[27] For a discussion of the range of potential interactions between social and legal sanctions, see
      Zasu 2007.

regulated by statute, and no sense that social sanctions should govern only "private" matters, however an Athenian might define that term. There were several cases of social sanctions aimed at behavior that was illegal as well, including homicide, theft and assault, unpaid debt, and treason.[28] It seems that the decision whether to pursue social or legal sanctions (or both) was a matter of the individual victim's preference. One passage suggests that the choice between using a legal or a social sanction may have had as much to do with the relationship between the parties as with the nature of the norm violation: Demosthenes states in *Against Meidias* that when someone commits a "terrible crime," his friends withdraw their friendship whereas his enemies bring lawsuits.[29] We have one example of a victim resorting to a lawsuit after his attempts to generate informal sanctions against his attacker failed. Aeschines reports that after Pittalacus was savagely whipped by Timarchus, his former lover, he sat in a prominent spot in the agora without a robe in the hope that other Athenians would be appalled by the beating and informally punish Timarchus.[30] Timarchus was so panicked that the entire city would learn of his behavior that he induced Pittalacus to leave the agora with promises of compensation. When Timarchus never carried through on his promise, Pittalacus finally brought suit.

While gossip is omnipresent in court speeches, reports of concrete social sanctions such as public ridicule or social exclusion are rare. In her thoughtful chapter on the politics of reputation in Athens, Virginia Hunter lists more than one hundred examples of "gossip" in the court speeches.[31] She argues that gossip was an important form of social control in Athens, "oversee[ing] people's lives down to the smallest detail."[32] But she assumes that talk inevitably led to public ridicule.[33] Of course, the allegations of wrongdoing in open court before hundreds of jurors *do* constitute a form of public ridicule – in fact, one theme of Chapter 4 is that

---

[28] Lys. 6.45; fr. 1.3; Dem. 25.60; Din. 2.9–10; Is. 9.16–20.

[29] Dem. 21.118.

[30] Aesch. 1.59–62.

[31] Hunter 1994:118–119. There is some question about whether character attacks by one litigant on another in court should be characterized as "gossip," but that issue is irrelevant for our purposes here.

[32] Hunter 1994:116.

[33] Hunter 1994: 116: "'Gossip and its outcome, ridicule, are in a certain manner the external sanctions which support the internal sanctions of individual actions, self-regard, and the sense of shame.'" (Quoting J.K. Campbell, *Honour, Family, and Prestige: A Study of Institutions and Moral Values in a Greek Mountain Community* [1964]).

informal sanctions were dependent on formal legal institutions in exactly this way. But it also seems that gossip that did not find its way into a court case may well not have resulted in public ridicule or social sanctions. Although many of the ubiquitous character attacks in the speeches must have originated in community gossip, it is notable that examples of actual social sanctions are quite rare in the surviving speeches.[34] It is possible that speakers do not mention social sanctions when attacking their opponents on the assumption that the imposition of a sanction would be assumed by the audience. But it seems more likely that a speaker would, whenever possible, tell the jury that his opponent had not merely violated a norm, but had actually been ridiculed, cast out, or shunned by his neighbors or business associates.

In fact, most of the surviving examples of social sanctions involve serious norm violations. The cases of confirmed social sanctions involve informal punishments for stealing from fellow prison inmates and attacking one of them so violently as to swallow the other man's nose;[35] homicide;[36] collaboration under the Thirty Tyrants;[37] participation in the Arginusae debacle;[38] and treason.[39] These are not minor deviations from community standards. The one example of the imposition of a social sanction for a relatively mundane offense – debt – is presented as an extreme and incorrigible case. The offender has so many debts to neighbors, retail traders, and even maritime lenders in the Piraeus that "so many people come to his

---

34 Clear examples of social sanctions: Aesch. 2.97; Lys. 13.79–80; Lys. fr. 1.3; Dem. 25.60/Din.2.9–10 (both discussing the case of Aristogeiton); Is. 9.16–20 (involving a man refusing to speak to the son of the man who killed his father); Xen. *Hellenica* 1.7.35. Lyc. 1.122, the stoning of Lycidas, should probably also be included, though it should be noted that the punishment was not entirely private in that it was initiated by a public body, the Council (though Lycurgus tells us that they took off their wreaths before commencing the stoning). Dem. 33.6 and Isoc. 18.9 report attempts by creditors to blacken the reputation of debtors in an attempt to prevent others from lending to them; Aesch. 1.59 reports the attempt of the slave Pittalacus to encourage others to impose social sanctions on Timarchus for his mistreatment of him. Dem. 47.70 and Isoc. 17.1 contemplate the possibility of future social sanctions; Lys. 6.45 recounts how an informer under the Thirty who was protected by the Amnesty nevertheless fled out of fear (possibly of private punishments, possibly of prosecutions in violation of the Amnesty); Dem. 21.118 states that when someone commits a "terrible crime," his friends withdraw friendship while his enemies bring court cases. And Dem. 19.243 describes widespread talk, but does not mention ridicule.

35 Dem. 25.60; Din. 2.9–10.

36 Is. 9.16–20.

37 Lys. 13.79–80.

38 Xen. *Hellenica* 1.7.35.

39 Lyc. 1.122; Aesch. 2.97.

house at dawn demanding what is owed to them that the passersby believe that the man has died, and they have come for a funeral."[40] In an interesting twist, when he repeatedly fails to pay back his *eranos* loans, his neighbors do not refuse to continue lending to him or otherwise shun him. Rather, the *neighbors* abandon their own houses and rent other ones far away to avoid having to interact with him![41]

While it is impossible to reach any certainty given the paucity of our sources, the fact that all our confirmed cases of social sanctions involve serious offenses may suggest that social sanctions were largely used as a last resort, when an offense was too serious to ignore. We simply do not see any evidence of relatively minor infractions of the sort that were regularly raised as character attacks in the speeches resulting in any concrete social sanctions.[42] It may be that the very interdependence of social life made Athenians hesitate to disturb social relations by punishing minor norm violations.

In fact, as Wallace recounts, we have several examples of Athenians who not only escaped social sanction but managed to have significant political careers despite widespread gossip about their behavior such as their sexual habits (Timarchus) or cowardice on the battlefield (Kleonymous). As Wallace states with regard to Timarchus, "even in deciding questions of direct political concern to the community, most people did not take too seriously the rumors of Timarchos' youthful debaucheries, even while they were happily scandalized to hear them."[43] In Xenophon's *Symposium*, Charmides lists as one of the benefits of his newfound poverty that he is no longer subject to criticism for his connection to Socrates because no one cares what he does.[44] If it is right that the behavior of poor Athenians was less likely to invite gossip and criticism than the rich,[45] then ordinary

---

40 Lys. fr. 1.3–5.

41 Lys. fr. 1.4.

42 We do have a few cases involving enemies publicizing allegations for ordinary debt and theft in an attempt to encourage others to impose social sanctions (Dem. 33.6; Isoc. 18.9). In neither case is it clear whether the attempt resulted in significant social sanctions; in fact, in both cases it is the person whose reputation is being damaged who reports the incident, with the implication that it is improper.

43 Wallace 2007:125–126.

44 Xen. *Symposium* 4.30–33.

45 For a hypothesis on why elites might be the primary victims of informal sanctions, see Forsdyke 2012:157–167.

Athenians may have been even less constrained by the prospect of social sanctions than the evidence from the court speeches suggests.

Some Practical Limits on the Power of Social Sanctions

Why weren't social sanctions more powerful? Until relatively recently it was widely thought that most of an Athenian's social and economic interactions would take place in the deme, which was characterized as a close-knit, face-to-face community.[46] Recent research has cast doubt on this assumption.

An Athenian's life was not limited to his local community: many Athenians moved away from their hereditary demes; upper-class citizens might have holdings in several demes; and some married outside their deme.[47] The average Athenian would likely interact with strangers on regular visits to the city center to attend the Assembly and festivals.[48] Harris, emphasizing the high degree of specialization of labor suggested by evidence of more than 170 distinct occupations, argues that the average Athenian "would need to acquire goods and services outside his immediate circle of friends, neighbors, and family."[49] The speaker in Demosthenes 25 states that every citizen in the city does business in the market,[50] and Theophrastus' *agroikos* ("country man") goes to the city to shop and get his hair cut. Vélissaropoulos-Karakostas points to evidence from the fourth century that small farmers and merchants would regularly carry out one-off small business dealings in the fourth century.[51]

If Athenians were regularly interacting with strangers, particularly if they were engaging in one-time transactions, the deterrence effect of diminished prestige or social sanctions would be greatly reduced. In such a case an Athenian could suffer a diminished reputation or social sanctions only if his mistreatment of the stranger came to the attention of the offenders' friends, neighbors, or business associates and those friends and associates accepted the stranger's version of events over the account given by their friend. We will see in Chapter 4 that the use of character evidence in court

---

[46] E.g., Hunter 1994:97.
[47] Osborne 1985b.
[48] Countrymen in the Assembly: Theophr., *Characters* 4.3; Xen. *Memorabilia* 3.7.6.
[49] E. Harris 2002:68, 72–74.
[50] Dem. 25.51.
[51] Vélissaropoulos-Karakos 2002:132.

speeches may have helped to publicize norm violations to an offenders' local community and thereby facilitated the economy of reputation and social sanctions. In this way, much of the compliance that may appear to result from purely informal modes of discipline may actually have been dependent on the operation of Athens' formal legal institutions.[52]

Some scholars have gone even farther in challenging the traditional view of Athenian social life. Edward Cohen argues that even the territorial deme may not have been as close-knit as we once thought, with less sustained social interaction among neighbors and less development of local knowledge.[53] He points to evidence of dispersed patterns of settlement rather than a centralized village for each deme[54] and the prevalence of "absentee owners, mobile inhabitants, and frequent turnover of short-term leases"[55] to suggest that some Athenians may have barely known, let alone had close and sustained relationships, with some inhabitants of their territorial deme.[56] In a similar vein, Christ convincingly argues that helping behavior such as lending money and providing other assistance in times of need appears to have been limited to an intimate circle of relatives and close friends; this mutual interdependence and commitment did not apply to all neighbors and demesmen.[57] If this revised view that not all neighbor and deme relationships were particularly close-knit is correct, then social sanctions may have been significantly less important than previously thought. Neighbors and demesmen outside the intimate circle might be less likely to learn of and less motivated to sanction norm violations. Moreover, diminished esteem and social sanctions within the deme might have had less impact because the affected individual had the possibility of social and economic interactions beyond the local community.

---

52 Ober (2007:68; 2008a:135–140) argues that extensive interconnected social networks may have helped maintain social cohesion even though each Athenian would only know a small percentage of the total population. Ober similarly emphasizes the importance of formal institutions – in particular political institutions, especially service in the Boule – in compensating for the lack of face-to-face interaction.

53 E. Cohen 2000a:106–129.

54 E. Cohen 2000a:121 (citing archaeological findings that "most demes lacked a single residential center, and were populated either through isolated houses spread widely over the deme territory … or through multiple small settlements at some distance from each other").

55 E. Cohen 2000a:128; Osborne 1988.

56 There are, of course, also many passages suggesting quite close interactions between neighbors. See, e.g., Is. 3.13; Aesch. 3.174; Dem. 53; Lys. 7.

57 Christ 2010b:254.

It is important not to overstate the argument. No doubt fear of negative talk (and, perhaps even more important, desire for positive talk) could play an important disciplinary role, particularly given the centrality of reputation and honor in Athenian culture.[58] Notwithstanding recent research emphasizing the breadth of Athenians' dealings with strangers, it is still clear that Athenians relied extensively on close friends and neighbors. Friends and neighbors were a source of interest-free loans; lending of food, tools, and animals; and companions in communal meals.[59] But implicit in the scholarship that emphasizes informal social control is the idea that Athenians who violated community norms risked not only the possibility of gossip and diminished reputation, but also the much more material and dire consequences of exclusion from neighborly aid or being driven out of business. In reality, the consequences of minor norm violations may not have been nearly as severe.

Ideological Limits on the Power of Social Sanctions

An additional limitation on the impact of reputation and social sanctions on behavior may have been ideological. Athenians were clearly uncomfortable with the idea of citizens' passing judgment on each other's private lives or imposing social sanctions. Pericles' funeral oration includes a famous, and doubtless highly idealized, boast about the Athenians' open-mindedness:

> We conduct our lives in the spirit of free men. In our day-to-day dealings with one another we are not suspicious or angry at a neighbor if he does something that gives him pleasure; we do not pull a sour face that, though it does not harm him, does give him pain.[60]

While this passage suggests that reputation and social sanctions played no important role in Athens, the speaker in *Against Aristogeiton* offers a more complicated picture. He draws an analogy between community life and a multigenerational family:

> Where there is a father and his sons are adults — and perhaps they too have children — it's bound to happen that they will have different wishes. Youth and old age, you know, do not speak and act the same way. Still,

58 See, e.g., Dodds 1951:18.
59 Theophr., *Characters* 9.7; 10.11; 15.5; 17.9; Dem. 50.56; 53.4, 7; Lys. 19.22. For discussion, see Gallant 1991:157–158, 171–175; Millett 1991.
60 Thuc. 2.37.2.

all young men, if they are sensible, act so as to avoid being noticed, and if that isn't possible, it's clear that that was their intention. Then again, the older men, if they see lavish spending, or drinking, or out-of-bounds fooling around, observe these actions in such a way that they don't *seem* to have noticed.... In the same way, fellow Athenians, you manage the city, in the manner of kind relatives. Some men, as the proverb goes, observe the actions of the unfortunate like this: though they see, they *don't* see, and when they hear, they *don't* hear; while the others act with care and a sense of shame.[61]

In this passage, restraint on the part of both parties is critical to maintaining the peace; some measure of deviation from established norms is tolerated, so long as the youths are discreet and do not go too far. Unlike Pericles in the Funeral Oration, for the speaker in Demosthenes 25 reputation and social sanctions *do* play an important disciplinary role. Fear of shame keeps the citizens in check since they know that their neighbors are always lurking in the background, ready to step in if an individual strays too far from acceptable behavior. But the community tries to avoid expressing disapproval or imposing social sanctions if at all possible.

So though they differ in degree, the Funeral Oration and Demosthenes 25 both suggest a culture of toleration that must have been at least somewhat inimical to the propagation of gossip or imposition of social sanctions. Social sanctions were likely disfavored not only because they were inconsistent with democratic ideology's commitment to allowing citizens to "live as one likes,"[62] but also because there was something distasteful, perhaps even smacking of *hubris*, about a citizen proclaiming his superiority over a fellow citizen by ridicule or shunning.[63] The reluctance to impose (or be seen to be imposing) social sanctions may be reflected in the tendency, pointed out by Lewis, to present *pheme* (rumor) as a spontaneous, quasisupernatural entity that "springs up and spreads of its own accord, as opposed to slander, which is deliberately passed from one person to another."[64] It seems that while the Athenians sometimes acknowledged that fear of shame and ridicule played a role in motivating behavior, they were ambivalent about these informal modes of discipline. Perhaps in part because of this ideological ambivalence, we have seen that surviving

---

61 Dem. 25.88–89.
62 For discussion, see Wallace 2007.
63 On the notion of *hubris* in Athens, see Fisher 1992.
64 Lewis 1996:12–13; see also Aesch. 1.127.

evidence suggests that the use of social sanctions may not have been as prevalent as one might guess, and that social sanctions may have been largely reserved for serious violations of norms.

In sum, the picture of Athens that emerges from the sources is neither the tolerant ideal depicted in the Funeral Oration nor the highly coercive environment imagined by some scholars.[65] It appears that the imposition of social sanctions was disfavored and was generally reserved for severe norm violations, leaving a space for minor deviations from community norms. At the same time, fear of reputational damage through gossip clearly had some deterrent effect, though the frequency of social and economic interactions with strangers suggests that informal social control cannot fully explain the high level of social order in Athens.

1.2. Internalized Norms

What regulating effect did internalized norms have? That is, did individual Athenians moderate their behavior based on their own sense of right and wrong, independent of any worry about getting caught? A comprehensive analysis of the Athenian moral universe is beyond the scope of this book.[66] In this section, I briefly suggest some reasons why internalized norms were unlikely to have been the key factor in maintaining order in Athens. There are three reasons to doubt that norms, in and of themselves, offer the solution to the puzzle of Athenian orderliness: (1) shame and concern for reputation appear to have had a greater influence on behavior than individuals' internal moral compass; (2) some of the norms related to public order may not have been as deeply internalized by all citizens as one might expect; and (3) the primary site of norm articulation and reproduction were not external to the formal legal system, but inhered in Athens' deliberative and adjudicative institutions.

First, Athenian culture may have been less compatible with internal discipline than modern society. In *The Greeks and the Irrational*, E.R. Dodds famously argued that we can discern in classical Greek drama the emergence of the notion of guilt and conscience in contrast to the shame culture reflected in the Homeric poems.[67] Without denying the existence of

[65] E.g., Hunter 1994:116; D. Cohen 1991a:88–94.
[66] Dover 1994 (originally published in 1974) is still an excellent place to start for such an inquiry.
[67] Dodds 1951:28–63.

guilt in Athens, both dramatic and forensic texts illustrate the predominance of concerns about shame and reputation rather than guilt at wrongdoing throughout the classical period.[68] As Dover points out, Athenians tended to use the locution that they desire to "be regarded as" or to "be seen to" be virtuous and to avoid "being regarded as" base rather focusing on whether they actually are virtuous or not.[69] Several characters in tragedy suggest that they would rather die than live in infamy, even when they know that they were falsely accused or that their intentions were pure.[70] While internalized norms undoubtedly played a role in compliance, it seems likely that this mechanism was a less important component of Athenian self-regulation than the concern for reputation discussed in the previous section.

A second reason for skepticism about the importance of internalized norms is that at least some of the norms encouraging order may not have been as traditional, as uncontested, or as universally shared as one might expect in such a small, relatively homogenous society. For example, cooperative norms of honesty and fair dealing appear to have been of recent vintage, part of the transition from a tribal Homeric society to a polis community. In the Homeric poems (particularly in the figure of Odysseus), trickery, lying, and relentless pursuit of advantage were celebrated, and it has been pointed out that the term *aischron* (disgraceful) began to be regularly associated with deception only in the late fifth century.[71] Moreover, the new cooperative values did not completely replace the traditional agonistic ethical code.[72] Rather, competing tribal and ethical codes coexisted uneasily with each other, which may explain why scholars on both sides of the debate over whether revenge or moderation were more highly prized in fourth-century Athens have been able to marshal evidence in support of their respective positions.[73] Thus cooperative values that would encourage fair dealing, compliance with law, and voluntary participation in polis

---

68 E.g., Isoc. 17.1; Dem. 1.27; 4.10; 22.76; 52.11; Is. 2.29; Eur. *Suppliants* 314–319; Eur. *Electra* 900–904; for discussion, see Dover 1994:226–242; D. Cohen 1991a:94–96; Cairns 1993.

69 E.g., Eur. *Hippolytus* 321; Dem. 34.30; Dem. 56.14; Is. 11.38; for discussion, see Dover 1994:226.

70 E.g., Eur. *Hercules Furens* 1286–1290; Soph. *Trachiniae* 719–732; Eur. *Iphigenia Taurica* 678–696; for discussion see Dover 1994:237.

71 Adkins 1975:172.

72 For discussion, see Ober 2007:148; Riess 2012:135–137.

73 Compare D. Cohen (1995:61–86), who describes Athens as an agonistic, feuding society with Herman (2006:190–215), who argues for an ideal, and reality, of moderation in the face of conflict. For further discussion, see Chapter 5.

institutions were unlikely to have been so deeply ingrained that they generated compliance without enforcement.

The coherence of the Athenian normative code was undermined not only by the gradual and incomplete transition from agonistic to cooperative values, but also by the sophistic revolution of the fifth century, which introduced a culture of skepticism, casting doubt on even the most basic cultural norms such as filial piety. For example, there is the scene in Aristophanes' *Clouds* in which a son beats his father and defends his actions at length on the basis of doctrines he learned in Socrates' "reflectory."[74] This is certainly exaggerated, but must contain a kernel of truth for the joke to work. Finally, as we will see in Chapter 3, it appears that at least with respect to some practices, such as homosexual pederasty, elite attitudes and norms could be quite different from those of ordinary Athenian citizens. In sum, just as Athenian society was not as close-knit as scholars used to think, Athenian culture and moral values were not as thickly coherent and universal as previously believed,[75] making it less likely that self-regulation through internalized norms was the driving force behind social order in Athens.

Finally, and most importantly, whatever role norms might have played, their influence must have been heavily dependent on the formal legal system. When an Athenian obeyed a norm because he thought it was right, that conviction must have been at least partially attributable to the formal legal system, where these norms were debated and reinforced. This is a topic I will discuss at length. For example, Chapter 3 examines how the process of enacting a statute in the Assembly may have shaped norms and behavior, independent of their enforcement. And we will explore in Chapter 5 how the Athenian courts were the natural site for contesting, articulating, reproducing, and transmitting norms that helped foster social order and compliance with law.[76]

There were certainly other fora for norm elaboration in Athens, but none of them was likely to be as influential as the formal legal institutions in addressing norms related to social order. Two of the major mechanisms for transmitting specific norms in modern societies – religion and public education – did not serve this purpose in classical

74 Ar. *Clouds* 1303–1475.
75 On Athens as a "thinly coherent" culture, see Ober 2007:25, 69–91.
76 On the importance of political institutions in Athenian civic education, see Ober 2007:130–141.

Athens. Athenian religion was not associated with a creed or fixed belief system, focusing instead on the performance of ritual acts.[77] To be sure, religious festivals, architecture, and sculpture reflected and reinforced Athens' democratic and imperial ideology. But there was no equivalent of the Ten Commandments or rabbinical law, no specific religious guidance that might, for example, constrain individuals from stealing or committing violence against one another. And Athens had no formal system of public education through most of the classical period.[78] Public honorary monuments and funeral orations honoring the war dead certainly offered examples of men and deeds worthy of emulation,[79] but these forms of moral education focused heavily (though not exclusively) on military exploits and offered less insight into ordinary domestic social and commercial norms.

What about Athenian drama as a source of norm elaboration? There is no question that Athenian tragedies raised moral questions. But the setting of nearly all surviving tragedies in the heroic period, with frequent appearances of the divine, limited the extent to which the plays offered concrete lessons for everyday life. Moreover, the central moral dilemmas of tragedy are often presented without clear resolution, where the protagonists have no clear rightful course of action. The tragic theater undoubtedly encouraged Athenians to contemplate and debate ethical questions, but the very fact that Athenian tragedy has been alternately interpreted as justifying the city's practices and norms and, by contrast, as offering a critique of the dominant norms and values, illustrates the limitations of theater as a site of collective norm articulation.[80] While comedy presented more realistic situations from which one might draw moral lessons, the presence of caricature, parody, and inversion may have made it difficult even for an Athenian to discern a clear message.[81]

---

77 For a recent treatment see Parker 1996.

78 In the late fourth century the reformed *ephebia* may have served this purpose. See Ober 2001:175–176.

79 For discussion of public monuments and funeral orations as a form of moral education, see Balot 2014:190, 300–308; Raaflaub 2001.

80 For discussion of the literature on Athenian tragedy, see Balot 2014:286–288. We will see that although the ability of court verdicts to express a clear moral message was limited because the jury's reasoning was unknown, the position of each court speaker is relatively clear, and the verdict at least clearly declared one side of the dispute as the winner.

81 On the difficulty of drama as a source of Athenian popular morality, see Dover 1994:14–22.

In short, Athens was a society where reputation was still much more important than conscience, and where notions of the proper course of action were clouded by the ongoing transition from agonistic values to moral concerns. There were no public schools, very little in the way of "media,"[82] and scarcely any relevant religious instruction; even drama presented morality as a series of paradoxes. Almost by default, the courts and the Assembly were the primary institutions in Athens capable of articulating and enforcing norms.

1.3. Self-Help and Private Discipline

So far, I have argued that social sanctions and internalized norms may not have been as powerful as commonly thought and that these "informal" mechanisms must have relied in critical respects on the formal legal system. I turn now to self-help and private discipline, which were powerful means of control, but only in a limited sphere: the household (*oikos*). "Self-help" refers to instances in which a victim of wrongdoing secures his own justice independent of the legal system; I do not include cases in which private initiative was required to initiate formal proceedings or to enforce a court judgment. It may be worth emphasizing the obvious defect of self-help as the primary explanation for social order in Athens: self-help would not reach victimless acts, offenses against the state,[83] or failure to carry out public duties. I also argue in the following text that in practice self-help appears to have been even more limited in Athens, focused largely on legally sanctioned self-help to protect the *oikos* from night burglars and sexual offenders. Before examining the evidence for self-help in Athens, I briefly discuss private discipline within the *oikos*. Like self-help, discipline within the *oikos* involved the imposition of a punishment determined and administered privately, without official involvement. Private discipline played a critical role in regulating the behavior of slaves, women, and minors, who were largely excluded from the various mechanisms through which the formal legal system enforced order explored in Chapters 2–6.

---

[82] What media there was – public monuments, honorary decrees, engraved laws, sculpture on public architecture – tended to emanate from the Assembly.

[83] An exception is the anti-tyranny law discussed in Andocides 1.95–98, which authorized any Athenian to kill anyone who "subverts the democracy" or participates in tyranny. This collective self-help provision required no official determination of subversion.

Private Discipline

The discipline of slaves is one area where the dominance of informal means of control is undisputed. Masters had complete discretion to determine when and how to punish their slaves, except that a master was prohibited from killing his slave unless he or she had been condemned by the state.[84] At least one source suggests that women as well as men could punish slaves in the household.[85] The most common private punishments in our sources were whipping and other physical abuse; the most common infractions leading to slave punishment were stealing, lying, and laziness of various sorts.[86] It seems that as a general matter only masters were legally permitted to discipline their slaves;[87] the proper recourse for an individual outside the *oikos* who was wronged by a slave was to bring suit to seek damages from the owner.[88] Presumably the master would in turn inflict punishment or, in the case of slaves operating independent businesses, use funds from the business to cover for any damages awarded in a suit. The master's prerogative to privately discipline his slaves extended to recapturing runaway slaves by force,[89] a right which could at times be exploited to attempt the forcible seizure of individuals whose legal status

---

[84] Ant. 5.48; 6.4; for discussion, see Klees 1975:42.

[85] Xen. *Oeconomicus* 9.14.

[86] E.g., Dem. 45.33; Lys. 1.18; Ar. *Wasps* 440–450; 1292–1296; *Frogs* 542–545; *Wealth* 190–192; 1139–1140; *Knights* 101–102; Men. *Samia* 306–307; *Heros* 1–5; Agora Inv. IL 1702 (text and translation in E. Harris 2006:271); for discussion see Hunter 1994:162–173; Cox 2002; Herman 2006:299–300; Hunt Forthcoming.

[87] [Xen.] *Constitution of the Athenians* ("Old Oligarch") 1.10 states that it was not permitted to hit a slave in Athens. Nevertheless, it is clear that disciplining another's slave was considered much less serious than harming a free person and may have occurred in practice with some regularity. One speaker recounts how his opponent deliberately sent a free boy onto his property to steal flowers in the hope that he would mistake the boy for a slave and hit him, inviting a suit for *hubris* (Dem. 53.16). The implication is that hitting a trespassing slave would not constitute *hubris*, or at least would not be considered serious enough to merit a lawsuit. Todd (1993:189) suggests that these two passages, taken together, imply that a free man was permitted to hit another's slave when there was clear justification; MacDowell (1993:81) views discipline of another's slave caught stealing produce as an exception to the general rule; Riess (2012:88–89) argues that citizens could hit others' slaves so long as they did not inflict permanent injuries on them, thereby damaging their owners' property.

[88] MacDowell 1993:81. The suit could be brought in the slave's name if the slave was acting without his owner's permission (Dem. 55.31), but the owner was still responsible for defending the suit in court and for any damages awarded.

[89] E.g., Dem. 53.6; 59.9.

and ownership were not entirely clear.[90] While private discipline was the primary means of regulating most slaves, there is evidence for a handful of public offenses – several of which involved business activities in the market and were directly enforced by magistrates[91] – which resulted in a penalty of whipping for slave offenders.[92] Official punishments such as these were likely limited primarily to public slaves (i.e., slaves owned by the city), to private slaves who operated businesses in the market, and to slaves who committed capital offenses.[93]

Women's compliance with norms was similarly achieved primarily through informal means. A woman could be directly sued only for capital offenses;[94] the head of the household (typically her husband or father) was responsible for privately disciplining a woman who failed to comply with norms.[95] Serious infractions of wives such as adultery or falsely pretending to be a citizen were expected to result in immediate divorce;[96] husbands who knowingly permitted their wives to commit such acts were themselves liable to prosecution and punishment.[97] Women, of course,

90 E.g., Lys. 23.9–11, where a man tries to seize an individual as a slave who disputes his slave status; Dem. 59.37–40, where Phyrnion tries to forcibly seize as his slave Neaera, who asserts that she is a free metic.

91 On the regulation of market activities, see Chapter 2.

92 The Athenian Law on Silver Coinage and the Coinage Decree are the most prominent examples of official punishments for public offenses committed by public and private slaves, respectively. For discussion, with citations to additional public offenses providing for punishment of slave offenders, see Hunter 1994:155–157. Two examples of laws providing for official punishment of slaves for offenses not related to the market are the prohibition on slaves becoming or attempting to become the lover of a free boy (Aesch. 1.39) and the prohibition on cutting wood in a particular sacred precinct (IG II² 1362).

93 As discussed earlier, it seems that slaves, like free women, could be prosecuted for capital offenses; in fact, masters could not impose the death penalty absent official sanction for the penalty (Ant. 5.48).

94 E.g., Ant.1 (homicide); Dem. 57.8 (impiety); for discussion, see Todd 1993:208.

95 Of course, women were also susceptible to the influence of social sanctions and the politics of reputation discussed earlier.

96 E.g., Dem. 59.51, 80–82, 87; Lys.14.28–29. Aesch. 1.182 reports a legend of an Athenian father killing his daughter for promiscuity.

97 The speaker in *Against Neaera* reports that when it was discovered that Theogenes' wife was not a citizen, the Areopagus Council initially punished Theogenes for "marrying such a woman and permitting her to perform the secret rituals for the city" [as the wife of the basileus], but pardoned him when he asserted that he was not aware of her deception and promised to immediately throw her out of his house (Dem. 59.81). The law quoted in Demosthenes 59.87 states that men who continued to live with a wife caught in adultery were disenfranchised, though there is some debate about the authenticity of this law. For discussion, see Canevaro 2013:190–196.

had much more informal power within the household than slaves,[98] and it is impossible to know how and how often *kyrioi* (heads of household) imposed discipline for infractions that were not so severe as to threaten the integrity and legitimacy of the family. There are a few hints of physical abuse of wives.[99] Alcibiades was said to have physically dragged his wife Hipparete back to his home after she attempted to leave,[100] and a few passages from Aristophanes include references to husbands using violence against their wives.[101] While our sources are largely silent on the acceptability of husbands physically punishing their wives,[102] it is clear that beating was a common and accepted form of private discipline for minor children within the household.[103]

In sum, due to their legal incapacity it was difficult to ensure compliance with norms from women, slaves, and minors through the operation of the formal legal system. These actors were kept in check almost exclusively through informal means of control, principally private discipline meted out by their *kyrios*.

Self-Help

Self-help – that is, private punishment meted out by the victim without official involvement in the determination of guilt or penalty – was explicitly permitted by law in three limited circumstances: catching a sexual offender caught in the act[104] or a thief at night,[105] or defending oneself or one's property from forcible attack or seizure.[106] Although these situations were not limited to events occurring within the house, they appear to have been designed in large part to protect the household from serious intrusions. While it is impossible to say for certain how often self-help was

---

98 On the gap between women's formal incapacities and social practice, see, e.g., Hunter 1994:9–42.

99 Omitowoju (Forthcoming) points out that mention of violence against women is largely absent from the court speeches.

100 Plu. *Alcibiades* 8.4; Lys. 14.42; Andoc. 4.10.

101 Ar. *Lysistrata* 160–166, 507–520; Ar. *Clouds* 1443–1446.

102 Fisher (1998:77), Ruiz (1994:174), and Llewellyn-Jones (2011) speculate that wife-beating was likely a regular practice, despite the understandable absence of explicit discussion of it in our sources.

103 Garland 1990:127–33; Fisher 1998:77; see also Golden 2003.

104 Dem. 23.53–54.

105 Dem. 24.113.

106 Dem. 23.60.

used in other circumstances, our evidence suggests that it was expected that those who had suffered other wrongs would seek revenge through official legal channels or informal dispute-resolution procedures rather than taking the law into their own hands.

Self-Help in Response to Nocturnal Theft and Violent Attack

The first major category of sanctioned self-help involved the permissible use of deadly force to protect against thieves and attackers in certain limited circumstances.[107] The speaker in Demosthenes 23 quotes from what he states is a portion of Draco's justifiable homicide statute. This provision permitted the use of deadly force to defend life or property against violent attack: "If a man at once and in defense kills someone who is unjustly and with violence seizing a man or his property, he is killed with impunity."[108] Another Athenian statute listed deadly self-help as one legitimate response to encountering a thief at night: "If, during the daytime hours, someone steals goods worth more than 50 drachmas, there may be *apagoge* to the Eleven [the procedure whereby the Eleven summarily executed admitted "wrongdoers" (*kakourgoi*)];[109] but if someone steals anything of whatever value at night, one is permitted to pursue the man and kill him, or to wound him, or to take him to the Eleven."[110] It is worth noting that this statute contemplates pursuing a fleeing thief: the law explicitly permitted violent defense of property, not simply self-defense in inherently dangerous situations.

Although the laws justifying deadly force in cases of forceful theft and nocturnal theft could apply to situations outside the household, it seems

---

[107] For discussion of the sources, see, e.g., Canevaro 2013:64–71; Youni 2001:117–121; Christ 1998b:522–525; D. Cohen 1983:113–118; Ruiz 1994:35–36.

[108] Dem. 23.60. Earlier in the speech, the speaker quotes from another portion of this law that lists various forms of justifiable homicide, including killing someone "on the road." Dem. 23.53–54. This clause has been the subject of much debate, with some scholars viewing it as inauthentic or so archaic as to be meaningless at the time of Aristotle. For discussion of the various scholarly interpretations, see Canevaro 2013:64–70. Antiphon's *Third Tetralogy* (4.b1) also suggests that deadly force was permitted in self-defense when attacked by another without provocation.

[109] On the summary *apagoge* procedure, see Chapter 2.

[110] Dem. 24.113. D. Cohen 1991a:118 argues that this law permitting killing only the nocturnal thief and not the daytime thief is a newer law that partially conflicts with the older justifiable homicide law that permitted killing any thief using force. He further argues that the Athenians never resolved the conflict.

likely that the archetypal case contemplated by these statutes was house burglary.[111] Nocturnal theft by stealth, without force, presumably applied most commonly to house burglars. The Draconian statute permitting homicide in response to any forcible theft would permit individuals to defend their household from violent theft in remote situations where it might be more difficult to call on help from passersby.

It is possible that self-help was not the most common response, even in the limited situations where deadly force against thieves was explicitly permitted by law. As Cohen has pointed out,[112] it seems likely that the law permitting the killing of nocturnal thieves was enacted after the Draconian justifiable homicide law that permitted killing in response to any violent theft. The provision for self-help in the more recent nocturnal theft law appears to have been narrower than the older justifiable homicide law: it provided that daytime theft of a significant sum should be handled through the official summary apagoge procedure, permitting self-help only in the case of nocturnal thefts.[113] Moreover, even in the case of nocturnal thieves the law provides for violent self-help as only one option alongside the official summary procedure.[114] The newer summary arrest procedure was also available for a range of crimes which might in some cases qualify as forcible theft, including those perpetrated by kidnappers, clothes-stealers, and thieves.[115] While the older law permitting self-help in response to violent theft, even in daytime, remained on the books throughout the classical period, the newer law may reflect a shift in norms and social practice away from exercising one's legal right to self-help against thieves in favor of the use of the official summary procedure.

Self-Help in Response to Adultery and Fornication

The second category of legally sanctioned self-help involved the treatment of sexual offenders – principally adulterers and fornicators – caught in the act. While many of the details of the laws addressing adultery and

---

[111] Cf. Christ 1998b:522 and D. Cohen 1991a:112–113 who also see these statutes as aimed at housebreakers.

[112] D. Cohen 1991a:118.

[113] Dem. 24.113.

[114] Dem. 24.113.

[115] *Ath. Pol.* 52.1; Aesch. 1.91; Ant. 5.9; Dem. 35.47; 54.1; Isoc. 15.90; Lys. 10.10; Xen. *Memorabilia* 1.2.62. For discussion of the summary arrest procedure, see Chapter 2.

fornication are uncertain,[116] this much seems clear: although Athenian law expressly permitted the killing of an adulterer taken in the act, in practice Athenians tended to favor non-deadly forms of self-help such as humiliation and demands for compensation.

Our sources refer to several potential forms of self-help against sexual offenders. The "Draconian" justifiable homicide statute discussed earlier also included a provision for killing adulterers and fornicators caught in the act: "If someone kills a man he finds having sexual intercourse with his wife, mother, or sister, or daughter, or with a concubine whom he keeps for begetting legitimate children, for these reasons it is not lawful to pursue and kill him [i.e., the man who kills the adulterer]."[117] As has often been pointed out, Euphiletus' apparent defensiveness when pleading that killing his wife's lover was not only permissible but indeed compelled by the city's laws[118] suggests that by the fourth century killing the adulterer was not the typical or accepted response in such a situation.[119]

Physical humiliation and compensation appear to have been more common. It is possible, but not certain, that a statute permitted the sexual offender caught in the act to be subjected to physical abuse and humiliation short of death.[120] Regardless of whether the law explicitly provided for physical abuse of sexual offenders caught in the act, our sources suggest that as a matter of social practice the Athenians condoned abuse and humiliation of the adulterer by means such as physical blows, "radishing" (inserting a radish into the anus), and depilation of pubic hair using hot ash.[121] Confining the sexual offender and demanding compensation is

---

[116] I do not summarize all the scholarly controversies here. For in-depth discussion of the debates over the Athenian treatment of adultery, see, e.g., Scafuro 1997:194–216; D. Cohen 1991a:98–132; Carey 1995; Kapparis 1995; Roy 1991; Forsdyke 2012:146–157.

[117] Dem. 23.53.

[118] Lys. 1.34.

[119] For the view that killing the adulterer was unusual, see, e.g., Cohen 1991a:98–132; Carey 1995; Kapparis 1995; Cantarella 2005:244; Scafuro 1997:214–215.

[120] The statement in Lys. 1.49 that the laws permit anyone taking a *moichos* to "treat him in any way he likes" does not explicitly prohibit killing the adulterer, but is sometimes read, in conjunction with the law limiting abuse of a convicted sexual offender (Dem. 59.66–67), as a paraphrase of a law that referred to humiliation and abuse short of death. For discussion, see, e.g., Kapparis 1995:110–116; D. Cohen 1991a:115–119; Scafuro 1997:198–199.

[121] Is. 8.44; Xen. *Memorabilia* 2.2.5; Lys. 1.25; Ar. *Clouds* 1083; Ar. *Wealth* 168. D. Cohen (1985:385–387) expresses doubts about comic evidence of radishing and depilation, but Carey (1993) and Kapparis (1996:66–67) argue that it was a common practice. Forsdyke (2012:153–157) emphasizes the public nature of these humiliations, which arguably blurs the line between private self-help carried out by the victim and social sanctions.

also attested,[122] though this practice does not appear to have been directly permitted by statute.[123] The law did, however, acknowledge and indirectly condone confinement of sexual offenders by providing a remedy in cases where a man alleges that he has been falsely taken as a sexual offender.[124] Under this law, if the complainant prevails, he and his sureties are released from their promise to pay compensation; if, however, the complainant is adjudged guilty of adultery or fornication, the man who arrested him is permitted to abuse the offender in court in whatever way he wishes, provided he does not use a knife.[125]

What of the woman taken in the act of adultery or fornication? As already noted, women were subject to private discipline, and likely divorce, by their husbands.[126] Some scholars have read the law cited in Demosthenes 59.87, and apparently paraphrased in Aeschines 1.183, as evidence that adulteresses were banned from public sanctuaries, and were subject to a severe form of social sanction if they flaunted this prohibition: anyone was permitted to tear her clothing, beat her, or subject her to any mistreatment short of death.[127] But Scafuro has argued that this law applies only to cases in which the male sexual offender had been convicted by a court, not self-help situations in which the offender was caught in the act.[128] If this is right, mistreatment of an adulteress in such a case was not a form of informal self-help but an example of the use of private initiative in enforcing a formal court verdict, similar to the provision that anyone sentenced to exile who returned to Athens could be killed with impunity.

While many of the details surrounding remedies for sexual offenses remain controversial, it is clear that the use of self-help was considered an acceptable response to discovering an adulterer or fornicator in the act. The rationale behind permitting the use of self-help in sexual offenses is similarly uncontroversial: it preserved the *kyrios'* prerogative to protect the

---

122 Lys. 1.25; Dem. 59.41–42, 64–66.

123 In fact, as Scafuro (1997:199, n. 26) points out, the speaker's statements in Lysias 1.28 suggest that the laws did not provide for compensation in response to taking an adulterer in the act.

124 Dem. 59.66.

125 Dem. 59.66. Physical abuse in court is not a form of self-help in our sense, but rather a court-ordered punishment.

126 The law quoted at Dem. 59.87 suggests that a husband who continued to live with a woman whom he had caught committing adultery was liable to disenfranchisement. For discussion of the authenticity of this law, see Canevaro 2013:190–196.

127 E.g., Forsdyke 2012:156.

128 Scafuro 1997:202–203. The argument hinges on the use of the verb *helein* ("to convict") rather than *labein* ("to take") in the law.

house (*oikos*) from intrusion. Adulterers posed a threat to the household by raising doubts about the children's legitimacy and inheritance rights, by disrupting family relations,[129] and by penetrating the house and therefore violating the head of the household's honor.[130]

Self-Help Beyond the Household

So far, we have seen that informal means of control played a major role in protecting the integrity of the household from internal and external threats. How often was self-help used outside the limited context of protecting the household? Hunter suggests that self-help played a vital role in policing Athens: "very often arguments were settled, violence quelled, and miscreants apprehended without the intervention of the authorities at all."[131] In fact, while there is extensive evidence of private initiative in conjunction with formal legal processes and bystander intervention to stop violence in process, there is relatively little evidence of individuals attempting to forcefully exact private punishment or enforce their rights outside the limited categories of permitted self-help discussed earlier.[132] Of course, self-help must have occurred in Athens just as it does in contemporary societies. However, our evidence does not suggest that self-help was a standard response to a violation of one's rights or that self-help and its deterrent effect were major factors in ensuring that Athenians complied with the law.

In the many descriptions of disputes over property, contracts, damages, and inheritances in our sources,[133] we often hear of Athenians attempting to peacefully (if angrily) demand recompense or settle the dispute with their opponent, pursuing their rights through private arbitration or formal

---

129 Hence the (much debated) statement in Lysias 1.32 that adultery was considered more serious than rape in Athenian law.

130 On protection of the *oikos* as the primary rationale behind the self-help remedies for adultery, see, e.g., Scafuro 1997:197–198; Cantarella 1991:293; Carey 1995:416; D. Cohen 1991a:112–114. On the rationale for including concubines (*pallakai*), see Scafuro 1997:197–198; Cantarella 1991:293; Carey 1995:416.

131 Hunter 1994:120.

132 In fact, we have seen that even within the categories of permitted self-help, such as responses to theft, there appears to have been a trend toward using formal legal procedures.

133 It is important to note that our evidence of disputes from court speeches is not limited to the dispute in each given case, which obviously resulted in the initiation of a legal procedure; many speeches include discussions of prior disputes between the parties unrelated to the current legal issue, and even disputes between parties not involved in the case.

legal process, or even letting a matter drop. But we do not hear of individuals violently attempting to enforce what they believe to be their rights or to exact private punishment in the absence of any official authorization to do so.[134] Interestingly, the three examples provided by Hunter of "self-help" (as opposed to private initiative as part of a formal legal procedure)[135] — Lysias 3, Lysias 23, and Demosthenes 59.37–40 — all involve attempts to seize a slave (or at least an alleged slave). In the latter two examples, an individual was claiming to seize his own slave, which, if true, would be a lawful exercise of the master's right of private discipline. In Lysias 3, Simon sought to violently enforce a contract for sexual services with a live-in rent boy, likely a slave.[136] Although the speech makes clear that Simon's violent attempt to get the boy back was illegal,[137] it may well be that the boy's inferior status made Simon more likely to attempt self-help.[138]

Hyperides' *Against Athenogenes* may provide an example of a more common response to a perceived legal wrong. Epicrates, in love with a slave boy, was tricked into purchasing the boy's father and his perfume business along with the boy. Despite Athenogenes' verbal assurance that the assets from the business were greater than the debts, Epicrates soon discovered that he now owed five talents. Incensed, he gathered a group of friends and relatives as witnesses and confronted the seller in the market.[139] They had a heated exchange, which attracted a crowd of bystanders. Although, according to Epicrates, the crowd took his side, excoriated Athenogenes, and

---

134 For discussion of private initiative in the enforcement of official judgments, see Hunter 1994:122–124, 140–141. In addition to a judgment by a court or arbitrator, an individual had legal authorization to take possession of property without pursuing a court action in three special circumstances: (1) legitimate sons and grandsons (but not those claiming inheritance by will or more distant relatives) could take possession of his father's or grandfather's property; (2) a lender could take possession of collateral if a debtor failed to pay; and (3) an individual who purchased land from the state could take possession. See Is. 3.62 (succession); Is. 5.22–24 (collateral); Dem. 24.54 (land purchased from the state). For discussion, see MacDowell 1993:153.

135 Hunter 1994:120–123.

136 Theodotus is most probably a slave, based on the mention of the possibility of torture; alternatively, it is possible that he was a free noncitizen. On the status of Theodotus, see, e.g., Hunter 1994:212 n.6. For a similar argument that the examples adduced by Hunter do not qualify as "self-help" see E. Harris 2007:160–161.

137 Lys. 3.22.

138 Cf. the suggestion in Dem. 53.16, discussed previously, that one might punish another's slave if he found him stealing despite the general prohibition on punishing slaves other than your own.

139 Hyp. 3.12.

even suggested that he use the summary arrest procedure, at no point did he or anyone in the crowd suggest that he forcefully seize compensation from Athenogenes or physically threaten him into voiding the contract.[140] Unable to peacefully get satisfaction from Athenogenes, Epicrates brought a lawsuit.

Perhaps the strongest evidence that self-help was not dominant in Athens is the apparent rarity of revenge killings in response to homicide; it seems that the predominant reaction to homicide was litigation.[141] What about self-help in response to personal insults and minor assaults? We do hear of instances in which men insulted or punched during a drunken party responded immediately with deadly force,[142] though we also hear of examples of immediate restraint in favor of later legal action in the face of severe affronts to a man's honor.[143] While some violent self-help, particularly in the context of drinking and/or perceived attacks on one's honor, was inevitable and perhaps even tolerated, our evidence suggests that self-help was not considered an acceptable response to assaults that fell short of the requirements for self-defense. In several cases of public violence, bystanders intervene to stop the attack, protect the victim, offer opinions on who is in the right, and serve as witnesses with a view to a later court hearing, but in none of these incidents does the victim or the crowd attempt to privately punish the aggressor.[144]

In sum, although it is impossible to quantify the prevalence of self-help in Athens, our surviving evidence suggests that self-help played an important role in situations involving the household, but is unlikely to have been a major factor in maintaining order and fostering compliance with norms outside this limited context.

---

[140] As Christ (2010b) points out, although bystanders sometimes act as witnesses for later use in a court proceeding or even join in the verbal argument over who was in the right, they almost never intervene physically.

[141] See Phillips 2008:29, 71. It appears that families sometimes reached settlement agreements prior to trial. Phillips 2008:80–82.

[142] Dem. 21.71–73.

[143] For example, Demosthenes' legal rather than physical response to Meidias' punching him in the face in front of thousands of spectators at the dramatic festival (Dem. 21.15–19). For the contrasting views of the norms surrounding such affronts, compare Herman 2006:155–183 with D. Cohen 1995:119–142. For further discussion of norms of interpersonal violence in Athenian court cases, see Chapter 5.

[144] E.g., Aesch. 1.60; Dem. 53.17; 54.3–6, 7–9; Lys. 3.6–7; 15–18. For discussion of the role of bystanders, compare Hunter 1994:137–139 with Christ 2010b.

1.4. Settlement and Private Arbitration

The final category of informal social control to be considered is alternative dispute resolution – that is, private settlement, mediation, and arbitration. It is impossible to reach any firm conclusions about the prevalence of attempts at informal dispute resolution and how often it was successful. But even if private settlement and arbitration were relatively common means of ending disputes in everyday life, it seems clear that these mechanisms on their own are unlikely to explain the high level of order in Athens. Like self-help, private arbitration did not reach victimless and public offenses. Moreover, in many cases private dispute resolution was not truly independent of the formal legal system because it relied on the operation of the court system both to encourage parties to participate in arbitration and to persuade the parties to abide by its outcome.

The court speeches and comic dramas provide a window into the various types of informal dispute resolution used in Athens. Our sources reveal instances of aggrieved Athenians, often with the support of friends or family members, approaching their opponent in an attempt to work out a private settlement agreement.[145] Informal family councils, including active participation by women, could be convened to resolve disputes within the family.[146] A somewhat more formal mechanism involved the voluntary engagement of one to five private arbitrators.[147] Both parties had to agree to the choice of arbitrators, who were generally family members or friends of the disputants. Athenian private arbitrators actually fulfilled the role of a modern mediator as well as an arbitrator: the arbitrator could either assist the parties in reaching a mutually acceptable reconciliation (*dialusis* or *diallage*), or could pronounce a verdict (*diaita*).[148] Unlike the process of public arbitration, which involved a hearing before a state official whose verdict could be freely appealed in a law court, private reconciliation agreements and arbitration awards were considered authoritative (*kurioi*). There is some debate over whether the reconciliation or arbitral award was enforceable in court, or whether only the written release (*aphesis*) or mutual settlement agreement (*apallage*) that the parties sometimes, but not always,

---

[145] E.g., Hyp. 3.10–12; Dem. 50.24.
[146] E.g., Dem. 44.19; Lys. 32.12–18; Dem. 45.4–5. For discussion, see Hunter 1994:38–55; Scafuro 1997:32–34.
[147] For an in-depth discussion of private arbitration in Athens, see Scafuro 1997:117–141.
[148] For an extensive discussion of arbitration, see Scafuro 1997:34–42.

voluntarily created to enshrine the reconciliation or arbitral award were enforceable.[149] It appears that even in the absence of a release or written settlement a party who suffered damage due to his opponent's violation of the reconciliation agreement or arbitration award could bring a suit for damages.[150] Thus it seems that one way or another a party could call on a court to enforce the terms of a private reconciliation or arbitral award.

How important was alternative dispute resolution in Athens? A firm answer is impossible given the limits of our sources. Scafuro reports eight successful private resolutions out of roughly twenty-two arbitrations mentioned in the speeches.[151] On one reading, this means that arbitration failed more than half of the time it was tried; on the other hand, these numbers may actually suggest a more positive conclusion when we remember that the court speeches are naturally skewed toward settlement attempts that failed and wound up in court. As several scholars have pointed out, it seems that settlement or private arbitration was considered the preferred method of resolving disputes, particularly in arguments involving family members. Litigants regularly claim to have tried to settle the case and accuse their opponents of forcing the case to court by being unreasonable.[152] Yet, the Athenians' reputation throughout Greece for litigiousness and the sheer volume of court cases[153] suggest that the preference for private settlement may have been more of an aspiration than a reality. But even if settlement and arbitration played a significant role in resolving private disputes, these mechanisms did not apply to victimless offenses or public offenses and therefore could not have played a major role in fostering order and promoting compliance with norms affecting the state as a whole, such as paying taxes, performing military and other services, and complying with laws against impiety and laws governing eligibility for citizenship and speaking in the Assembly.[154]

---

[149] For discussion of the evidence, see Scafuro 1997:117–131.

[150] For discussion, see Scafuro 1997:128–129.

[151] Scafuro 1997:37–38; 395–396.

[152] Dem. 21.74; 27.1; 29.58; 30.2; 40.1–2; 41.14–15; 42.11–12; 44.31–32; 47.81; 48.2,40; 54.24; Lyc. 1.16; Lys. 3.3; 9.7; Is. 5.28–30; for discussion see Hunter 1994:57; Dover 1994:187–192.

[153] On litigiousness, see, e.g., Thuc. 1.77; Ar. *Peace*, 505; *Clouds*, 206–208; *Wasps* passim; *Birds*. 35–45. For the volume of legal cases in Athens, see Chapter 4.

[154] We hear of sycophants threatening individuals with false public charges in the hope of securing a payoff, but in these cases the private settlement serves not to encourage compliance with public norms, but simply to compensate the malicious prosecutor.

Settlement and private arbitration are unlikely to independently account for Athens' orderliness, not only because these mechanisms were limited in scope, but also because they relied in critical respects on the formal courts to help initiate and enforce private resolutions. As Scafuro has pointed out, in many of the cases we have, requests to arbitrate come *after* initiation of a court case; it seems that charges were often brought primarily for the purpose of pressuring the other party into settling or agreeing to arbitrate the issue.[155] Reaching agreement on arbitrators must have often been difficult. The threat that the dispute might be decided by an unpredictable jury,[156] along with all the additional costs and risks involved in a court case, may have induced some disputants to attempt to settle or submit to private arbitration. Moreover, we have already seen that a disputant could call on a court to enforce a private settlement that resulted in a written agreement or a private arbitration award. Compliance with informal dispute-resolution outcomes, particularly arbitration verdicts handed down by an arbitrator, depended in large part on the possibility of enforcement by a court. In this sense, any compliance with norms stemming from private dispute-resolution procedures cannot be attributed to purely informal social control, but rather reflect interaction and reinforcement between informal and formal mechanisms.

***

Why was Athens an orderly place? In this chapter I have tried to argue that informal means of social control alone cannot give us all or even most of the answer: some applied only in narrow situations (self-help and private discipline); some were partially dependent on the courts for their articulation or enforcement (social sanctions, norms, and arbitration); some were simply less influential (social sanctions and norms) than one might think. In the next chapter we examine the extent to which compliance can be attributed to the straightforward enforcement of statutes through the formal legal system.

---

[155] Scafuro 1997:38–39.
[156] See Isoc. 18.9–10 (describing how the speakers' friends advised him to pay a settlement even though he was in the right to avoid the arbitrary decision making of the jury and the embarrassment of a court case).

TWO

Law Enforcement and Its Limits

What role did straightforward deterrence play in maintaining order in Athens? That is, did the imposition of penalties in court cases induce compliance with the norms expressed in Athenian statutes? We will see that the Athenians' reliance on private initiative to enforce the law resulted in sporadic enforcement, particularly with respect to victimless crimes. Moreover, Athenian courts did not predictably and reliably apply the statute under which a given case was brought. This uncertainty regarding prosecution, trial outcomes, and enforcement of judgments must have weakened the deterrent effect of Athenian statutes. At the same time, the Athenians provided special mechanisms to ensure more straightforward enforcement of laws in a few circumstances: selected market and shipping transactions, and offenses that threatened public order, including certain theft-related offenses and threats to the state. In this way, Athens ensured a minimum level of public order and economic security, making it possible for order to be maintained despite a more limited formal coercive apparatus in the rest of the system.

2.1. The Underenforcement of Athenian Statutes

Fear of statutory penalties undoubtedly played a role in inducing compliance with statutory norms. Indeed, Athenian court speakers, particularly prosecutors urging a conviction, often suggest that legal penalties deter wrongdoers.[1] But the sporadic and unpredictable enforcement of statutes

---

[1] E.g., Dem. 19.343; 22.68; 45.87; 54.43; 59.77; Lys. 14.15; 30.23–24; Aesch. 3.175–176.

must have weakened incentives to comply in some situations. Classic deterrence theory typically considers deterrence a function of the certainty of punishment and the severity of the sanction.[2] Modern legal theorists have pointed out that a high risk of conviction has a much stronger effect on deterrence than the severity of the penalty.[3] We will see that the absence of public prosecutors and the reliance in most cases on private initiative for prosecution and enforcement of judgments resulted in underenforcement of statutes, particularly in the case of "victimless" public offenses. By lowering the probability of punishment, the reliance on private initiative reduced deterrence. Moreover, the vagueness of Athenian statutes, absence of binding precedents, and broad notion of relevance meant that while Athenian courts enforced general norms of fairness and good citizenship, they did not reliably and predictably enforce the legal norms expressed in statutes. The broad uncertainty regarding trial outcomes also reduced the deterrent effect of statutes.[4]

There is evidence that the Athenians recognized that the deterrent effect of statutes was undermined by the reliance on volunteer prosecutors and unpredictable juries. Lycurgus laments the risks facing volunteer prosecutors and notes: "neither the law nor the judges' vote has any force without a prosecutor to bring wrongdoers before them."[5] And Demosthenes notes that the laws are ineffective unless juries enforce them in their verdicts: "What gives [the laws] strength? *You* do, if you confirm them and make them effective each time someone asks. So the laws get their power from you, and you from the laws."[6]

Before we explore the lack of reliable prosecution, trial outcomes, and enforcement of judgments in Athens in more detail, it may be worth asking whether the fear of high penalties, even if rarely enforced, may have been sufficient to provide a high level of deterrence. After all, the death penalty was a possibility for a relatively wide range of offenses, including not just homicide and treason but impiety, *hubris*, and some varieties of theft.[7] Again, increasing the severity of the penalty generally provides less

---

2 Polinsky and Shavell 2009. The swiftness of punishment is also often included as a factor.
3 Reiss and Roth 1993:6.
4 Hadfield 1994; Craswell and Calfee 1986.
5 Lyc. 1.4.
6 Dem. 21. 224–225.
7 In fact, Todd (1993:140–141) suggests that the high penalties in Athenian law may reflect an attempt to compensate for uncertainty in prosecution and punishment.

deterrent effect than enhancing the risk of conviction and punishment. In fact, in the modern context many studies have shown that attempts to boost deterrence by imposing very severe penalties may be counterproductive because extreme penalties actually make the imposition of punishment *less* likely. Witnesses are less willing to participate, prosecutors are less willing to file the most serious charges, and juries are less likely to convict if the penalty seems grossly disproportionate.[8] Something like this dynamic may have operated in Athens to reduce the likelihood that the most severe statutory penalties would be imposed. Defendants were permitted to go into voluntary exile to avoid trial, and we know of several examples of defendants facing potential capital charges who availed themselves of this option.[9] Moreover, the prevalence of defense arguments appealing to the jurors' pity based on the severity of the penalty[10] suggests that such arguments could sometimes sway a jury to acquit in order to spare a guilty defendant harsh punishment. Thus even Athenian statutes that provided for very harsh penalties (or the possibility of a harsh penalty in the cases subject to *timesis*) may not have had much of a deterrent effect if potential wrongdoers believed that they were very unlikely to suffer the most severe punishment even if a prosecutor brought charges against them.[11]

Reduced Probability of Prosecution and Enforcement of Judgments

Due to the absence of public prosecutors in most situations,[12] there was no guarantee that even men who were obviously guilty of serious public

---

8   For discussion, see Katyal 1997. In a similar vein, Green (1985) showed that early English juries acquitted defendants to prevent the imposition of the death penalty.

9   Todd (1993:140) discusses the prevalence of defendants in *eisangeliai* fleeing without facing trial (Hansen 1975:35–36), and notes that "the *stele* recording the confiscation of Theosebes' property for temple robbery regards it as a routine matter that he 'did not remain to stand trial.'"

10 See Lanni 2006:53–59.

11 In a similar vein, Scafuro (2014:320–325) provides several examples of provisions for extremely high financial penalties against magistrates, which she interprets as intended to deter but never to be actually carried out. She points out that some of these decrees included additional smaller, more realistic, penalties, likely because "the deterrence capability of [the high, ten thousand drachma penalty] had become so much of an obvious fiction by 425/4, that now, real and feasible penalties had to be tacked on" (Scafuro 2014:324).

12 As discussed subsequently, there were some important exceptions: magistrates might bring suit, typically against those who had committed offenses against them in their official capacity; a board of public advocates (*sunegoroi*) prosecuted officials for financial charges at *euthunai* and public prosecutors (*kategoroi*) could be appointed in treason cases. For discussion, see Todd 1993:92; MacDowell 1993:61–62.

offenses would be charged. This was particularly true in the case of "victimless" offenses, such as draft-dodging, tax and liturgy avoidance, failure to pay state debts (including fines imposed for previous public offenses), and a number of other public laws. Victimless offenses were generally pursued through public suits (*graphai*) brought by volunteer prosecutors. In an effort to prevent malicious prosecutions, the Athenians set up an incentive structure in most *graphai* that forced volunteer prosecutors to take on significant risks with no expectation of financial rewards. In most public suits, the state rather than the prosecutor collected any fines from the defendant.[13] Moreover, if the prosecutor dropped his suit or failed to win at least one-fifth of the jurors' votes at trial he faced a severe penalty: he was fined 1000 drachmas,[14] and barred either from bringing similar suits in the future or from bringing any public charges.[15] Given the uncertainty of Athenian jury verdicts, this penalty must have served as a significant deterrent to prosecution.[16] It seems that victimless crimes were prosecuted rather randomly, according to whether a personal enemy of the defendant or a man trying to make a public name for himself was willing to initiate a public suit despite the financial risks involved.[17]

The Athenians were clearly worried about uneven and unpredictable enforcement of public laws and took steps to encourage volunteer prosecutions in certain types of case. For most of our period the penalty for failing to win one-fifth of the votes was lifted for prosecutors in *eisangeliai*, public suits usually used to allege serious charges such as misconduct by public officials and treason.[18] Successful prosecutors in a few types of

---

13 MacDowell 1993:257. As discussed subsequently, in some special procedures, such as *phasis* and *apographe*, the prosecutor was entitled to a portion of the fine collected.

14 Dem. 23.80; 24.7; 58.6. For discussion of fines associated with dropping a public suit, see Wallace 2006.

15 Compare Hansen (1976:63–65), who argues that prosecutors who failed to get one-fifth of the votes were barred only from bringing similar charges, with E. Harris (2006:407–413), who argues that such prosecutors were barred from bringing any type of public charge. For a discussion of provisions to prevent abuse of the legal process, see Christ 1998a:28–32. For situations in which the penalty did not apply, see subsequent text.

16 But Rubinstein (2000:93) suggests that the possibility of joint prosecution teams may have lowered the burden for volunteer prosecutors and made prosecutions somewhat more likely.

17 On the motivations of public prosecutors, see Osborne 1985a; Christ 1998a:118–159; on the "uneven" and "patchy" enforcement of laws by volunteer prosecutors, see Rubinstein (Forthcoming:32).

18 Poll. 8.52; Hyp. 2.8,12. The penalty appears to have been reinstituted sometime in the 330s: Dem. 18.250; Lyc. 1.3; Harrison 1998:52; Hansen 1975. Two other types of *eisangelia* also seem to have been without risk to the prosecutor: prosecutions alleging mistreatment of

public suit were permitted to collect a portion of the judgment: prosecutors in suits recovering state property, including fines owed to the state (*apographe*), likely received one-third of the proceeds;[19] volunteer prosecutors received one-half the recovery in cases of *phasis*, a procedure used particularly in trading, mining, and commercial cases;[20] and prosecutors exposing individuals who were falsely representing themselves as citizens stood to collect one-third of the proceeds from the sale of the convicted defendant's property.[21] But there is little evidence that these financial rewards significantly enhanced the likelihood of prosecution. Osborne has shown that prosecutors using the *apographe* and *phasis* procedures in our attested cases rarely seem to be motivated by profit,[22] and Christ has noted that these actions were not thought to be any more prone to attract sycophants (vexatious litigants) than other sorts of public suit.[23] In fact, it seems that it was not unusual for public debtors to escape prosecution via *apographe*: the speaker in Demosthenes *Against Aristogeiton* suggests that some citizens "turn a blind eye" even to state debtors who ignore the automatic penalty for failure to pay and continue to exercise citizenship rights.[24] In this

orphans and heiresses (*Ath. Pol.* 56.6.), and misconduct by an arbitrator. For discussion see Harrison 1998:51–52.

[19] Dem. 32.2 suggests that the successful prosecutor in an *apographe* received a lavish three-quarters of the recovery, but several scholars have suggested that the text should be emended so that the actual reward was one-third of the proceeds (Lewis 1966:191 n.67; Osborne 1985a:44–47).

[20] Todd (1993:119) describes the grab bag of offenses that could be prosecuted via *phasis*: "Some are trading or mining offences; others concern encroachment on public property; but certain (unspecified) forms of impiety seem to have been included; and maltreatment of orphans appears to have been thrown in for good luck." For discussion of *phasis*, see MacDowell 1991; Osborne 1985a:47–48; Harrison 1998:218–221.

[21] For discussion, with references, see Christ 1998a:138–143.

[22] Osborne 1985a:44–48. Osborne (1985a:44–47) notes, e.g., that in several of the attested *apographe* cases the prosecutor does not in fact collect any reward because the proceeds of the confiscated property did not exceed the debt owed to the state.

[23] Christ 1998a:139–143.

[24] Dem. 25.85–91. Hansen (1999:262) notes that the sanctions for state debt were "extremely severe in principle but were administered somewhat randomly." See also Hansen 1976:59–60; Wallace 1998; Wallace 2012:118. Hunter (2000b:30–35) demonstrates that the attitude and treatment of state debtors varied enormously depending on the source of the debt: defaulting trierarchs and others who incurred a debt while performing a public service were treated very leniently and often continued to exercise full citizenship rights despite being formally *atimoi*; judgment debtors who observed the rules of *atimia* were rarely imprisoned and generally only faced property confiscation if a private citizen (often an enemy) took it upon themselves to initiate an action; while those who defaulted on tax or rent contracts were treated most severely, often facing immediate imprisonment pending payment and possibly (at least according to *Ath. Pol.* 48.1) direct enforcement by the Boule.

way, the financial rewards offered to volunteer prosecutors seem to have reflected, not rectified, underenforcement in those types of suit.

Even when a volunteer prosecutor stepped forward and secured a conviction in a public suit, some judgments would go unenforced. While physical penalties were enforced by the state, the collection of fines was less predictable. Public officials, the *praktores*, would attempt to collect the fine and inscribe the name of defaulters on the list of public debtors, but do not appear to have forcibly confiscated property.[25] Enforcement required a volunteer prosecutor to take the further step of initiating an *apographe* action to denounce the debtor's property, which we have already seen was far from certain.

Prosecutions were likely sporadic even where there was a clear injured party with an incentive to sue to enforce the law. Where an individual violated a law ordinarily redressed by a public suit, for example *hubris* (roughly, "assault accompanied by insult") or false arrest, the victim might be deterred from bringing suit because he, like any prosecutor in a public case, risked penalties and did not stand to gain financially from the verdict. In both private and public cases, victims with considerably less money and social clout than their opponent might be particularly reluctant to prosecute. A richer party had several advantages in court: he could afford a better speechwriter, would be likely to be a better public speaker by virtue of his education, and would have performed more public services, which might win over the jury.[26] In theory, where a public procedure was available a volunteer prosecutor could step in to protect a weak third-party victim; in describing Solon's invention of the *graphe*, the *Constitution of the Athenians* contemplates a volunteer prosecutor assisting a wronged third party,[27] and Plutarch, writing well after the classical period, explicitly links the *graphe* to protection of the weak.[28] But Christ has demonstrated that third-party prosecution, even on behalf of friends and family members, was rare in Athens.[29]

---

25 Dem. 25.28; 43.71; 58.19–20. For discussion of the process of collecting a public debt, see Hunter 2000b:26–34.
26 Christ 1998a:33. Rubinstein (2000:91–93) suggests that the use of *sunegoroi* (supporting speakers), who were not subject to the risks faced by volunteer prosecutors, may have made it easier for weaker victims to bring suit in both public and private cases.
27 *Ath. Pol.* 9.1.
28 Plu. *Solon* 18.5–6.
29 Christ 1998a:119–130; but see E. Cohen 2000b:120–123. Christ (1998a:130–134) points out that it was also relatively uncommon for victims to bring public suits on their own behalf. Most *graphai* allege a public wrong, though in these cases the prosecutor is usually not a

The Athenians' reliance on injured parties (or their families in cases of homicide) to prosecute reduced deterrence by lowering the probability of prosecution and enforcement. How large an impact did this have? After all, modern legal systems also rely on private parties to bring noncriminal cases, and money can confer a significant advantage in litigation today just as it did in Athens. But there are two important differences between the reliance on private litigation in the ancient and modern world: (1) in modern systems public prosecutors ensure more regular enforcement of what we think of as criminal offenses, while in Athens even prosecution of analogous cases depended on private initiative; and (2) in the modern world, in situations involving structural inequality between victims and responsible parties, litigation remedies are often supplemented by regulations enforced by state actors — some examples include consumer protection, occupational safety, and environmental regulations.[30] We will see subsequently that Athenian magistrates could summarily impose small fines for deceitful market practices and violations of building and sanitation regulations. But Athenian regulation likely fell well short of fully correcting for the failures of litigation remedies: a handful of magistrates — just five magistrates were charged with maintaining order and supervising sales in the city market — could not systematically inspect or issue licenses, but simply responded haphazardly to individual complaints.

The reliance on the private initiative of victims also reduced the probability that judgments would be enforced. Even if a "little guy" prevailed in court, the limited state mechanisms for enforcing private judgments meant that a verdict might come to nothing if he didn't have a group of friends to help him claim his due. We hear of several cases in which successful litigants attempted to forcibly collect on a judgment, a process that was sometimes met with violent resistance and could even turn deadly.[31] If a judgment debtor refused to pay, the successful plaintiff had the option of initiating another lawsuit, a *dike exoules*. If successful, the ejectment suit would result in a fine, thereby subjecting the defendant to the risk of losing his citizenship rights as a state debtor. It seems that a successful ejectment

---

public-spirited volunteer but an enemy of the defendant or person who stands to gain from the defendant's conviction.

30 The Athenian situation might be analogous to the United States before the rise of the regulatory state in the early twentieth century: the tort system alone did little to prevent or provide redress for workplace accidents, consumer swindles, or product defects.

31 Dem. 47.21–44; 45–66; 53.14–15; Dem. 30.2,8. For discussion see Hunter 1994:141–143.

suit also gave the plaintiff official license to collect on the judgment by force.[32] It is unclear whether the demarch (the top official in each deme) could assist in the collection of private debts: the demarch did collect debts owed to the deme,[33] and it is possible that he also assisted private creditors who requested help in collecting debts within his deme.[34] In any case, the surviving court speeches describe private attempts at enforcement but never mention the possibility of enlisting the assistance of a public official. Even a man as well connected as Demosthenes could have trouble getting justice. He was unable to collect from Meidias after he won a suit for slander and initiated an ejectment suit;[35] and even after establishing his former guardians' mismanagement in court, he had to resort to a *dike exoules* to collect part of the judgment and in fact never recovered the full amount owed to him.[36]

We have seen that the reliance on private initiative reduced deterrence by lowering the probability of prosecution and enforcement of judgments. Can we offer a more fine-grained analysis of which types of litigants and offenses were least likely to be successfully prosecuted? Private offenses against victims of lower social standing may often have gone unprosecuted. Demosthenes claims, for example, that Meidias wronged many men with impunity because they were too intimidated to prosecute him.[37] Nonwealthy metics may have been at a particular disadvantage: they often engaged in commercial transactions that might generate disputes but had few connections or character evidence to draw on in pursuing a case or enforcing a judgment.[38] On the other end of the spectrum, it is likely that prosecutions in homicide cases were unusually reliable, regardless of social status: both cultural and religious norms created an expectation that relatives of a homicide victim bring suit.[39]

---

32 For discussion, see Todd 1993:144–145; Hunter 1994:141–143.
33 Dem. 57.63–64; IG II² 2492.7–9.
34 The primary evidence for the demarch's role in collecting private debts comes from comedy: a character in Aristopanes' *Clouds* (30–37) suggests that the demarch might come to collect on his son's debts. For discussion of this difficult question, see Whitehead 1986:125–127; Hunter 2000b:142–143; E. Harris 2013:36 and n.67.
35 Dem. 21.81.
36 Dem. 30, 31.
37 Dem. 21.141.
38 On the difficulties faced by metics in court, see Patterson 2000.
39 IG i² 115.20–23.

As already noted, public prosecutions for victimless offenses against the state may have been the least predictable, dependent primarily on whether an enemy or political rival was willing to bring suit rather than the seriousness or visibility of the infraction. Ironically, less wealthy and lower-status individuals may have had an advantage here, since they were less likely than elites to have political rivals and may have been able to avoid prosecution for victimless public offenses. Moreover, to the extent that prosecutors were motivated by financial rewards in suits like *apographe*, they may have been less eager to pursue defendants who did not offer the prospect of a large recovery. Christ's study of suits for draft evasion and various forms of cowardice (the *graphe astrateias*, *lipotaxiou*, and *deilias*) support this hypothesis: the few suits that were brought for these offenses tend to involve prominent citizens prosecuted by wealthy personal and political rivals, while these laws do not seem to have been regularly enforced against ordinary Athenians.[40] But we should not exaggerate the ability of ordinary Athenians to avoid prosecution. Nonelite Athenians did use the court system,[41] and even humble citizens could have personal enemies willing prosecute them. Demosthenes 53, *Against Nicostratus*, for example, involves an *apographe* brought by a farmer embroiled in a feud with his neighbor, and Lysias 24, *For the Disabled Man*, arose because someone came forward to challenge the speaker's eligibility for a disability pension at a *dokimasia*, the annual review of such privileges conducted by the Council. In sum, the lowered probability of prosecution and enforcement must have weakened – but of course not eliminated – the deterrent effect of Athenian statutes.

Uncertainty about Trial Outcomes

Another factor that weakened formal deterrence – even once a prosecution was initiated, and putting aside the subsequent problem with collecting a judgment – was the unpredictability of the jury's decision on the merits. The cornerstone of deterrence is the widespread belief that sanctions will follow from a violation of legal norms. But the ad hoc, discretionary nature of Athenian jury decision making meant that in many cases it might be impossible to predict ex ante whether a jury would find a violation of the statute in a particular situation. This sort of broad uncertainty

---

40 Christ 2006:60–61; 119; 140.
41 For discussion see Chapter 4.

surrounding trial outcomes reduced deterrence[42] and thereby must have limited the ability of the legal system to foster order and compliance with legal norms.

Athenian statutes were notoriously vague. As a result, many statutes did not provide much guidance about how to conform one's conduct to the law. As has often been pointed out, Athenian laws generally simply state the name of the offense, the procedure for bringing suit under the law, and in some cases the prescribed penalty; our surviving laws and decrees rarely define the offense or describe the essential characteristics of the behavior governed by the law. The surviving law of *hubris*, for example, offers no definition of this subjective term,[43] and the range of situations charged as impiety (*asabeia*)[44] and bribery (*dorodokia*)[45] suggest that these offenses may not have been clearly understood. To be sure, in some cases vague statutes may lead to overdeterrence as actors avoid any activity that could plausibly be interpreted as falling within a loosely worded statute, particularly where embarrassing charges, like those related to sexual misconduct, are involved.[46] But it seems likely that in most situations lack of statutory definition would lead to less, rather than more, deterrence. For politicians, statutory ambiguity may have resulted in more lawsuits, while simultaneously reducing incentives to comply with specific statutes: if a motivated enemy could always concoct some kind of charge from an array of broadly written statutes – the *graphe paranomon* and *eisangelia* procedures were favorite weapons in political prosecutions[47] – there was little an individual

---

42 In the modern context, studies suggest that broad uncertainty reduces compliance, though as discussed subsequently minor uncertainty caused, e.g., by an ambiguous legal standard, can lead to overcompliance. Hadfield 1994:544; Craswell and Calfee 1986:281.

43 Dem. 21.47. For a book-length treatment of the meaning of *hubris*, see Fisher 1992.

44 For discussion, see D. Cohen 1983:203–210. Carey (1998) has shown that laws relating to family and religion often include an unusual amount of substantive detail.

45 Conover 2010:21–64.

46 We will see in Chapter 3, e.g., a similar phenomenon related to the lack of clarity about what constituted *hetairesis* (roughly, "prostitution"). In the modern context, studies suggest that while broad uncertainty reduces compliance, uncertain legal standards that are not too broad can lead to overcompliance as individuals avoid legal behavior that might be construed to fall under the uncertain legal standard (Hadfield 1994:544; Craswell and Calfee 1986:281). This may explain why the significant uncertainty surrounding trial outcomes in Athens likely reduced deterrence, but the somewhat vague standard for *hetairesis* may have induced overcompliance.

47 Demosthenes (18.250), e.g., reports that after Chaeronea he was forced to constantly defend himself from political charges. The *graphe paranomon* required an allegation that a decree was unconstitutional, though it seems that this could encompass arguments of a "breach of the (democratic) principles underlying the laws, and so ... the mere accusation of undesirability."

could do to protect himself from potential charges. For an ordinary citizen, uncertainty about whether his behavior had even contravened a law, when combined with the possibility that, even if he were guilty, he might never be prosecuted, must have reduced the deterrence effect of statutes.

In the absence of legislative history or juristic commentary, litigants and jurors were left with little guidance on how to interpret vague statutes. At times litigants, doubtless assisted by speechwriters, made ingenious arguments supporting their interpretation of the law based on the putative intent of the lawgiver[48] or on analogous statutes.[49] Juries may have been swayed by these arguments on occasion. But it is difficult to imagine that a citizen contemplating a course of action would engage in this sort of legal reasoning to attempt – let alone succeed – in predicting how a jury might apply the law to his situation.

Did shared norms and values significantly reduce legal indeterminacy? We must consider the possibility that Athenian statutes might not have been nearly as vague to the Athenians as they seem to us. Common values might have provided the average citizen with a general sense of what sort of behavior might, for example, put him in danger for a suit for *hubris* even though the term is not defined by statute. But our evidence suggests that shared values did not entirely compensate for the vagueness of statutes. The Athenian statute on defamation (*kakegoria*) provides an example. In Lysias, *Against Theomnestus*, the defendant is charged with defamation for stating that the speaker killed his father. The defendant apparently argued that he was not guilty because he did not use the precise word prohibited by the defamation statute (*androphonos*, "manslayer"), but rather simply said that he had "killed" his father.[50] The prosecutor rejects this defense as hair-splitting, arguing that it is not the text of the statute but the purpose

Hansen 1999:206; see also Lanni 2010. The *graphe paranomon* appears to have been a common weapon in political rivalries, and we hear of politicians being charged multiple times under this procedure (Hansen 1999:208–211). The law governing *eisangelia* (Hyp. 3.7–8) included more detail than most, but the sheer number of cases brought (130 cases between 492–322 BCE; 35 of our 143 known generals in the period of 432–355 faced prosecution by *eisangelia*) suggests that the definitions of treason and corruption in the statute were deemed capacious enough to permit political rivals to concoct prosecutions. For discussion of how the broad definitions in Athenian statutes "allowed litigants to turn virtually any matter into a legal issue," see Gagarin 2012:311.

48 For discussion of the rhetorical uses of the intent of the lawgiver, see Johnstone 1999:25–33.

49 E.g., Is. 8.31–34; Hyp. 3.15–18. For discussion, see Lanni 2006:69–70; Johnstone 1999:28; E. Harris 2000:47–54.

50 Lys. 10.6–7.

of the law that matters. One would expect that there would be a clear consensus among Athenians on whether defamation involved only the use of particularly offensive words enumerated by the statute or should be interpreted broadly to include a variety of insults having the same effect. That both litigants apparently thought their respective interpretation of the statute could persuade the jury[51] suggests that shared norms did not eliminate uncertainty concerning the meaning of statutes in Athens. Indeed, Aristotle's call for precise definitions of offenses like theft (*klope*) and adultery (*moicheia*), as well as *hubris*, in the *Rhetoric* suggests that the Athenians lacked a clear idea of the criteria for even straightforward offenses.[52] Moreover, some norms – for example, norms related to interpersonal violence and revenge – were subject to enough disagreement to support differing interpretations of the laws that implicated these norms, such as the statutes on assault, *hubris*, and self-defense.[53] Finally, the interpretation of some statutes may have changed significantly over time, as Conover has shown for *dorodokia* (bribery).[54] This process must have created uncertainty in trial outcomes, particularly during and right after the transition to a new understanding of the statute.

It may be worth mentioning here that some scholars have recently argued that Athenian litigants were less focused on interpreting and applying the applicable statute than on proving or disproving the specific allegations in the written indictment (called a *graphe* in public suits, *enklema* in private cases), which sometimes included a detailed list of alleged wrongs in addition to, and sometimes instead of, the statutory charge.[55] This may well be right, though I am not convinced of the further argument that litigants and jurors restricted themselves to arguments related to the indictment.[56] Even

---

51 As Johnstone (1999:25) points out, the defendant's arguments are not as absurd as the speaker portrays them, and in fact at the pretrial stage the arbitrator ruled for the defendant, not the speaker.

52 Arist. *Rhetoric* 1374a8. For discussion of the vagueness of laws, see D. Cohen 1983:6–7; 203–210.

53 For discussion, see Chapter 5.

54 Conover 2010:21–64.

55 Thür 2008:66–72; Gagarin 2012; E. Harris 2013:114–136. From the few examples that survive, it seems that some indictments did not include much detail beyond the name of the offense and proposed penalty (e.g., Dem. 45.46), while others included a detailed narrative (e.g., Plu. *Alcibiades* 22; Dem. 37.22–25). The indictment of Socrates did not mention that the case was being brought under a *graphe asebeia* (D.L. 2.40).

56 The routine use of extralegal arguments discussed subsequently, such as character evidence and appeals to pity are hard to square with a view that the jurors focused narrowly on the factual allegations in the indictment. For a contrasting interpretation, see E. Harris 2013:114–136.

if we assume that jury decisions were tightly focused on determining the defendant's guilt under the allegations in the indictment, this might make the resolution of particular cases more predictable once the indictment was known, but would not provide ex ante guidance to behavior, and thus deterrence, because indictments were individualized allegations specific to the case.[57]

Perhaps even more problematic than undefined statutory terms from the standpoint of predictability and deterrence was the lack of statutory guidance regarding exceptions, defenses, and aggravating and mitigating factors. The presence of these types of arguments in our surviving speeches suggests that Athenian jurors sometimes considered them in reaching their verdicts,[58] and there is some evidence suggesting that jurors in particular cases were swayed by these arguments.[59] The difficulty is that there were no clear rules, written or unwritten, about when particular defenses or mitigating factors might trump the straightforward application of the statute. The case of Euaion described in Demosthenes *Against Meidias* provides an example. While at a drinking party, a drunken friend of Euaion punched him in front of several companions, and Euaion retaliated by killing him.

---

57 Gagarin (2012:310–311) points out, e.g., that the lack of definitions in statutes meant that plaintiffs could include a wide variety of alleged wrongs under the broad categories of behavior like *hubris* or *asebeia* listed in the statute. There may be one exception. In occasional public cases, indictments in previous suits might offer some guidance on the types of specific behaviors that might be alleged under certain poorly defined statutory offenses. The indictment of Socrates, e.g., might serve warning that at least one volunteer prosecutor had interpreted impiety (*asebeia*) to include introducing new divinities and corrupting the youth. But it is unlikely that indictments served a major role in elucidating the meaning of statutes. First, indictments in private cases (*enklema*) do not appear to have been publicized in any way. Public indictments (*graphai*) were temporarily displayed in the agora and may even have been retained in the Metroon, but were not easily accessible once a case was heard. Most important, most *graphai* were likely either too general or too specific to offer any guidance for future litigants: an indictment that simply named the offense would not offer any information beyond the statute, while more detailed allegations – e.g., lists of the specific allegedly unconstitutional decrees proposed by the defendant – were too case-specific to offer any guidance. And, of course, the fact that a single volunteer prosecutor interpreted the statute to prohibit the allegations in the indictment does not mean that an Athenian jury would necessarily agree with this interpretation.

58 E.g., the speaker in Hyp. 3, *Against Athenogenes*, suggests an exception to the general rule that contracts should be binding. Riess (2012:22–101) sketches various aggravating and mitigating factors regarding violence that seem to have affected jurors, including public vs. hidden violence, inebriation vs. sobriety, old age vs. youth, and escalation vs. de-escalation. E. Harris (2013:285–291) lists several examples of equitable arguments in the surviving speeches.

59 Din. 1.55–57; Dem. 21.71–76; for discussion see E. Harris 2013:292–300.

Demosthenes tells us that Euaion was convicted of intentional homicide by only one vote, and describes different jurors' contrasting interpretations of the case: according to Demosthenes,[60] a narrow majority convicted on the theory that a mere punch did not justify retaliating with deadly force, while a sizable minority voted to acquit because the humiliating circumstances surrounding the punch excused his escalation of the fight.[61] The lack of clarity about how a court would respond to what must have been a fairly common occurrence like a drunken fight at a party illustrates why the straightforward enforcement of statutes is unlikely to have been the primary factor driving Athenian compliance with norms.

So far, we have been discussing the relatively high level of uncertainty regarding the application of what a modern would recognize as traditional "legal" considerations in Athenian courts – that is, the rules defining the offense and any defenses. But the predictability of verdicts was further hampered by the jury's consideration of what a modern would consider to be factors unrelated to whether the offense was committed.[62] From an Athenian point of view, of course, these arguments were just as relevant as statutory or mitigating arguments to reaching a just resolution of the case. I point out that moderns would view them as "extralegal" considerations simply to highlight the fact that the number and types of factors that might influence an Athenian verdict was much larger than in a modern court. Athenian litigants routinely presented a highly contextualized picture of the dispute, describing the relationship and past interaction of the parties, including their behavior in the course of litigation; the character and public services performed by the litigants and their families; and the effect that a penalty would have on the defendant and his family.[63] Moreover, litigants in cases that might appear to turn on a specific factual or technical question – for example, did a witness in a prior lawsuit perjure himself, had the statute of limitations run, was the suit barred in a *paragraphe* action – typically attempt to convince the jury not only that the

---

60 There was of course no official recording of the jurors' reasoning.
61 Dem. 21.71–76.
62 For a more complete discussion, with references to primary sources, see Lanni 2006:42–64. On Athenians jurors' consideration of extralegal considerations, see also Christ 1998a:40–44; Wallace 2012:121.
63 Lanni 2006:42–64.

narrow issue should be resolved in their favor but that they are in the right in the underlying substantive dispute as well.[64]

We cannot know for certain how the average juror conceived of his task, but our surviving speeches suggest that even the relative importance of legal and contextual evidence in any individual case was open to dispute.[65] Individual Athenian court verdicts were the untraceable result of many individual jurors' complicated weighing of a variety of factors, both statutory and extrastatutory. This form of ad hoc, multifactored decision making meant that the courts rarely enforced the statute under which the case was brought in a straightforward or predictable manner.

Past court decisions may have been a more promising source of deterrence than statutes. Indeed, we will see in Chapter 5 that high-profile court arguments and verdicts may have affected behavior by reinforcing existing norms and signaling norm shifts. But there were important limits on the ability of court-imposed penalties to deter future wrongdoing. Individuals could not be confident that a verdict was an accurate indication of future decisions. There was no doctrine of binding precedent obligating jurors to abide by previous verdicts. Records of past decisions were not easily available to litigants who wished to use them in their speeches, and even where litigants do cite previous verdicts they rarely compare the cases in a way that would allow the jury to extract and apply a rule of decision from the prior case.[66] Perhaps most important, the presence of multiple statutory and extrastatutory arguments would make it difficult for an individual attempting to conform his behavior to the law to glean guidance from court verdicts. Decisions could be interpreted in various ways, depending on which legal or extrastatutory factor one thought played the decisive role in the jury's verdict.

Of course, fear of court-imposed sanctions must have played some role in promoting order and compliance with legal norms. But the overall picture is one of underenforcement and substantial legal uncertainty about trial outcomes, both of which must have weakened the deterrent effect of statutes and court decisions. We turn in the next section to explore a few exceptional domains in which the Athenians did provide for more straightforward enforcement of statutes.

[64] Lanni 2006:66–67.
[65] For discussion, see Lanni 2006:72.
[66] For discussion, see Lanni 2006:118–128.

2.2. Spheres of Enhanced Deterrence

The general observation that deterrence based on fear of formal legal sanctions was relatively weak does not apply to four distinctive areas of Athenian regulation: certain market and shipping transactions, some theft-related offenses, disorderly conduct at public gatherings, and treason and political corruption.[67] In these exceptional areas, legal uncertainty was reduced in some, but not necessarily all, stages of enforcement. We will see, for example, that the summary execution process for some theft-related offenses provided for more predictable guilt determinations and enforcement than the popular courts, but in most cases private initiative was still needed to arrest the offender. And in cases of suspected treason, political bodies like the Council might take responsibility for investigating and appointing prosecutors, but enforcement was still subject to the uncertainties of the jury trial process. Nevertheless, the more reliable law enforcement in these limited spheres must have gone a long way toward establishing a base level of physical and economic security for ordinary Athenians.

Economic Security

The use of magistrates to enforce a variety of rules related to market transactions is the most important exception to the Athenians' general reliance on private initiative in law enforcement. In many cases magistrates could determine guilt and impose summary fines up to a certain amount. This approach enhanced deterrence by eliminating the need for victims to initiate a formal lawsuit and by reducing the uncertainty related to jury trial outcomes. Of course, the enforcement of summary fines, just as in the case of fines imposed by court verdicts, remained unpredictable and dependent on private initiative. There is evidence that at least in some situations magistrates controlled enforcement as well. It seems that some officials could impose immediate physical punishments on slaves, and possibly even on free noncitizens, and we have at least one example in which immediate confiscation could be used as a penalty. Athens'

---

[67] E. Harris (2013:21–58) discusses summary enforcement in these areas, suggesting they were the predominant form of law enforcement in Athens rather than the anomalies. Rubinstein (Forthcoming) discusses examples of summary enforcement in the market and public spaces throughout the Greek world.

various market measures provided ordinary Athenians with some protection against fraud and deceit in day-to-day consumer transactions. At the other end of the spectrum – overseas commerce – Athens provided special procedures for disputes involving maritime contracts that facilitated trade by providing more predictable verdicts and reliable mechanisms for enforcing judgments.

The ten agoranomoi ("market controllers"), five of whom served in the city and five in the port of the Piraeus, supervised the sale of goods in the market and were responsible for ensuring that merchandise was pure and that transactions were carried out without deceit.[68] Ten magistrates, even with the help of slave assistants, were not nearly enough to effectively police the market through independent inspections and investigations. In most cases, they likely heard complaints from consumers[69] who believed they had been cheated in some way, for example, that they had been sold adulterated or defective goods,[70] or that a seller had lied in the course of the transaction,[71] or, less certainly, that the seller had disregarded price regulations.[72] The agoranomoi also helped maintain order in the market: in Aristophanes' Wasps a female bread seller summons Philocleon before the market official because he damaged her goods.[73]

The agoranomoi were permitted to impose fines on their own initiative.[74] Our sources do not mention the upper limit for summary fines by market officials. Athenian officials maintaining public order in other contexts

---

68 Ath. Pol. 51.1; Harp., Lexicon of the Ten Orators s.v. kata ten agoran apseudei (quoting Theophrastus). For discussion of the powers and duties of the agoranomoi, see, e.g., Rhodes 1993:575–576; MacDowell 1993:157; Stanley 1979; E. Harris 2007:162–163; Herman 2006:387. For discussion of the use of summary fines throughout the Greek world, see Rubinstein (Forthcoming); for discussion of market inspectors under Islamic law in Mamluk Egypt, see Stilt 2011:38–72, 127–193.

69 The prohibition on false statements applied to buyers as well as sellers, but as Johnstone (2011:12–13) points out, the use of coinage results in asymmetry in information, putting buyers at a disadvantage.

70 Ath. Pol. 51.1; Hyp. 3.15; Xen. Symposium 2.20, involving the weight of bread; cf. Athenaeus 6.225c, which describes a law forbidding fish-sellers from sprinkling fish with water, presumably to make it look fresher than it was; Dio Chrys. X.9.14, which discusses the right to return defective goods. For discussion see Stanley 1979:16–18.

71 For the law prohibiting making false statements in the agora, see Dem. 20.9; Hyp. 3.15.

72 We do not have direct classical evidence for the regulation of prices in Athens. For discussion of price regulation in other texts, see Pl. Laws 917b; Arist. Nichomachean Ethics 1133b14–15; Plaut. Miles Gloriosus 727–729; for discussion see Harrison 1998:25–26; Stanley 1979:17; Bresson 2000:151–208.

73 Ar. Wasps 1407.

74 Xen. Symposium 2.20.

could impose fines of up to 50 drachmas,[75] while other magistrates, including the Forty who decided minor cases, were limited to fines of 10 drachmas.[76] The daily wage in the later fourth century has been estimated at about 1.5 drachmas for an unskilled worker[77] and 2 to 2.5 drachmas for a skilled worker.[78] A 50-drachma fine was thus a significant sum for most ordinary Athenians, and even a 10-drachma fine represented several days' pay. There is also some suggestion in our sources that the *agoranomoi* might be permitted to whip offenders.[79] Presumably this punishment was not allowed in the case of citizens and was limited to slaves, and possibly also noncitizens.[80] Where the alleged offense merited a penalty beyond the limits of the magistrate's summary jurisdiction, it appears that officials were permitted to prosecute the case themselves in court,[81] though in practice it seems likely that the complaining party or informer usually served as the prosecutor.

Ten *metronomoi* ("controllers of measures"), five in the city and five in the Piraeus, were charged with ensuring that sellers used standard weights and measures.[82] Some fourth-century weights and measures found in the agora appear to have official stamps, which suggests that the *metronomoi* may have carried out periodic inspections and issued approval of the weights and measures being used in the market as well as receiving complaints from disgruntled buyers.[83] Although we have no direct evidence from classical Athens regarding how these officials enforced the law, it seems likely that they could impose fines up to a specified limit and bring suits just like other market officials. An inscription from the second century BCE suggests that the *metronomoi* may also have been able to impose immediate

75 Aesch. 1.35; MacDowell 1993:235–236.
76 *Ath. Pol.* 53. For a list of sources referring to fines imposed by magistrates, see Allen 2000a:343 n.17.
77 Allen 2000a:41.
78 Carey 2000:xxx.
79 Poll. 10.177; see also Ar. *Acharnians.* 723–724, 824–828, which refers to leather whips in connection with the *agoranomoi*; Stanley 1979:18. In the fifth century, the presence of Scythian archers may have helped some magistrates intimidate offenders into compliance, and passages in Aristophanes suggest that Scythians could manhandle offenders and assist magistrates in making arrests. Ar. *Acharnians* 54; *Lysistrata* 434, 445; *Thesmophoriazusae* 923.
80 On the use of physical punishments as a mechanism of separating slave from free, see Hunter 1994:154–184. Rhodes (1993:575–576) and Stanley (1979:18) suggest that market officials might also be permitted to use corporal punishment against free foreigners.
81 Todd 1993:92; MacDowell 1993:235–236.
82 *Ath. Pol* 51.2; MacDowell 1993:158; E. Harris 2013:31–32; Stanley 1979:18–19.
83 Lang and Crosby 1964:21, 22, 40; Stanley 1979:18.

punishment on violators: the inscription provides for the magistrate to destroy any undersized container and confiscate its contents.[84]

The regulation of Athenian silver coinage provides another example of the more straightforward deterrence regime employed in matters related to the market. Nikophron's law of 375/4, found on a stele in the agora, provides a detailed description of the process.[85] The law provides for two public slaves to serve as coin testers (*dokimastes*), one in the agora, and one in the Piraeus. Any seller who doubts the quality of a buyer's silver coins can present them to the tester. Any coins that are rejected are immediately confiscated from the buyer and taken out of circulation; coins that are approved must be accepted by the seller. If a seller refuses to accept approved coins, the buyer may report him to the relevant market official, who is empowered to decide cases worth up to 10 drachmas. Larger transactions are transferred to a court and are prosecuted by the private individual who reported the violation to the magistrate. In this way, the law not only prevented buyers from attempting to pass off counterfeit coins, but also deterred sellers from demanding an unfairly high price on the grounds that some of the buyer's coins might be suspect.[86]

Due to Athens' heavy dependence on imported grain, both wholesale trade and retail sale of grain and bread was heavily regulated to ensure sufficient supply and fair prices. The *sitophylakes* (guardians of grain) were charged with making sure that grain was sold in the market at a fair price, and that millers and bread-sellers did not impose too high a mark-up in setting their prices.[87] It seems that *sitophylakes* could impose summary fines of up to 10 drachmas.[88] The *Constitution of the Athenians* reports that the number of *sitophylakes* was raised from five in the city and five in the Piraeus to twenty in the city and fifteen for the Piraeus.[89] The fact that four times as many officials were devoted to supervising grain prices than were assigned to supervise all other sales in the city market suggests that the *sitophylakes* may have taken a proactive role in enforcing fair prices rather than simply responding to complaints.

---

[84] IG ii² 1013, lines 27–29; for discussion, see E. Harris 2013:31–32.

[85] For a complete translation and extensive discussion of the law, see Ober 2008a:220–245.

[86] On why the penalties in the law seem targeted at sellers, see Johnstone 2011:30–33.

[87] *Ath. Pol.* 51.3; Rhodes 1993:577–578; E. Cohen 2005:297–300; Gauthier 1981.

[88] SEG 26:72.22–26; Gauthier 1971:44–79.

[89] *Ath. Pol.* 51.3.

As Rubinstein has pointed out, the use of summary fines to enforce a variety of small-scale market regulations, attested in both democratic and oligarchic city-states throughout the Greek world, can most likely be traced to practical considerations.[90] We have seen that uncertainty regarding trial outcomes and the difficulty of enforcing judgments may have discouraged prosecutions even where a significant amount of money was at stake; it is hard to imagine anyone bothering to bring formal prosecutions for consumer fraud amounting to less than 10 or 50 drachmas.[91] Yet in the aggregate these minor offenses were costly to buyers and reduced trust in the market, thereby discouraging mutually beneficial economic transactions with unknown vendors. The fact that many market traders were not Athenian citizens also meant that they were largely immune from the various non-Austinian mechanisms through which formal legal institutions fostered compliance with norms discussed in Chapters 3–6. For all these reasons, summary fines were needed to deter minor fraud in the market and provide the minimal assurances of economic security necessary for everyday market transactions.

The final example of enhanced deterrence in market transactions is of a different character from the others. While low-level market disputes were referred to magistrates with summary jurisdiction, the special procedures for maritime commercial suits (*dikai emporikai*) offered speed and more predictable decisions and enforcement within the context of a formal court process.[92] The *dike emporike*, introduced in the middle of the fourth century BCE, was a special procedure that was available in cases involving a written contract for shipment to and from Athens.[93] These maritime suits were tried in the popular courts before ordinary juries, but had a variety of distinctive features, including equal standing for foreigners and metics and expedited procedures to make it more convenient for wronged traders to bring suit.[94] Even more important for our purposes, the *dikai emporikai* required foreigners to post bail before trial to prevent flight and stipulated that the losing party be imprisoned until the judgment was paid.[95]

90 Rubinstein (Forthcoming:31–37).
91 Rubinstein (Forthcoming:32) points out that the low status, and often foreign extraction, of most traders also made them unlikely targets for volunteer prosecutors motivated by political rivalry or personal enmity.
92 On the *dikai emporikai*, see Lanni 2006:149–174.
93 Lanni 2006:151.
94 Lanni 2006:152–155.
95 Dem. 32.29; 33.1. E. Cohen 2005:301–302.

Jury verdicts may also have been more predictable as well, since litigants in maritime suits tended to focus their arguments on the terms of the written contract between the parties and relied less on the extralegal argumentation common in ordinary popular court trials.[96] In this way, the special features of the commercial maritime procedures enhanced deterrence by making prosecution and enforcement more likely and reducing uncertainty surrounding verdicts. The special maritime procedures were likely introduced with the explicit aim of attracting foreign merchants to Athens by providing them with a reliable and predictable mechanism for enforcing their contracts.[97]

Maintaining Order in Public Spaces

Just as in the case of minor market violations, magistrates used their powers to issue summary fines to address disorderly conduct in the city, including both rowdy behavior at public gatherings and violations of building and sanitation regulations. It seems likely that most of these offenses were resolved in a straightforward manner by a magistrate's warning or small fine and never reached the court system, though in principle a magistrate who believed a higher penalty was warranted could prosecute the offender in court.[98]

Ten *astynomoi* ("city controllers"), five in the city and five in the Piraeus, enforced a variety of regulations aimed at maintaining a minimal level of public order in the city.[99] The *Constitution of the Athenians* reports that their duties included ensuring that the dung collectors properly removed dung from the city, that buildings were constructed in a way that did not encroach on the street or empty waste into the road, and that corpses were removed from the streets.[100] Other officials enforced similar sorts of regulations in public sanctuaries.[101] A fifth-century Athenian inscription, for example, authorizes treasurers to fine anyone who lights fires, camps, or fails to dispose of animal dung on the Acropolis.[102]

---

96 Lanni 2006:161–171.
97 For discussion, see Lanni 2006:171–174.
98 MacDowell 1993:159, 235–236.
99 For discussion, see MacDowell 1993:159; E. Harris 2013:30; Rhodes 1993:573–574.
100 *Ath. Pol.* 50.2. As MacDowell (1993:159) points out, this list of responsibilities is probably not comprehensive.
101 For other examples, see E. Harris 2013:33.
102 IG i³ 4, lines B6–16; E. Harris 2007:174 (listing other examples); E. Harris 2013:33; Rubinstein (Forthcoming) (discussing similar provisions outside of Athens).

Disorderly conduct in public spaces was also dealt with summarily. In the fifth century, public slaves, known as the Scythian archers, helped maintain order at public gatherings in the city: in Aristophanes' comedies they are shown physically removing or whipping drunken and disruptive individuals in the market, at the Assembly, and in the Council, often at the behest of a magistrate.[103] It seems that the use of Scythian archers was abandoned early in the fourth century.[104] Public slaves assisted magistrates throughout the fourth century, but our sources do not mention these slaves engaging in crowd control. As we have already seen in the case of the *agoranomoi* ("market controllers"), magistrates who supervised public areas or public events were often permitted to issue summary fines to maintain order. For example, the chairmen (*proedroi*) who presided at the Council and Assembly meetings in the fourth century were empowered to impose a fine of up to 50 drachmas on any speaker who disregarded the agenda or was abusive or disruptive.[105] The magistrates responsible for organizing festivals were similarly permitted to summarily fine disruptive individuals for up to 50 drachmas.[106]

Just as in the case of minor market violations, the elaborate popular court process was ill-suited to address drunk and disorderly conduct and minor violations of building and sanitation regulations.[107] These minor infractions had the potential to cause significant harm by disrupting the political process, causing destruction and injury at festivals and other public events, or interfering with the city's water supply. Yet it is hard to imagine volunteer prosecutors ever taking on such cases. Small fines imposed summarily by magistrates may have been the only viable option for enforcing these regulations.[108]

---

[103] Ar. *Acharnians* 54–57; *Ecclesiazusae* 143; *Knights* 258–259; see also Xen. *Memorabilia* 3.6.1; Pl., *Protagoras* 319c; Poll. 8.131–132. It is generally assumed that they also exercised crowd control at festivals, though there is no specific mention of this in the sources. For discussion, see Hunter 1994:145–147; E. Harris 2013:39; Yakobson 2011.

[104] Hunter 1994:147, 235 n.61.

[105] Aesch. 1.35; *Ath. Pol.* 44.1; MacDowell 1993:235.

[106] Dem. 21.179; IG i² 84.26–30; MacDowell 1993:235–236.

[107] Rubinstein (Forthcoming:31–37).

[108] A similar explanation may be behind a somewhat anomalous exception to the reliance on private initiative in the Athenian legal system: the eponymous archon had the power to fine individuals who wronged orphans, heiresses, and pregnant widows (*Ath. Pol.* 56.7), presumably because these victims often did not have anyone to pursue grievances on their behalf.

Security from Theft

Both citizens and noncitizens who manifestly committed certain theft-related offenses could be condemned to death without trial through extraordinary summary procedures. The most common form of summary process eliminated the uncertainty surrounding jury verdicts and enforcement by providing for summary execution by a board of magistrates, but retained the necessity of private initiative by requiring the victim to personally arrest the offender and drag him before the Board of Eleven. A related procedure further enhanced deterrence by permitting victims to request that a magistrate arrest the offender.

The *apagoge kakourgon* procedure permitted victims to summarily arrest *kakourgoi* ("wrongdoers") and haul them before the Eleven. Several sources indicate that the category of *kakourgoi* included thieves (*kleptai*),[109] kidnappers (*andrapodistai*), and cloak-stealers (*lopodytai*).[110] There is some uncertainty about which other offenses were subject to *apagoge*, but it seems likely that house burglars (*toichorychoi*), cutpurses (*ballantiotomoi*), bandits (*lestai*), and temple-robbers (*hierosyloi*) were also included.[111] Summary arrest of *kakourgoi* was permitted only if the offender had been caught *ep'autophoro*, which is sometimes translated "in the act," but probably also included situations where guilt was manifest, as, for example, where a thief was found with the stolen goods on his person.[112] If the accused admitted his guilt – or perhaps if he simply was unable to offer a plausible explanation for his possession of the stolen goods[113] – the Eleven immediately executed him without trial. If the accused denied guilt, the Eleven held him for trial in the popular courts.[114]

---

109 Dem. 24.113 suggests that only thieves who stole at night or who stole goods worth more than 50 drachmas were subject to *apagoge*. This limitation on the value of the stolen goods may not be significant if cutpurses (*ballantiotomoi*) were included among the *kakourgoi* since presumably cutpurses often netted less than 50 drachmas from each victim.

110 E.g., *Ath. Pol.* 52.1. For a list of the sources referring to *kakourgoi*, with discussion, see Hansen 1976:36–48.

111 Dem. 35.47; Pl., *Republic* 552d1–6, 575b6–7; Xen. *Memorabilia* 1.2.62; Lys. 13.78; Dem. 7.14. For discussion of these and other possible additions, including adulterers, homicides, and theft in *gymnasia* and harbors, see, e.g., Hansen 1976:36–48; D. Cohen 1983:52–62; Hunter 1994:135–136; E. Harris 1994b:181–182; Hunter 2007:9–10; Fisher 1999:61–62; Gagarin 2003:185.

112 Lys. 13.86; Dem. 45.8; Aesch. 1.91; for discussion see Hansen 1976:48–53; E. Harris 1994b; cf. Carawan 1984.

113 *Ath. Pol.* 52.1; Dem. 45.81; Todd 1993:80–81.

114 *Ath. Pol.* 52.1.

A related summary procedure, *ephegesis*, was similar to *apagoge* except that a magistrate carried out the arrest at the request of the victim and dragged the wrongdoer before the Eleven.[115] Even this summary procedure required some private initiative, since in most cases of *ephegesis* the victim and his friends were required to physically detain the offender while the magistrate was summoned; in others the victim may have been able to lead the magistrate to the wrongdoer's location.[116] While several sources refer to the use of the *apagoge* summary arrest procedure, there are very few references to summary arrest by a magistrate through *ephegesis*. As Hunter points out, it is impossible to know whether the lack of evidence for *ephegesis* suggests that this procedure was rarely used, or merely that it was used by helpless individuals whose activities rarely show up in our surviving sources.[117]

Why did the Athenians use such extraordinary procedures for certain theft-related offenses, permitting the imposition of the death penalty without authorization from a jury or a popular Assembly? Gagarin points out that *apagoge* is unusual in that it names a category of offenders (*kakourgoi*) rather than offenses, and suggests that the law was directed at "career criminals" who were not thought to deserve the benefits of the full legal process.[118] Common criminals with few close community ties were also presumably likely to flee prior to trial, which made summary process more attractive.[119] And the requirement that the offender's guilt be obvious may have made a trial seem unnecessary, particularly since *kakourgoi* were unlikely to have significant extralegal arguments to draw on, and must have diminished any unease created by giving magistrates power to impose such a harsh penalty. What is most important for our purposes is the undeniable effect of the existence of such summary procedures. The possibility of immediate arrest and summary execution must have augmented the deterrent effect of these theft-related statutes. The awareness that robbers and thieves who were caught would be immediately dealt with must have greatly enhanced Athenians' perception of personal security and public

---

115 Dem. 22.26; Hansen 1976:24–28; Hunter 1994:136–137.
116 Fisher 1999:62.
117 Hunter 1994:136–137.
118 Gagarin 2003:185–187.
119 Perhaps for this reason, it appears that the Eleven imprisoned *kakourgoi* who denied guilt prior to trial (*Ath. Pol.* 52.1).

order, despite the lack of predictability surrounding the enforcement of statutes in other areas.[120]

Securing the Democracy

The final exception to the Athenians' reliance on private initiative involved threats to the democracy. This category includes two types of case: one extraordinary and one routine. In cases of alleged treason and subverting the democracy, Athens' political institutions could investigate allegations and appoint public prosecutors, thereby enhancing deterrence by making prosecution for these crimes more reliable. Second, the Council regularly inspected the financial accounts of magistrates both during and after their term in office to deter corruption.

Although the details are sometimes obscure, it is clear that when Athens' political bodies became aware of potential acts of treason the state could take the initiative to investigate allegations and bring charges.[121] The most famous example is the reaction to the mutilation of the Herms and the profanation of the Mysteries in 415 BCE, religious crimes that were widely interpreted as attempts to sabotage the Athenians' naval expedition to Sicily and overthrow the democracy.[122] The Assembly authorized the Council to make arrests and conduct a wide-ranging investigation that resulted in several court trials.[123] It seems likely that throughout the classical period the Council had the power to investigate and make arrests in response to any allegations of treason made by individual informers.[124] It is also possible that when the Council or Assembly referred treason cases under the *eisangelia* procedure for trial, they could appoint a team of public prosecutors (*kategoroi*) in addition to, or instead of, the volunteer who had initially brought the accusation.[125] The *apophasis* procedure, introduced

---

[120] This was all the more true when we consider the legal right to use self-help to respond to violent attacks and night thieves discussed in Chapter 1.

[121] There are also a couple of instances of the Council contemplating or carrying out summary executions in times of emergency, but it seems likely that in these cases the Council exceeded its authority. For discussion, see Rhodes 1972:179–207; MacDowell 1993:189–190; cf. Hansen 1999:257.

[122] Finley 1983:21; Hunter 1994:120; MacDowell 1993:182; Rhodes 1972:186–188.

[123] And. 1.11–15; Rhodes 1972:186–188.

[124] Lys. 13.21–23, 30–35, 55–56; Dem. 24.11, 63, 144–146; Din. 1.5; MacDowell 1993:181–183.

[125] For discussion of the evidence and modern debate, see Rubinstein 2000:115–122; see also MacDowell 1993:61–62.

around 340 BCE, was used for allegations of treason, subversion of the democracy, and political bribery.[126] Under this procedure, the Areopagus could investigate allegations at the request of the Assembly or on its own initiative and present a report to the Assembly.[127] If the Assembly determined that the case should be pursued, it passed a decree outlining the charges and potential penalty and appointing public prosecutors (*kategoroi*) to prosecute the case in court.[128]

The final exception to the reliance on private initiative is the Council's regular inspections of officials' accounts both during and after their tenure in office. Ten members of the Council served as a board of auditors (*logistai*) charged with inspecting each magistrate's account every month to detect financial malfeasance.[129] If they discovered evidence of wrongdoing, the Council could fine the magistrate up to 500 drachmas or could appoint prosecutors and refer the case to a popular court to seek a higher penalty.[130] Upon leaving office, each magistrate also underwent an extensive accounting (*euthyna*).[131] The first stage of this procedure involved inspection of the official's financial accounts for evidence of embezzlement, bribery, or financial mismanagement by a board of auditors (also called *logistai*) chosen by lot from the people. The auditors convened a popular court to determine whether the magistrate had passed this portion of the audit. At this court hearing, public prosecutors (*sunegoroi*) presented any charges that arose out of the audit, and members of the public were invited to bring forward accusations for the jury's consideration as well. In this way, the state not only encouraged informers to report wrongdoing but used state officials to actively seek out and prosecute financial misconduct by magistrates.

The exceptional use of state coercion in response to the existential threat of treason hardly needs an explanation, but the reason for the Athenians' unusually proactive approach to policing official corruption may be less obvious. Without active investigation, many instances of embezzlement

---

126 Din. 1.63; Din. 1.3, 58, 63 112; Hyp. 1.2, 38; Dem. 18.133. For discussion, see Wallace 1989:113–119; Hansen 1999:292–294; MacDowell 1993:190–191.

127 Dem. 18.133; Din. 1.4, 58, 63.

128 Din. 1.50–51, 58; Hyp. 1.38; for discussion see Rubinstein 2000:113–114.

129 *Ath. Pol.* 48.3; 45.2; Ant. 6.35, 49; for discussion see Hansen 1999:220–221; Hansen 1975:21–28; Rhodes 1972:147–162; MacDowell 1993:169–170.

130 MacDowell 1993:170.

131 For discussion, see MacDowell 1993:170–171; Hansen 1999:222–224.

and bribery might be difficult to detect,[132] even where a personal or political enemy stood willing to serve as a volunteer prosecutor. In fact, while the regular examination of the accounts must have helped deter embezzlement, even the accounting may not have turned up evidence of cases where an Athenian willingly bribed a magistrate.[133] Nevertheless, the invitation for anyone who might know of such an arrangement to make an accusation without bearing the responsibility of bringing a prosecution may have generated some deterrence. In addition to practical considerations, political ideology may also have played a role. Since accountability of public officials was considered a defining feature of the democracy,[134] the elaborate and public accounting procedures may have served as an important democratic symbol.

✳✳✳

The use of summary jurisdiction by magistrates, particularly in regulating the market, maintaining order in public spaces, and responding to certain theft offenses, must have significantly enhanced deterrence in these areas. Despite the uncertainty and lack of predictability that plagued the popular court process, these exceptional procedures provided the basic economic and physical security needed for the city and market to function. Summary jurisdiction was particularly important for disciplining foreigners who were largely unaffected by the various non-Austinian mechanisms of maintaining order discussed in Chapters 3–6. The exercise of summary jurisdiction must have loomed large in the everyday experience of ordinary Athenians; as Rubinstein points out, for many Athenians, summary fines inflicted by magistrates may well have represented the "main personal encounter with the administration of penal justice."[135]

But these areas of relatively straightforward crime and punishment should not obscure the many other offenses where the punishment was uncertain. Market fines – limited in most cases to 10 drachmas and in no case higher than 50 drachmas – would apply to daily consumer purchases,

---

[132] The difficulty of detecting magistrates' wrongdoing may be one reason why the Athenians used collective sanctions against boards of magistrates, thereby encouraging members of the board to deter, detect, and punish malfeasance by other board members. For discussion, see Lanni (Forthcoming); Rubinstein (2012); Johnstone 2011:127–147.

[133] In fact, bribery charges were not primarily addressed through the *euthyna* but were commonly brought through regular court procedures.

[134] E.g., Hdt. 3.80.

[135] Rubinstein (Forthcoming:37). E. Harris (2013:28–59) goes much further, suggesting that enforcement by officials was the main form of policing in Athens, not the exception.

but not larger economic transactions; in fact, we will look in detail at a popular court trial involving a claim of fraud in a market sale in Chapter 5. Moreover, the small number of magistrates – for instance, a mere five *agoranomoi* were charged with maintaining order, ensuring that goods sold were unadulterated, and preventing fraud in the city market – meant that officials could not possibly address more than a small percentage of violations. And, of course, the magistrates' summary jurisdiction did not include all the sorts of personal and property disputes that kept the courts busy enough to give Athens a reputation for litigiousness. Perhaps most important for our purposes, summary enforcement did not address many of the victimless offenses that we have seen were only sporadically enforced through straightforward enforcement in court. In the remainder of this book, I will explore the various mechanisms through which Athens' formal legal institutions fostered compliance with the norms not reached through summary jurisdiction.

PART TWO

THREE

The Expressive Effect of Statutes

Given that the Athenian courts did not predictably enforce statutes, a traditional Austinian view of law would suggest that Athenian laws played little role in maintaining order. But a law's impact is not limited to the direct effect produced by the sanction or incentive created by a law; law can serve a variety of other roles — symbolic,[1] constitutive,[2] for example — that have profound effects on society. Some scholars working on modern law have tried to describe some of the mechanisms through which a law may strengthen, weaken, or change social norms and thereby indirectly affect individuals' behavior.[3] To cite a simple example, an antilittering ordinance may have a significant impact even if it is rarely (or never) officially enforced.[4] The law may serve an "expressive function,"[5] communicating that the community disapproves of those who litter, and emboldening individuals to enforce the law informally, thereby changing both the norms and behavior surrounding the disposal of waste. Other modern examples of statutes that have significant symbolic content and may have important independent expressive effects include antidiscrimination laws, drunk driving laws, and hate crime legislation.

---

[1] The symbolic role of law is most commonly used in the sense that law can make a powerful statement about the social values and priorities of the sovereign/people.

[2] The notion here is that law and legal categories play a constitutive role by shaping identities, social relationships, and baseline expectations. See, e.g., Geertz 1983:167–236; Gordon 1984:109–110.

[3] Lessig 1998:661; Sunstein 1996a:2024–2025.

[4] Cooter 2000:11.

[5] Sunstein 1996a:2024 defines the expressive function of law as the "function of law in 'making statements'" as opposed to controlling behavior directly."

In this chapter I argue that Athenian statutes played an important role in fostering compliance with law even though they were not predictably enforced through the courts. I try to show that Athenian statutes had important effects on Athenian social life quite apart from any direct effects of the sanction provided in the law. Drawing on recent research by legal scholars and sociologists on the mechanisms of social influence, I first discuss the theory of the expressive function of law and the benefits of applying these insights to ancient Athens. I also try to identify some features of Athenian life (such as the greater popular participation in government and the judicial process) that may have made the expressive power of laws greater in Athens than it is today in the United States. I then provide case studies of two sets of Athenian statutes whose impact extended well beyond the relatively few cases in which they were enforced through the court system.

In the first case study, I examine the expressive effects of the statute prohibiting *hubris* ("outrage" or intentionally treating someone with dishonor).[6] This statute was unusual, perhaps unique, in that it protected slaves as well as freepersons. But because slaves did not have standing to bring suits, this law was rarely enforced in court. The *hubris* law played a prominent role in Athenian public discourse because deterrence of *hubris* was thought vital to social stability in the democracy. The expressive effect of the *hubris* law may explain the Athenians' unusual solicitude toward others' slaves, particularly in the agora. In this way, the *hubris* law may have reduced violence and promoted security in business transactions.

The second case study concerns laws that barred high-level political participation by male citizens who had previously worked as prostitutes,[7] and the effect these laws may have had on social norms and practices related to homosexual pederasty.[8] According to the current scholarly consensus, these laws reflect an Athenian conception of a private sphere in which homoerotic and other sexual activity was free from regulation so long as it did not infringe on the political life of the city.[9] Under this

6 I discuss the contours of the offense of *hubris* subsequently.
7 "Prostitution" is an imperfect translation for *hetairesis*. I discuss the details of the laws and the meaning of this term later in this chapter.
8 Pederasty, deriving from the Greek word *pederasteia*, is the standard term used by classicists for a particular set of ancient Greek sexual practices which will be described in more detail subsequently. This term is far from perfect given the potential for unfortunate and misleading associations with contemporary notions of pedophilia. But it has the virtue of emphasizing to the reader that we are discussing a cultural context entirely different from our own, and in this respect is less misleading than a term like "Greek homosexuality."
9 D. Cohen 1991a:222–223; Wallace 1997; Fisher 2001:39.

view, the law's practical effect was limited to a very small number of elites who might anticipate taking an active role in the city's politics.[10] But my argument is that when the expressive function of the laws is taken into account, the laws may have had a much broader practical impact, one that influenced norms regarding purely private conduct and reached beyond the handful of politically active citizens.

I should say at the outset that it is always difficult to establish definitively that any change in norms is attributable to a particular law (rather than the other way around), and doing so for ancient Athens is impossible. Law is part of culture and the relationship between law and society is recursive, not unidirectional. Nonetheless, we will see that because of the structure of Athens' democratic institutions, the passage of a statute in the Athenian Assembly crystallized and publicized the community's shared cultural values in a way that modern legislation does not, making it particularly likely that the statement made by the law (as opposed to the cultural norms that produced the law) would have an effect on behavior. Moreover, the second case study provides some evidence that Athenian laws had real independent effects on behavior.

The two case studies involve statutes that regulate norms and practices that generated a lot of literary evidence, in large part because they were controversial. For this reason, we will see that the expressive effects of these laws were varied and at times unintended and counterproductive. The expressive effects of ordinary statutes reflecting uncontroversial norms — statutes prohibiting theft, mistreatment of parents, or false statements in the agora, for example — were more predictable and straightforward, though less dramatic because these statutes reinforced and lent moral authority to well-established norms rather than changing them. In doing so, they may have helped foster compliance with these laws. In this way, Athenian statutes may have played a larger role in Athens' success as a well-ordered society than has been previously supposed.

3.1. The Expressive Function of Law

There is a large interdisciplinary literature on the mechanisms of social influence and the interaction between laws, norms, and practices. A detailed discussion of this field is beyond the scope of this book; in this section

---

10 Winkler 1990:46, 56–59; D. Cohen 1991a:222–223; Halperin 1990:98–99.

I highlight just one of the possible mechanisms through which a statute may have an expressive effect on behavior in a democratic society. In what follows, I combine theoretical discussion from the law review literature with the empirical findings in the sociological literature on the mechanisms of social influence.

One theory about how law may influence norms in a democratic society is by signaling a popular consensus about a social practice.[11] In some cases, a statute simply publicizes and lends moral authority to a widely held norm.[12] In other cases, where public opinion about an issue is divided or is in flux, individuals may not know what the majority view is, especially since people tend to associate with like-minded individuals and exaggerate the typicality of their own views.[13] In these situations, the passing of a statute reveals the wider community's majority view about a given issue. In both cases, the passage of a law may embolden individuals in the majority to informally sanction those who do not comply.[14] And individuals in the minority may feel pressure to conform for a variety of reasons: (1) they fear informal sanctions that may be visited upon them by members of the majority; (2) they desire social approval; and (3) they experience psychological pressures to conform, most notably cognitive "dissonance associated with conduct that is inconsistent with an actor's identity or social roles."[15] In this way, legislation alone, it is argued, can shape or significantly strengthen social norms. Over time, those who were in the minority and those who were undecided may even internalize the norm, though this is not necessary to foster compliance with the law.[16]

Pooper-scooper, antilittering, and antismoking ordinances are often cited as examples of laws that have altered social norms by publicizing a changing public consensus regarding these practices and by encouraging informal enforcement by the public.[17] Under the right conditions, laws

---

[11] The discussion in this paragraph draws heavily on McAdams' theory (1997:400–408) of how laws can change norms and on the summary of mechanisms of social influence provided in Goodman and Jinks 2004:638–644.

[12] Robinson and Darley 1997:473–475.

[13] McAdams 1997:400–408.

[14] McAdams 1997:400–408. Sometimes, as in the case of gay marriage bans, the passage of a statute indicates not widespread consensus, but a growing minority view, which leads the majority to pass legislation clarifying that they still are in the majority, which may bolster and embolden their members.

[15] Goodman and Jinks 2004:640.

[16] McAdams 1997:404.

[17] Cooter 2000:11; McAdams 1997:400–408.

can thus promote a desired behavior apart from, and perhaps even in the absence of, formal enforcement of the law. Under this theory, individuals will only feel the sting of potential social sanctions for noncompliance if they view the majority who support the law as a reference group whose approval or disapproval matters to them.[18] When a group norm is expressed through legislation, the law's ability to influence behavior also depends on the law's "perceived legitimacy," that is, whether the target individual accepts the law as a source of moral authority.[19]

For these reasons, in some cases the expressive effect of a law may make that law counterproductive by weakening the very norms that its sanctions seek to enforce.[20] This can happen if members of the subgroup targeted by the law are impervious to, or are even encouraged and radicalized by, the public statement of disapproval expressed in the law. Laws banning Internet file-sharing, for example, appear to have been ineffective, and possibly even counterproductive, among young adults in Sweden.[21] A law that provokes resistance from a subgroup affected by the law may not only undermine the specific norm but may also weaken the legitimacy of the legal system as a whole in the eyes of members of that subgroup. Some scholars have suggested that the harsh penalties associated with the war on drugs have led to precisely this result.[22]

It is probably not an accident that the examples that seem to suggest a relatively straightforward enhanced compliance effect – littering, smoking, and so on – involve changing norms that are not central to the actor's identity; the expressive power of law is less likely to completely reverse a practice in which an actor or group is deeply invested. But that is not to say that the expressive power of law cannot influence practices that implicate important norms. For one thing, there may be norms regarding practices that are important from a societal point of view – for example, attitudes toward drunk driving – that most individuals are not deeply invested in,

---

[18] Social impact theory suggests a number of factors that influence the ability of a law to exert the kind of social and cognitive pressures to conform described earlier. According to social impact theory, compliance in response to social pressures to conform to a group norm becomes more likely (1) the more important the group is to the individual; (2) the more important the norm is to the group; and (3) the more interaction the individual has with the group (Goodman and Jinks 2004:642).

[19] Robinson and Darley 1997:474–475; Tyler 1990:64–68.

[20] Lessig 1998:669.

[21] Lewin 2008:188–191.

[22] Meares 1997.

and are thus open to change. And even where the expressive power of law runs up against deeply held norms, it may not result in the type of dramatic reversal of practices that we've seen in smoking, but it may still alter behavior by, for example, driving the practice underground. Perhaps most important for the question of how underenforced laws may have helped foster order in Athens, the expressive power of law may play an important role in strengthening uncontroversial existing norms and thereby encouraging compliance.

Before discussing the expressive effect of law in Athens, a few words on methodology and the limits of our evidence are in order. Much modern norms scholarship in the law review literature operates primarily on a theoretical level.[23] Many studies adopt a particular interpretation of a statute's communicative content without offering specific evidence supporting these assertions.[24] Critics of these types of studies have pointed out that there are often several plausible hypotheses for the expressive effect of a law.[25] Moreover, different individuals and subcultures might well interpret and react to a law in different ways. The dynamics by which laws may penetrate, shape, and be assimilated or resisted by informal norms or practices is highly contingent on the particular social and cultural context. Because of the lack of evidence and apparent non-falsifiability of much law review work on the expressive effects of laws, some legal scholars are skeptical about the usefulness of norms scholarship. In response to these criticisms, several scholars with a grounding in empirical sociology of law have called for a more in-depth, qualitative, and context-specific approach to analyzing the expressive effect of laws.[26]

Of course, we cannot interview the Athenians about their reactions to the passage of various laws. But we are not limited to a purely theoretical and speculative exercise. Our literary and forensic evidence often tells us a good deal about the message that prominent laws were perceived to convey, how the social meaning of various practices changed over time, and how different social classes were likely to react to statements of approval

---

[23] For discussion and criticism of purely theoretical norms scholarship, see Harcourt 2000; Goodman 2001:545–646; Tushnet 1998.

[24] For discussion, see Harcourt 2000.

[25] Weisberg 2003; Harcourt 2000; Tushnet 1998.

[26] Goodman 2001; Harcourt 2000; Tushnet 1998. One study that illustrates the gold standard for such an approach examines the effects of South Africa's unenforced sodomy laws through in-depth interviews of gays and lesbians conducted both before and after the repeal of these laws (Goodman 2001).

or disapproval from the popular Assembly. We can use this evidence to formulate hypotheses about the possible expressive effects of the two laws under discussion in our case studies. And while we cannot verify these hypotheses conclusively, we will see that they are supported by what our sources tell us about Athenian social practices. The case studies in this chapter thus attempt to provide a "thick description" of the expressive effects of two Athenian laws. The difficulty of separating out the effects of the law as opposed to broader cultural norms remains. But we will see that at least in our second case study there is reason to believe that the effects we observe are linked to the specific expressive message communicated by the statute rather than to the popular attitudes that led to the enactment of the statute.

The Expressive Role of Law in Athens

The particular mechanism through which law may influence behavior described previously presupposes a democracy in which statutes are perceived to reflect the views of the majority of the community. For this reason, this mechanism cannot be applied to many ancient societies and city-states,[27] but it can be safely applied to a direct democracy like Athens. In fact, the expressive function of law may have served an even more important role in ancient Athens than it does today. Laws passed in the Athenian Assembly were comparatively direct, well-publicized expressions of community sentiment. The symbolic function of law may have been particularly powerful in ancient Athens because it offered a more direct expression of community sentiment than contemporary legislation. Today in the United States, it is not always clear that a law accurately expresses the majority view on an issue – for example, legislation can reflect the preferences of powerful interest groups or the idiosyncratic preferences of individual members of Congress.[28] A law provides at best only a noisy

---

[27] This is not to say that statutes enacted under monarchies have no symbolic or expressive power. In fact, the most famous ancient set of laws – the law collection of Hammurabi – appears not to have been enforced in actual cases, leading some scholars to argue that it was purely symbolic legislation (e.g., Westbrook 1989; Roth 2000). But the specific mechanisms through which law enacted by a sovereign might (or might not) have an expressive effect on actual behavior would be different from those described earlier, which presume informal sanctions imposed by ordinary citizens.

[28] McAdams (1997:403) points out that in a representative democracy laws will often not reflect a consensus of the public at large.

signal as to the current consensus or majority viewpoint. This difficulty was significantly reduced in Athens. There were no political parties or organized interest groups. In the fifth century, all Athenian statutes were voted on directly by thousands of citizens in the popular assembly.[29] The agenda for the Assembly was set by the Council, a group of 500 citizens selected by lot for a one-year term. In the fourth century, a more complicated procedure was adopted for passing new laws (*nomoi*, as opposed to more temporary measures still passed in the Assembly), but this process also involved a vote in the Assembly to change the existing law followed by a trial before a panel of hundreds of citizens drawn from the pool of jurors.[30] The procedure for voting in the Assembly – a show of hands in which the minority is never counted, and may even have been encouraged to change their vote when it became clear they were in the minority[31] – may have helped create an impression that a law represented a statement of the unified demos rather than a majority of a divided populace. Indeed, as Ober has shown, *homonoia* ("same-mindedness" or consensus) was celebrated as a democratic virtue in fourth-century Athens.[32] To be sure, there are famous examples from Thucydides where rhetoric and group dynamics arguably distorted decisions taken by the Athenian Assembly.[33] But compared to modern lawmaking, Athenian statutes appear to be relatively direct expressions of community sentiment.

The Athenian process of legislation also ensured that the laws were well-publicized. For those who were not present in the Assembly when a law was passed, the laws were inscribed on stelai and displayed in public. It appears that in the classical period functional literacy extended beyond members of the elite, and several passages in the orators refer to Athenians of different social classes reading the laws.[34] Hundreds of jurors at a time were exposed to Athenian statutes when litigants had them read out during court cases. This familiarity with laws was all the greater because litigation was endemic in Athens, and litigants often call for several laws to be read

---

[29] Hansen (1999:90–93, 130) estimates that at least 6,000 people, or about one-fifth of the adult male citizen population, would ordinarily be present in the Assembly.

[30] Hansen 1999:165–175.

[31] Schwartzberg 2010.

[32] E.g., Dem. 25.89–90; Hyp. 4.37; Din. 3.19; for discussion see Ober 1989:297.

[33] The Athenians' quick change of heart after condemning the Mytileneans is the most prominent example (Thuc. 3.36–50).

[34] Gagarin 2008:176–177; Missiou 2011:11–35; 143–149. For a more skeptical view, see W. Harris 1991.

out in addition to the statute under which the case was brought.[35] Because much modern legislation is technical and largely unfamiliar to the general public, only a small percentage of laws are likely to have an expressive effect.[36] In Athens, by contrast, the expressive function of law was potentially implicated in every decision of the Assembly.

Plato, at least, was aware of the expressive power of law and attempted to harness this power in his model constitution, the *Laws*.[37] He argues that it is better to use law to persuade citizens to obey, making direct sanctions unnecessary.[38] To enhance the expressive power of the law, Plato adds preambles explaining various statutes to citizens. Although Plato describes the preambles as intended to rationally persuade educated citizens of the justice of the law,[39] Yunis has pointed out that the vast majority of the preambles in the *Laws* take the form of preachy admonitions that had the effect of lending moral and emotional force to the law rather than offering reasoned argument.[40] The notion that statutes could play a symbolic role and could have an important effect on behavior even in the absence of direct enforcement was thus familiar to Athenians in the classical period.

3.2. The Law Prohibiting *Hubris* and the Treatment of Slaves

This section presents the first of two case studies on the expressive effect Athenian statutes had on social norms and practices. What appears to be an accurate text of the law prohibiting *hubris* ("outrage") is preserved in Demosthenes' *Against Meidias*:

> If anyone commits *hubris* against anyone, either a child or a woman or a man, whether slave or free, or does anything improper (*paranomon*) to any of these people, let anyone who is willing of the eligible Athenians bring a *graphe* before the Thesmothetai....[41]

---

35 E.g., Aesch. 1; Dem. 54; Hyp.3.
36 McAdams 1997:403–404.
37 Discussions in the law court speeches tend to emphasize the importance of the deterrent and educative effect of direct sanctions enforced through the courts (e.g., Dem. 25.17; Lyc. 1.117–119; Dem. 24.68). This is not surprising since these statements tend to come from prosecutors trying to convince the jury to convict.
38 Pl. *Laws* 854C; 870E. For discussion, see Yunis 1996:211–236.
39 Pl. *Laws* 720A-E; see also Pl. *Laws* 718D3-4.
40 The exception is impiety. For discussion, see Yunis 1996:228–234.
41 Dem. 21.47. I follow Fisher in translating *paranomon* as "improper"; for discussion, and the implications for the dating of the law, see Fisher 1992:54–55; cf. Gagarin 1979. The text of

Among the many remarkable features of this statute is that it offers the same substantive protection to slaves as to freepersons.[42] But since slaves could not bring suit and third parties rarely had incentives to serve as a volunteer prosecutor on behalf of a slave, this protection appears to have been primarily symbolic. In this section I argue that the *hubris* law, though rarely (if ever) enforced on behalf of slaves, changed norms and practices surrounding the treatment of others' slaves. I first place the *hubris* law's protection of slaves in the context of Athenian law's otherwise strict demarcation between slave and free. I then discuss the message the law was thought to convey: not concern for slaves, but the belief that hubristic behavior, even against slaves, posed a serious threat to the democracy. Finally, I discuss how the expressive effects of the statute may explain why, according to several classical sources, Athenian slaves enjoyed unusual liberty and security.

Legal Treatment of Slaves

The protection of slaves alongside free persons in the first clause of the *hubris* law stands in stark contrast to the many Athenian laws that explicitly mark slaves as inferior to citizens.[43] Several Athenian laws contain different penalty provisions depending on the status of the victim or the offender. While the penalty for intentionally killing a citizen was death, the law imposed a lesser penalty, probably exile, for the killing of a slave.[44] Several laws, such as the law on silver coinage, provide different penalties for those convicted of breaking the law: fines for citizens, whipping for slaves.[45] In fact, one orator suggests that freedom from corporal punishment was the primary fact that set free men apart from slaves: "If you wish to examine the difference between a free man and a slave, you will find the greatest

this law is accepted by most, but not all, scholars as genuine (e.g., Fisher 1992:36; MacDowell 1990:43–47; cf. E. Harris 1992:75–78).

[42] If the later clauses of the law are accepted as genuine (on which, see Fisher 1992:36 n.1; MacDowell 1990 ad loc.), the law did include a procedural distinction based on the status of the victim: a man convicted and assessed a fine was imprisoned until he paid the fine only if the victim was a free person. Dem. 21.47.

[43] Many laws governing private wrongs (e.g., the *dike blabes*) presumably applied equally to slave and free victims, but these statutes almost certainly did not explicitly place slaves on a par with freepersons. In any case these wrongs were seen primarily as a financial injury to the slave's master, especially since the master would be the one bringing suit on behalf of the slave.

[44] For discussion of the evidence, see MacDowell 1963:126–127.

[45] SEG XXVI.72; Stroud 1974; Rhodes and Osborne 2007: no. 25. For other examples and discussion, see Hunter 2000a:7–15.

distinction: the bodies of slaves are subject to punishment for all their crimes, but free men can keep theirs safe from harm even in the worst disasters."[46]

Whipping and other physical affronts were also the methods of choice for masters administering private punishments to their slaves.[47] A master was free to punish his slave without interference in whatever way he saw fit, with only one limitation: no slave could be killed without being condemned by the state.[48] This minimal protection was exceedingly difficult to enforce: slaves could not bring charges and homicide was a private suit, so a slave murdered by his master could only be avenged in court if a member of the master's *oikos* or a free relative of the slave took on the case.[49]

The physical vulnerability of the slave can also be seen in the peculiar requirement that the testimony of a slave witness was admissible in court only if it had been extracted under torture.[50] The rationale for this rule appears to have been that a slave subject to his master's later discipline would say whatever his master wished unless the fear of immediate pain induced him to tell the truth to stop the torture.[51] There is some debate about how often, if at all, slaves were actually tortured to obtain testimony. Although our court speeches frequently refer to one litigant challenging the other to have a slave tortured,[52] there are no attested instances in which the challenge was taken up. Some scholars view the challenge to torture as a purely rhetorical device;[53] others argue that the absence of confirmed examples of torture in the court speeches is unsurprising since slave evidence obtained through torture likely resolved the case.[54] Whether

---

46 Dem. 22.55.
47 Examples of threatened and actual physical punishments of slaves for offenses such as lying, stealing, laziness, and incompetence are more common in comedy than in our forensic sources. Dem. 45.33; Lys. 1.18; Ar. *Wasps* 1292–1296; *Frogs* 542–545; Men. *Samia* 306–307; *Heros* 1–5; for discussion, see Hunter 1994:162–173; Cox 2002.
48 Ant. 5.47; 6.4. For discussion, see Morrow 1937; Klees 1975:42.
49 Plato's *Euthyphro* includes what may be a fictitious story of a master being charged by his own son for killing a slave, though Socrates' reaction to the suit indicates that bringing such a case would be considered highly unusual and possibly impious. Pl. *Euthyphro* 4b; for discussion see Morrow 1937:220–222.
50 There is one exception: for religious crimes, and perhaps also for treason or theft of public property, slaves were permitted to inform against their masters without being tortured. MacDowell 1993:181–183; Osborne 2000.
51 Ant. 6.25; Lys. 4.16; Lyc. 1.30. For discussion, see Mirhady 2000.
52 Hunter (1994:93–94) lists the twenty-three surviving examples.
53 E.g., Gagarin 1996; cf. Thür 1996, 1977 (seeing torture as a relic by the time of the orators).
54 Mirhady 1996; 2000; Hunter 1994:89–93.

rhetorical or real, the rule's frequent citation in court speeches underscored the strict distinction between slaves and free men in classical Athenian law.

The Hubris *Law in Context*

The inclusion of slaves in the *hubris* law was an anomaly, and was perceived as such by the Athenians of the classical period. We will see that this part of the statute was interpreted not as an attempt to protect slaves from mistreatment, but as a means of deterring all forms of hubristic behavior, which was viewed as a serious threat to the democratic order. Before we examine the motives that led to the enactment of the statute and the message that the law conveyed to later Athenians, it may be helpful to briefly discuss what we know about the meaning and scope of *hubris*, particularly as it applied to slaves.

The statute does not define *hubris*. Based on an exhaustive study of the use of the term in forensic oratory, Fisher argues convincingly that the central feature of *hubris* was intentionally treating another person in a manner that did not befit that person's legitimate status or honor (*time*).[55] *Hubris* most often involved violence intended to dishonor the victim,[56] and a surprising number of instances (82 of our 500 references in prose authors)[57] include sexual assault. The speaker in Demosthenes 54 recounts what he considers paradigmatic hubristic behavior on the part of his opponents: on one occasion he beat the speaker's slaves, emptied chamber pots on them, and urinated on them, while on another occasion he seriously assaulted the speaker and stood over his broken body crowing and flapping his elbows like a victorious fighting cock.[58]

What did it mean for a free man to insult a slave's honor, and was it even possible for a slave's own master to do so? As we will see, our classical sources view the inclusion of slaves in the *hubris* law as remarkable, yet they leave no doubt that slaves could be the victims of *hubris*.[59] Discussions of how to manage and properly motivate slaves in classical sources recognize that even slaves had some claim on honor and that some

---

55 Fisher 1992:1–5, 36–85; 1995:45; for other views, see, e.g., Gagarin 1979; Cairns 1996.
56 Fisher 1992:1; cf. Gagarin (1979:230), who argues that the injury had to be physical to qualify as *hubris* under the statute.
57 E. Cohen 2007a:218; for the importance of sexual assault in the law of *hubris*, see D. Cohen 1991b.
58 Dem. 54.3,9.
59 Dem. 21.46–50; Aesch. 1.17.

slaves rightly enjoyed a higher status than others (agricultural overseers, and also, presumably, trusted household slaves and slaves entrusted to run businesses).[60] Beatings of slaves carried out by someone other than the master are described in our sources as examples of *hubris*,[61] as are instances of sexual assault of slave *hetairai* (courtesans), musicians, and other entertainers at *symposia*.[62]

Some scholars view such outrages committed upon slaves as within the master's prerogative. They discount statements in court speeches and the plain language of the statute, and argue (or simply assume) that the *hubris* law could not have applied to slave masters' treatment of their own slaves because of the very nature of classical slavery.[63] This is true up to a point: the behavior prohibited by the law depended on the relative honor (*time*) and relationship between the parties. Any act by the master that could be interpreted as legitimate punishment did not unjustly dishonor the slave and therefore did not fall within the definition of *hubris*, but unprovoked physical cruelty might well have. And despite some modern scholars' assumption that masters sexually exploited the female slave members of their household at will, Cohen has pointed out that there is very little evidence to support this claim.[64] To be sure, the range of treatment by a master that might be viewed as *hubris* was undoubtedly small, and the likelihood of a jury finding against a master in a *hubris* case was even smaller.[65] But it seems probable that in theory, at least, this law regulated masters' treatment of slaves.

The protection of slaves in the *hubris* law was interpreted not as a reflection of concern for slaves' well-being, but rather as an indication of the danger posed to the social stability of the polis by hubristic personalities. This was true both in the classical period, and, as far as we can tell, at the time the law was enacted. We cannot date the *hubris* law with certainty, but it seems most likely that it was part of Solon's reform legislation in the

---

[60] E.g., Xen. *Oeconomicus* 14.7. For discussion, see Fisher 1995:55–62.

[61] Dem. 54.3; Aesch. 1.54ff.

[62] Dem. 19.196; Aesch. 2.4, 153–155; Din. 2.23: a Rhodian lyre-girl, who was probably, but not certainly, a slave; Dem. 21.36–38: a flute-girl whose identity is similarly uncertain.

[63] E.g., Todd 1993:189; Harrison 1998:172. But others agree with the analysis here that a master *could* commit *hubris* against his own slave: Morrow 1937:222–223; Fisher 1995; E. Cohen 2007a:217; 2000:166.

[64] E. Cohen 2000a:166–167.

[65] On the difficulties of enforcing the *hubris* law against masters, see the subsequent discussion.

early sixth century BCE.[66] And we know that Solon was not a champion of slaves. One of his major reforms – the abolition of debt bondage of the free – attempted to create civic cohesion among citizens by sharpening the distinction between free and slave. We also know that Solon believed that hubristic behavior by rich Athenians was the primary cause of the class conflict[67] that produced his reforms. In his poems, Solon rails against the evils of *hubris*, particularly the excesses and *koros* (insolence) of the wealthy, and their unjust enslavement of poor citizens.[68] He argues that *stasis* and civil war naturally follow when *hubris* is left unchecked.[69] The broad prohibition of *hubris* of any sort, even against slaves, may reflect this belief that individuals' unjust assertion of superiority posed a dire threat to Athens' social structure.

In the fourth century, Athenians continued to see the *hubris* law as addressing these same concerns. We are fortunate to have two passages from forensic oratory that explicitly discuss the law's protection of slaves. Both see the inclusion of slaves as an unusual provision aimed primarily at condemning and deterring all forms of *hubris* rather than protecting slaves. In his prosecution of Timarchus under a different law, Aeschines has the law against *hubris* read out and then states that *hubris* is so reprehensible that it is punishable regardless of its victim:

> It may be that someone at first hearing might wonder why on earth this term, slaves, was added in the law of *hubris*. But if you consider it, men of Athens, you will find that it is the best provision of all. For the legislator was not concerned about slaves; but because he wanted to accustom you to keep far away from *hubris* on free persons, he added the protection against committing *hubris* even against slaves. Quite simply, he thought that in a democracy, the man who commits *hubris* against anyone at all was not fit to share the rights of citizenship.[70]

---

66 Most convincing for me is the close fit between the law and Solon's reform program, particularly the creation of the *graphe*, as discussed by Fisher (1995:63–65). For other arguments for a Solonian date, see Murray 1990; Morrow 1937:226; cf. MacDowell 1976 (suggesting the law is of sixth century, but not necessarily Solonian, provenance). Gagarin 1979 dates the law to the fifth century. Although Solon drafted the legislation, his laws were likely put before the assembled people for ratification (Hdt 1.29). For the view that the sovereignty of the Assembly had been established by the time of Solon, see, e.g., de Ste. Croix 2004:74.

67 Sol. fr. 5 (West); *Ath. Pol.* 2.1–2.3. Some scholars emphasize rivalry among aristocrats as the primary source of the crisis.

68 Sol. fr. 13 West; Sol. fr. 4 West; Sol. fr.15 West. For discussion, see Fisher 1992:69–76.

69 Fr. 4 West.

70 Aesch. 1.17.

In his prosecution of Meidias, Demosthenes does state that the protection of slaves reflects an admirable *philanthropia* on the part of the Athenians,[71] but his primary explanation, like that of Aeschines, emphasizes the seriousness of the offense:

> The lawgiver went even further so that even if someone commits *hubris* against a slave, he provided that there would be a *graphe* in the same way on his [i.e., the slave's] behalf. In his opinion, it was necessary to consider not the identity of the victim, but the nature of the action that took place. When he found a type of behavior inappropriate, he did not permit it toward a slave or anyone else. There is nothing, men of Athens, nothing at all more intolerable than *hubris*....[72]

Hubris was intolerable because it threatened the democratic order; in fact, classical sources directly associate *hubris* with the overthrow of the democracy.[73] The survival of a direct democracy depended on the ability of all citizens, particularly those who were wealthy and/or of noble birth, to behave in a manner that recognized even the poorest citizens as political equals. Several sources assume that the wealthy are the most likely to try to establish superiority through acts of *hubris*.[74] As the passage from Aeschines quoted earlier suggests, hubristic behavior was thought to indicate something fundamental about a person that made the offender "unfit" for democratic citizenship. Ober summarizes why *hubris* was considered perhaps the most serious crime an Athenian could commit: "Athenian democratic ideology construed the threat to public order ... as the hubristic individual – he who was strong enough and arrogant enough to seek to establish preeminence via the humiliation of others within the *polis*."[75]

The wealth of classical sources discussing Athenians' understanding of the *hubris* law is not an accident. Discussions of the law and the nature of the offense abound in the surviving court speeches, presumably because the prohibition of *hubris* occupied such a central place in Athenian democratic ideology. But despite the law's apparent "high profile"[76] in Athenian discourse, relatively few cases appear to have been

[71] Dem. 21.48–50.
[72] Dem. 21.46.
[73] Ar. *Eccesiazusae* 453; Thuc. 3.81.4. For discussion, see Ober 2007:123–124; Fisher 2005:68–75.
[74] Ar. *Rhetoric* 1378b; Lys. 24.15; Dem. 21.98, 100.
[75] Ober 2007:123.
[76] Fisher 1990:123.

brought under the *hubris* statute.[77] A likely explanation is that most *hubris* cases could be styled as a private suit (*dike*) — for assault, rape, or slander, for example — a choice that offered the prosecutor the possibility of winning money damages without the financial and social risks of making such a serious public charge.[78]

It seems likely that suits for *hubris* committed against slaves were even less common.[79] A master or third party could pursue a suit for *hubris* on behalf of a slave, but such prosecutions were probably rare given the risks associated with the *graphe* procedure, the availability of less serious private charges, masters' limited incentives to bring such cases, and the difficulty of amassing witness testimony since slaves could testify only under torture.[80] There are three possible references to *hubris* cases brought on behalf of slaves, but in all of these cases there is either uncertainty about whether the victim was a slave (as opposed to a former slave), or it is unclear whether the case actually came to trial under the charge of *hubris*.[81] Moreover, two of these cases involve victimization of a slave *hetaera* (courtesan) or entertainer at a symposium or festival, a special situation where one might imagine the

77 We know of one definite *hubris* trial and one suit that was begun but then dropped. Fisher 1990:125–126; Osborne 1985a:55–58. In a handful of cases in which we do not know the charge, the prosecutor *may* have used the *hubris* procedure, though we have seen that prosecutors often chose alternative procedures even when the facts appear to merit a conviction for *hubris*. For discussion, see Fisher 1990:125–126.

78 Prosecutors in private suits collected any damages and were not subject to a fine for failing to win one-fifth of the jurors' votes. Perhaps more importantly, bringing such a serious public charge would, for good or ill, attract a great deal of public attention. The speaker in Demosthenes 54.1 claims that although his opponent was guilty of *hubris*, modesty and inexperience induced him to bring a private suit for assault. For discussion, see Osborne 1985a; Fisher 1990:133–136.

79 The standard scholarly view is that the protection of slaves in the *hubris* law was rarely enforced. See, e.g., Morrow 1937:218; Fisher 1995:65–71; 1990. For the contrary argument that this law *was* commonly enforced in court, see E. Cohen 2000b:120–121.

80 Demosthenes' claim in his prosecution of Meidias that many men had been executed for committing *hubris* against slaves is transparently unreliable, part of a thought experiment in which barbarians whose people were enslaved by the Athenians are imagined to appoint the Athenians as their political advocates (*proxenoi*) abroad. Dem. 21.49. As Todd (1993:189) notes, it is telling that Demosthenes cannot produce an example of a case, in contrast to the discussion of specific cases to support other points in the speech (Dem. 21.58–65; 71–73).

81 One case (Dem. 19.196; Aesch. 2.4, 153–55) involves an Olynthian woman at a symposium, but it is unclear whether a lawsuit was brought. The victims in other two cases (Din. 1.23), one involving a Rhodian lyre-girl mistreated at a festival and the other an Olynthian woman put in a brothel, were probably, but not certainly, slaves. For discussion of the evidence, see Fisher 1995:69–70; E. Cohen 2007a:215.

slave's master or sexual partner viewing the abuse as an affront to his own honor as well as that of the slave.[82] More pointedly, the surviving court speeches include several examples of clear instances of *hubris* committed against slaves that did *not* lead to a legal action.[83] If it was uncommon for a master to bring suit for *hubris* on behalf of his slave, it seems likely that it was virtually unheard of for a volunteer prosecutor to charge a master for *hubris* committed against his own slave.[84] Plato offers a pithy statement of the legal vulnerability of the Athenian slave: "when he is treated with injustice (*adikoumenos*) and contempt (*propalakizomenos*: literally, 'splattered with mud'), he is unable to defend himself or anyone else for whom he feels concern."[85]

In short, the *hubris* statute presents something of a paradox. Suits against *hubris* were difficult to prosecute and rarely litigated, particularly on behalf of slaves. Yet Athenians clearly believed the law was important because of the threat to democracy posed by hubristic citizens.

The Expressive Effects of the Law Against Hubris

The *hubris* statute's protection of slaves presents an ideal case to explore the potential expressive effect of law in Athens. The *hubris* statute was largely unenforceable with respect to slaves yet played a prominent role in Athenian discourse. Did the law nevertheless have an effect on behavior — that is, an effect attributable primarily to the *expressive* power of the law?[86] I think we can glimpse the possibility of such an effect in the treatment of Athenian slaves: that is, they enjoyed a security from mistreatment by nonowners that was unique among Greek *poleis*, notwithstanding their

---

82 Fisher 1995:69–70.

83 E.g., Dem. 54.3; Dem. 19.196. For discussion, see Klees 1998:364–365.

84 Thomas Hubbard has suggested to me that independent slaves might have been able to hire a citizen to prosecute on his behalf. This is certainly possible, though there is no evidence to confirm it.

85 Pl. *Gorgias* 483b.

86 Fisher (1995:72–75) briefly suggests that the protection of slaves in the *hubris* law may have had some beneficial effects on slave owners despite being rarely enforced, but does not discuss the expressive effect of the law or analyze the mechanism through which the law might have influenced behavior. Ober (2007:107–118) discusses the inclusion of slaves in the *hubris* law and the evidence for relatively mild treatment of slaves in Athens in the course of arguing that Athenian slaves enjoyed some negative liberties. Forsdyke (Forthcoming b) discusses the beneficial effect of Athenian democratic values more generally on the practice of slavery in Athens.

inability to bring suit for *hubris* and their otherwise low status under Athenian law.[87]

How might the expressive function of the *hubris* law have operated? The law communicated a clear message: hubristic behavior of any sort was a serious crime that threatened the social order and was incompatible with democratic citizenship. Committing *hubris*, even against a slave, marked a man as an immediate danger to the community and perhaps even an enemy of the democracy. It is not surprising that in his prosecution of Aeschines for betraying the democracy to Philip II, Demosthenes makes much of the story that Aeschines had committed *hubris* against a slave at a symposium held in Macedon.[88] Aeschines was so worried about the effect of this story on his reputation and on the jurors' verdict that he takes care to deny this charge at the outset of his defense speech, and to explain his side of the story in some detail later on in his presentation.[89]

The expressive effect of the *hubris* statute deterred potential violators not only because they feared that committing *hubris* would damage their reputation and result in social sanctions. Perhaps more importantly, committing *hubris*, even against a slave, was incompatible with most Athenians' identity as valued members of the community and loyal democratic citizens. To be sure, a small minority of Athenians who were openly hostile to the democracy may have resisted the idea that they should treat men they thought of as their inferiors with respect; both Plato and the treatise-writer known as the "Old Oligarch" criticize the solicitude shown to slaves in Athens.[90] But most Athenians, even those of aristocratic birth, would be reluctant to engage in behavior that was perceived to pose a threat to the democracy.

---

87 Of course, another way to measure the expressive effect of the law would be to ask whether the law reduced hubristic behavior of all sorts, not limited to the treatment of slaves. The difficulty here is that we do not have any evidence about the relative levels of *hubris* among Athenians and non-Athenians, and given the possibility of prosecuting other types of *hubris* it would be impossible to distinguish between the deterrence effect of the legal sanction as opposed to the expressive effect of the law. The value of looking at the treatment of slaves as a measure of the expressive effect of the law is that (1) avoidance of hubristic behavior toward slaves runs counter to general cultural beliefs and practices that emphasize slaves' inferiority; (2) the effective unenforceability of the law means that any effects can be attributed to expressive effects; and (3) we have direct evidence remarking on the relative freedom of Athenian slaves.

88 Dem. 19.196–198.

89 Aesch. 2.4, 153–155. Ariston similarly seeks to blacken Conon's character by describing the *hubris* he committed against Ariston's slaves (Dem. 54.3).

90 Pl. *Republic* 563b; [Xen.] *Constitution of the Athenians* ("Old Oligarch") 1.10–11.

Athenian elites may have had their own subculture and norms relating to cultural and social activities,[91] but civic engagement and leadership in democratic institutions was part of the mainstream elite's sense of identity and central to achieving status within elite circles.[92] As a result, the frequent public proclamation of the evils of *hubris* may have deterred Athenians from mistreating others' slaves even though there was little risk of being prosecuted for this offense.

Our surviving sources provide some evidence for this expressive effect of the *hubris* law. Several sources remark that slaves in classical Athens enjoy unparalleled freedom and security. Demosthenes states that in Athens "one can see many slaves among you with more power to say whatever they want than citizens in other city-states,"[93] and in the *Republic* Socrates suggests, disapprovingly, that in radical democracies like Athens slaves "are just as free as their owners who paid for them."[94] The treatise-writer known as the Old Oligarch discusses the "uppityness" (*akolasia*) of Athenian slaves and attributes this attitude to the laws protecting slaves from mistreatment: "In Athens slaves and metics exhibit the greatest uppityness (*akolasia*): it is not permitted to hit them, and a slave will not step aside for you."[95] Unlike in Sparta, he says, Athenian slaves are not afraid of men who are not their masters.[96]

The *hubris* law's effects were likely most prominent in the case of wealthy slaves who worked outside their master's household and interacted with citizens on a regular basis.[97] Some slaves were hired out by their master or operated a shop or business on his behalf; others, the *douloi khoris oikountes*, lived independently and ran their own business for profit in return

---

91 On which, see the subsequent text.

92 Carter (1986:1–27) discusses the centrality of political engagement in Athenian identity; Ober (1989) explores how the elite desire for political honor bestowed by the masses operated as a sort of discipline; D. Cohen's (1995) notion that elites competed for prestige in Athenian courts certainly captures one of, if not the full picture of, litigants' motivations; and Herman (2006:258–309) describes how the democracy harnessed aristocratic competition and desire for honor for its own ends.

93 Dem. 9.3.

94 Pl. *Republic* 563b. See also Eur. *Ion* 854–856; Plautus *Stichus* 447–450.

95 [Xen.] *Constitution of the Athenians* ("Old Oligarch") 1.10. I am adopting Ober's (2007:111) translation of *akolasia* as "uppity" behavior. For discussion of this passage, and an argument that the Old Oligarch's depiction of the treatment of slaves in Athens is supported by their protection in the *hubris* law, see Ober 2007:111–116.

96 [Xen.] *Constitution of the Athenians* ("Old Oligarch") 1.10–12.

97 In fact, the Old Oligarch suggests that the need for such slaves to carry on business with citizens was one reason for the rule ([Xen.] *Constitution of the Athenians* ("Old Oligarch") 1.11).

for regular payments to their master.[98] Such business arrangements would not have been possible if citizens regularly refused to treat such slaves with respect despite these slaves' limited practical legal recourse for mistreatment. We hear, for example, of a slave working in a bank responding to an urgent inquiry by a prominent man with a nonchalant, "Why are you asking?"[99] Similarly, we know that ordinary household slaves regularly shopped and did errands for their masters in the city, apparently without any fear that they would be mistreated by free men.[100] This is not to say that Athenian slaves were perceived (or perceived themselves) to be the equals of free men: their many legal disabilities were a constant reminder of their inferior status in Athenian society. But our evidence suggests that Athenian slaves were unusual in that they expected and were accorded a modicum of respect and protection from mistreatment in public.

Given the evidence for the unusual solicitude shown to Athenian slaves, it seems reasonable to suppose that even though the protections offered to slaves in the *hubris* law were rarely enforced in court, the law nevertheless had an expressive effect that deterred citizens from mistreating others' slaves. Should the treatment of Athenian slaves be attributed to the deterrent effect of masters' bringing non-*hubris* private charges for mistreatment of their slaves, for example for damaging their property? The possibility of these sorts of suits might protect slaves from serious and permanent physical injury, but they don't explain the apparent reluctance of Athenians to insult or cuff others' slaves, offenses that were unlikely to be prosecuted by the slave's master. Nor does it explain the "uppityness" of Athenian slaves remarked on by our sources. The Athenians knew that such minor insults against another's slave were unlikely to lead to litigation; direct legal sanctions cannot explain the unusual treatment of slaves in Athens. It is also unlikely that the security enjoyed by Athenian slaves reflects broader cultural attitudes toward slaves unrelated to the message communicated by the *hubris* law. We have seen that in all other respects Athenian law strictly demarcated slaves as inferior to free men, and that the unusual inclusion of slaves in the *hubris* law did not reflect a concern for the well-being of the

---

98 On wealthy and independent slaves in Athens, see E. Cohen 1998; 2007b; 2007a. E. Cohen (e.g., 2007b) argues that the *hubris* law deterred potential violators through fear of enforcement of the law's sanctions; my own view is that since enforcement was unlikely, and known to be so, the *hubris* statute altered behavior through the expressive function of law.

99 Dem. 52.5. For discussion, see E. Cohen 1998:116.

100 E.g., Lys. 1.8; Xen. *Oeconomicus* 8.22.

unfree. Moreover, the Old Oligarch explicitly draws a connection between the prohibition on hitting slaves – generally taken to be a reference to the *hubris* law – and the unique *akolasia* of Athenian slaves. The *hubris* law thus seems to have played an important role in reducing violence and maintaining order in interactions between slave and freepersons even though its provisions protecting slaves were practically unenforceable.[101]

Did the law also affect how masters treated their own slaves?[102] Our evidence on this question is extremely thin. Passages in comedy suggest that even higher-status household slaves were routinely beaten by their masters for petty offenses,[103] though scholars have noted that we don't see the kind of random, wanton cruelty toward Athenian slaves characteristic of other ancient slave societies such as Sparta or Rome.[104] The apparent relative rarity of outright savagery in Athenian master–slave relations may reflect an expressive effect of the *hubris* law, though there are other social and economic factors that may explain this difference.[105] In any case, any effect of the law seems to have been relatively small: Athenian slaves do not appear to have enjoyed the kind of respectful treatment or exhibited the *akolasia*

[101] The *hubris* law applied to metics and foreigners (and women) as well as slaves. The law may have had similar expressive effects that helped reduce violence aimed at these groups as well and made it easier for metics and foreigners to engage in business and trade in Athens. I focus here on the effects of the law on the treatment of slaves only because the statute was particularly unlikely to be enforced on behalf of a slave victim and because we have literary evidence suggesting that Athenian slaves enjoyed considerably more freedom and security than slaves in other city-states.

[102] For a tentative suggestion along these lines, without discussion of the expressive function of law, see Fisher 1993:63–64; 1995:66–75.

[103] E.g., Ar. *Wasps* 449–450; 1292–1296; *Birds* 1323–1327; *Plutus* 1139–1145; Men. *Samia* 679–680. For discussion of these and other passages, as well as the difficulties of relying on comic evidence, see Hunter 1994:162–170.

[104] Hunter 1994:170; de Ste. Croix 1981:48.

[105] Other possible explanations: (1) Athenian farms tended to be small holdings, with relatively few slaves per household, which led to a more intimate, personal relationship with masters very different from the plantation-type slaveholding familiar in the American South (Hunter 1994:170); (2) Athenian slave-management literature stressed the importance of employing fair rewards and punishments as a way of motivating slaves (Xen. *Oeconomicus* 9.13); (3) philosophical literature condemned punishing slaves in anger or while drunk because such actions jeopardized the master's self-control (D.L. 8.20; 3.38; Xen. *Hellenica* 5.3.7; Plu. *Moralia* 155c–d; 551a–b; Klees 1998:201ff) ; and (4) the absence of manumission with continued duties, combined with the social stigma attached to citizens engaging in business, resulted in a class of wealthy slaves who naturally were accorded respect from their masters in accordance with their skills and practical independence (E. Cohen 1998). Of course, the slaves that appear in our sources tend to be household slaves or particularly privileged slaves; our picture of the absence of wanton cruelty might not reflect the experience of slaves in the silver mines, for example.

("uppityness") evident in their interactions in the agora when they interacted with their own masters. It seems that the ban on *hubris* had only marginal, if any, effects on master–slave relations, in contrast to what appears to be the law's significant effect on relations between slaves and the owners of *other* slaves.

Why the difference? First, we would expect the expressive effect of the *hubris* law to be weaker in the case of a master's behavior toward his own slaves because (1) many interactions within the *oikos* were private and thus less likely to generate fear of reputational damage or social sanctions and (2) a master's mistreatment of a slave could often be rationalized as legitimate motivation or punishment, reducing the chance of cognitive dissonance. Perhaps most important, masters were much more deeply invested in the power to treat their own slaves however they wished than citizens were in the power to abuse others' slaves in the agora. As we noted at the outset, the expressive power of law is unlikely to completely overturn norms and practices in which actors are heavily invested. This is why unenforced laws could not eliminate segregation in the Jim Crow era; segregationist whites had too large a stake in the system to be easily moved by the expressive power of law. But Mothers Against Drunk Driving could revolutionize norms with respect to drunk driving, even though the number of prison sentences for vehicular homicide remained tiny. No culture was built on the foundation of drunk driving; no one had as large a stake in it as Southern whites' stake in Jim Crow. So too with the Athenians and their slaves. Masters had an enormous stake in the treatment of their own slaves; citizens had much smaller stakes in their treatment of other men's human property. Thus while the *hubris* law appears to have had a significant effect on the treatment of Athenian slaves by nonowners, the law left master–slave relations largely unaffected.

3.3. Homosexual Pederasty and the Prostitution Laws

My second example of the expressive effect of the law is the statutes banning men who had engaged in prostitution from active political participation. I argue that although the direct effect of these laws was limited to those who intended a political career, the laws changed the social meaning, and thus the social practices, surrounding the elite Athenian tradition of homosexual pederasty. Unlike the inclusion of slaves in the *hubris* law, the prostitution laws did not promote "order" in the sense of limiting violence or facilitating the smooth operation of business and social interactions. But the prostitution laws are particularly revealing for this study for two reasons. First, an analysis of these laws demonstrates that formal legal institutions did participate in the regulation of private, indeed intimate, behavior despite the Athenian ideology of a "private sphere" free from government interference. Second, the prostitution laws appear to be an example of the rare case where it may be possible to separate the expressive effects of a statute from the effects of the larger cultural shift in norms that led to the passage of that statute.

Sorting out how the prostitution laws may have changed the social meaning and practices of pederasty requires some understanding of Athenian sexual mores. After discussing the social meaning of homosexual pederasty in Athens from the seventh through the fourth century BCE, I describe the texts of the laws and the motivations behind their passage. I then explore various ways in which Athenians may have reacted to these laws.

This study suggests that the expressive effect of the prostitution laws may have reached far beyond the limited number of citizens who were in danger of being prosecuted under these laws. These laws appear to have changed the way Athenians thought about homosexual pederasty more generally (even where no prostitution was involved). Because the line between pederasty and the practice of *hetairesis* (the male equivalent of being a courtesan)[106] addressed in the law was not always clear, enemies could easily paint a former young lover (*eromenos*) as a prostitute. The laws banning those who had engaged in *hetairesis* from speaking in the Assembly or holding public office transformed pederasty from a rite of passage for future politicians to a practice that was incompatible with political honor. By changing the social meaning of pederasty, the laws may have affected elites who did not intend a political career and who might not otherwise respond to direct expressions of popular disapproval. In this way, the indirect sanction imposed by these laws may have actually been *more* effective than a direct ban on pederasty.

Literary sources suggest that the prostitution laws may have altered elite social norms and practices relating to homosexual pederasty in a variety of ways. Some men appear to have become more careful about courting in public; the prostitution laws may have created, in effect, an Athenian "closet." Others adopted a conception of "chaste pederasty" that would

---

106 I discuss the meaning of *hetairesis* in more detail later in the chapter.

not run afoul of the law. The laws may also have provoked resistance among a particular subset of elites, the *apragmones*, contributing to this group's deliberate disengagement from public affairs.

The Cultural Context of Pederasty

Athenian homosexuality is a large and controversial topic. I will attempt in this section to give only an outline of how the norms and social meaning surrounding this practice changed from the archaic period through the fourth century. In the archaic and early classical period, homosexual pederasty, far from being dishonorable, gave a boost to aspiring politicians, provided certain proprieties were observed: this pedagogical (as well as sexual) relationship with an older mentor was a primary mechanism through which young elites trained to be political leaders. Beginning in the middle of the fifth century, we see evidence of a growing ambivalence and anxiety toward pederasty, particularly in sources aimed at nonelite audiences. It is in the context of this growing ambivalence that the laws banning Athenians who had prostituted themselves from active politics were passed, probably sometime in the mid-to-late fifth century BCE.

Literary and artistic sources of the archaic period depict homosexual pederasty as a well-established practice. The typical homosexual relationship in Athens involved an active adult lover (*erastes*) and a passive youth or boy (*eromenos*). "Righteous love" (*dikaios eros*) had a distinctly elitist, even aristocratic cast to it.[107] Depictions of courtship in literature and vase painting are often set in the gymnasium, where rich boys with money and free time went to train.[108] Elaborate and complicated norms surrounded the process of homosexual courtship.[109] Prospective lovers competed for the most attractive youths in part by giving them expensive gifts. For the younger partner, the relationship was ideally as much pedagogical as it was sexual, part of one's training to become a civic leader.[110] For this reason, it was disgraceful for the *eromenos* to appear to give in too quickly to

[107] Davidson 2007:484–485.
[108] On Greek homosexuality's "profound and ubiquitous association" with the gymnasium, and its resulting "elitist or even aristocratic colouring" see Davidson 2007:484–485.
[109] For discussion, see Fisher 2001:25–27, 36–53; Halperin 1990:93–95; Dover 1989:81–110; Cantarella 1992:17–54; 1989.
[110] Lear and Cantarella 2008 trace the pedagogical emphasis in archaic literary and artistic depictions of Athenian homosexuality and its decline in the classical period.

a lover's advances. The choice of lovers was to be made after a lengthy courtship based on affection, respect, and the prospect of intellectual or professional enhancement rather than sexual attraction. The pedagogical nature of pederasty is highlighted in two verses in which Theognis describes the noble virtues that he will teach his *eromenos*: "with kind intention, Cyrnus, I will give you advice such as I while still a boy learned from noble men (*agathoi*).[111] And again: As father to son, I myself will give you good advice."[112] Promiscuity as well as appearing to be living with (and thus off of) one's lover brought shame on the youth. There is some evidence suggesting that the *eromenos* should ideally permit only intercrural sex (i.e., between the thighs),[113] but scholars disagree about how central this norm was, and in any case comic sources suggest that in practice anal penetration may have been common.[114]

It seems that, at least from the seventh through the early fifth century, participation in a homosexual relationship brought no shame upon the younger partner as long as he observed these norms.[115] In fact, homosexuality appears to have been positively regarded in this period. Lyric poets from various places in archaic Greece celebrate the practice.[116] Athenian vase paintings frankly depicting pederastic courtship are common.[117] Many of these vases connect the lovers with an admirable elite activity such as hunting, athletic activity, and military service.[118] Perhaps most telling is the lionization of Harmodius and Aristogeiton, a pederastic couple who played a role in ousting the Peisistratid tyranny by killing one of

---

111 Theog. 27–28.

112 Theog. 1049–1051.

113 For discussion see Winkler 1990:54; Halperin 1990:96–97; Dover 1989:103–109, 140.

114 For the argument that the preoccupation with anal sex has been exaggerated by modern scholars, see Davidson 2007:100ff.

115 E.g., Cantarella 1992:21; Fisher 2001:26; Dover 1989:60–68; 81–109; Halperin 1990:47. D. Cohen (1991a:182–183, 201) has challenged this view, arguing that submission to an *erastes* always entailed some loss of honor, and that Athenian society experienced ambivalence and anxiety about pederasty without directly prohibiting it. He (1991a:183) points in particular to laws protecting very young boys from pimps and seducers.

116 E.g., Anac. fr. 357–360 PMG; Ibyc. fr. 287 PMG; Theog. 695–696. The poetry of Archilochus (e.g., fr. 294W) is a notable exception. Although there are important differences in pederastic practices among different *poleis*, there is no reason to suspect that the generally positive depiction of pederasty in archaic lyric throughout the archaic Greek world does not reflect Athenian attitudes of the period.

117 For a survey, see Lear and Cantarella 2008:38–62.

118 Lear and Cantarella 2008:86–105. This connection is made both through the type of courtship gifts and through the other scenes on these vases.

Peisistratus' sons. The lovers became a democratic symbol, and as such were honored in literature, popular drinking songs, and a prominent statue in the agora.[119]

As several scholars have pointed out,[120] popular Athenian attitudes toward homosexual pederasty appear to have changed beginning around the middle of the fifth century. We can detect a definite anxiety and ambivalence about this institution, particularly in comedy and oratory, two genres whose audiences were likely dominated by ordinary Athenians. Aristophanes' comedies are famously filled with attacks on those who submitted to anal penetration.[121] The comedies also include passages suggesting that being an *eromenos* was shameful in itself, quite apart from the question of anal penetration. To cite one example, a character in the *Birds* imagines an ideal city where a father would welcome older men courting his son:

> [HOOPOE]: Then, what sort of city would you most like to live in?
>
> ...
>
> [EUELPIDES]: A city where, on meeting me, the father of a boy in his bloom would scold me, as if he had been done wrong: "Mr. Gleaming, you sure did my boy a good turn when you met him coming out of the gymnasium, freshly bathed. You didn't kiss him; you didn't say hello; you didn't draw him close to you; you didn't fiddle with his balls — and *you*, my old family friend!"[122]

The clear implication is that in Athens fathers would attempt to protect their sons from such advances. More controversially, Hubbard has argued that the comedies also heap criticism on the active partner in pederastic relationships.[123] The treatment of Harmodius and Aristogeiton is again a bellwether of Athenian attitudes. Thucydides and Aristotle present a very different account from the traditional story, one that minimizes the role of the lovers in the overthrow of the tyranny and that recasts them from public-spirited heroes to self-interested players in a squalid lovers' quarrel.[124]

---

119 For discussion, see Lear and Cantarella 2008:15–16; Hubbard 2000:7; Monoson 2000.

120 Hubbard 1998; Lear and Cantarella 2008:17–22.

121 E.g., Ar. *Knights* 364–365; *Clouds* 949–1113. For discussion, see Dover 1989:135–153.

122 Ar. *Birds* 127–142.

123 Hubbard 1998.

124 Thuc. 6.54–59; *Ath. Pol.* 18.1–19.1; for discussion see Monoson 2000. We may also detect evidence of ambivalence in our surviving vase paintings. Around the middle of the fifth century, the forthright depictions of homosexual courtship of the archaic period are largely replaced

Unsurprisingly, the changing attitudes toward pederasty did not completely affect elite circles. Within the confines of interactions among Socrates' exclusive set, admiration of boys and pederastic courtships appear common and unremarkable.[125] Yet even elite writers and thinkers express some ambivalence about the practice in this period. It has been suggested that the notion of Platonic or chaste pederasty developed in Plato's *Symposium* and *Phaedrus* and echoed in Aeschines and Aristotle represents an attempt to rehabilitate the institution by minimizing or eliminating the sexual component and elevating the pedagogical and intellectual aspects of the relationship.[126] As I discuss subsequently, it is possible that the development of the elite ideal of chaste love was as much a specific reaction to the expressive effect of the Athenian prostitution laws as to the general shift in popular attitudes toward pederasty.

I should also respond to two potential counterarguments to my story that pederasty acquired a negative valence among ordinary Athenians beginning in the middle of the fifth century. First, some scholars have argued that, notwithstanding the apparent growing literary bias against pederasty, the practice of pederasty became more common, and thus more accepted, among nonelites in the fourth century.[127] Leaving aside the possibility of simple pederastic sex and explicit homosexual prostitution,[128] it seems unlikely that many ordinary Athenians would have the money and leisure time to participate in the full panoply of gymnastic, sympotic, and courtship practices associated with the traditional institution of "righteous love." In any event, the ambivalence toward pederasty continues throughout our fourth-century forensic sources. Lawcourt speakers commonly ridicule and deride those who have served as both the active and passive partner in a pederastic relationship.[129] To cite one example, the defendant in one speech

---

by covert interactions that scholars once viewed as nonerotic gymnasium scenes (Lear and Cantarella 2008:175; Davidson 2007:426). But we cannot place too much weight on this observation because vases depicting heterosexual sex also declined in the period, which may suggest a larger aesthetic or cultural shift unrelated to specific attitudes toward pederasty (Lear and Cantarella 2008:175).

[125] Xen. *Symposium* 8.2; Plato, *Charmides* 153a–155d; Plato *Lysis* 203a–207c.

[126] Hubbard 2003:9; Lear and Cantarella 2008:17–21.

[127] E.g., Fisher 2001:26–27.

[128] On the apparent rise in the fourth century of pederastic sex, often with hired slave boys, that did not conform to the courtship and other norms associated with "righteous love," see Davidson 2007:446–463.

[129] Lys. *Against Teisis*, fr. 17.2.1–2; Lys. 14.25–27; Is.10.25; Aesch. 2.179; 3.162; Hyp. fr. 215C.

is clearly embarrassed to admit his amorous involvement with a slave boy, though his embarrassment may stem in large part from his age.[130]

Second, there is part of one prominent lawcourt speech that is arguably an exception to this generally negative view of pederasty in the surviving speeches. In *Against Timarchus*, Aeschines attempts to distinguish between the prostitution allegedly committed by the defendant and "righteous love" (*dikaios eros*).[131] Some scholars contend that Aeschines' defense of traditional pederastic practices suggests that the jurors would be familiar with and approve of pederasty.[132] But it has been pointed out that Aeschines insinuates throughout his speech that Timarchus' homosexual lifestyle is disgusting and feminine, quite apart from its mercenary character.[133] It has even been suggested that the discussion of righteous love near the end of the speech represents an attempt to appeal to the minority of upper-class jurors, or even a postdelivery insertion for the benefit of the elite reading public.[134] In any case, when looked at as a whole, our surviving speeches suggest that having engaged in pederasty was a liability rather than an asset in court.

The tendency of our comic and forensic sources to conflate homosexual pederasty with prostitution is particularly interesting for our purposes because it suggests that *eromenoi* in traditional pederastic relationships could reasonably fear that the prostitution laws could be construed to apply to them. As several scholars have pointed out, the line between pederasty and prostitution was not entirely clear. The gifts, entertainment, and mentoring of homosexual pederasty could easily be construed as evidence of a mercenary relationship.[135] Indeed, a character in Aristophanes' *Wealth* suggests that routinely giving *eromenoi* expensive gifts like horses and hunting dogs is tantamount to prostitution.[136] Even a dinner invitation was suspect: "Whenever a young fellow learns to go and dine on another man's dinner, and puts his hand on the food without contributing anything, you may take it that he's paying the bill overnight."[137] Lawcourt

130 Lys. 3.3–4.
131 Aesch. 1.132–159.
132 Fisher 2001:58–61; Halperin 1990:91.
133 Aesch 1.110–111; Sissa 2002:156–157; Hubbard 1998:64–67.
134 Sissa 2002:156; Hubbard 1998:67–68.
135 Hubbard 1998:64; Dover 1989:107; Fisher 2001:49–50; Hindley 1991:173 n.29.
136 Ar. *Wealth* 153–159; on the greed of *eromenoi* see also Ar. *Birds* 704ff; Callim. *Epigrams* 7 PF. (G-P. 7).
137 Ephippus, *Sappho* fr.20 PCG.

speakers slander their opponent as a prostitute based only on evidence that he had been an *eromenos*.[138] Most famously, Aeschines had no evidence that Timarchus ever took payment of any kind from his lovers. He successfully painted Timarchus as a prostitute based on his promiscuity and his having submitted his body to shameful things, which may be an allusion to anal intercourse.[139]

These passages are a far cry from the noble institution depicted in the lyric poetry and vase paintings of the archaic period. In the popular sources pederasty is associated most visibly with anal sex and prostitution, not pedagogy and elite values. We can see in Aristophanes' plays a particular fixation with the possibility that many politicians who were *eromenoi* in their youth submitted to anal penetration or engaged in prostitution, and anxiety that this behavior might lead to corruption.[140] The laws banning former prostitutes from holding office or speaking in the Assembly were likely passed in the context of the ambivalence surrounding homosexual pederasty that began to appear in the middle of the fifth century.

The Athenian Prostitution Laws and Modern Interpretations

Athenian law did not prohibit prostitution.[141] In fact, the state condoned this practice by taxing prostitutes and treating contracts for sexual services just like any other enforceable contract.[142] But two separate laws prohibited citizens from actively engaging in political activity once they had prostituted themselves.

The first law, known as the *graphe hetaireseos*, banned those who had engaged in *hetairesis* from holding public office or speaking in the Boule or the Assembly.[143] The law does not define *hetairesis*, and the term may have been somewhat ambiguous even to the Athenians.[144] *Hetairesis* seems to connote the male equivalent of a *hetaira*: a "companion" or "escort" who

[138] Lys. 14.25–27; Dem. 22.21–22, 58.
[139] Aesch. 1.40, 41, 52–55, 70.
[140] E.g., Ar. *Knights* 417–428; *Clouds* 949–1113; for discussion see Davidson 2007:464.
[141] However, if a relative or guardian hired out a boy as a prostitute, both the relative/guardian and the customer could be prosecuted under a *graphe* (Aesch. 1.13–14). A separate law provided that acting as a pimp for a free boy was punishable by death (Aesch. 1.14).
[142] Aesch. 1.119; Lys. 3.22–26; Aesch. 1.160–161; E. Cohen 2000b.
[143] Aesch. 1.19–20. For discussion of the laws related to prostitution, see Dover 1989:19–31; MacDowell 2000; D. Cohen 1991a:175–186; Fisher 2001:36–52; Todd 1993:107.
[144] Todd 1993:107.

provides sexual favors for material benefit on a long-term, and perhaps exclusive, basis, as opposed to *porneia*, which referred to discrete sex acts in exchange for money.[145] As Todd notes, *hetairesis* was viewed as considerably more dignified and less commercial than *porneia*.[146] If the arguments Aeschines uses in his prosecution of Timarchus are any guide, evidence of a pederastic relationship without proof of money payments could be construed as *hetairesis* under the laws. The law imposed no penalties or restrictions on the client, and the prostitute was subject to prosecution under this law only if he attempted to engage in one of the prohibited political activities. Aeschines states that the lawgiver imposed the "heaviest penalties" for the offense.[147] Taken literally, this passage suggests that the statute provided for the death penalty, but some commentators have suggested that death was simply one of the possible penalties available through *timesis*.[148]

The second law provided for a procedure called *dokimasia ton rhetoron*, the "scrutiny of public speakers," through which any citizen could initiate a jury trial to determine whether a *rhetor* was unfit to speak in the Assembly because of his past behavior.[149] The acts that disqualified a speaker included abusing or failing to support one's parents, desertion from the military, squandering one's paternal estate, and prostituting oneself by serving as a common prostitute (*porneuesthai*) or as a companion (*hetairein*).[150] Loss of citizenship rights (*atimia*) was the penalty for conviction.[151] This second law was thus both broader and narrower than the *graphe hetaireseos*: the disqualifying behavior was broader than simply prostitution, but the prohibition applied only to speaking in the Assembly (as opposed to the *graphe hetaireseos'* prohibition on speaking in the Assembly, Council, or holding public office), and the penalty for conviction appears to have been more lenient. It was not unusual for Athenian laws to provide for overlapping procedures and even different penalties for the same conduct, depending on the type of action the prosecutor decided to bring.[152]

The precise rationale for prohibiting those who had prostituted themselves from active political life eludes us, but it seems clear that concerns

---

[145] E.g., Fisher 2001:40–44; MacDowell 2000:14; Dover 1989:20; Todd 2007:328–329.
[146] Todd 2007:328 n.33.
[147] Aesch. 1.20.
[148] Fisher 2001:136.
[149] Aesch. 1.28–32.
[150] Aesch. 1.28–32.
[151] Aesch. 1.134, Dem. 19.257, 284.
[152] Osborne 1985a.

over such a man's independence, moral status, and self-control all played a part. Aeschines mentions the worry that a man who had sold his body was apt to sell out the city as well.[153] Moreover, a man who agreed to surrender himself to another man's sexual desires, particularly if those desires included anal intercourse, had adopted a position of submission more suited to a woman or slave than to citizen capable of leading others.[154] Finally, the notion that engaging in prostitution evinced an insatiable appetite for sex and/or money incompatible with the self-control required of a self-governing citizenry may have played a role.[155]

We do not know precisely when the prostitution laws were enacted, but a reference in Aristophanes' *Knights* indicates that a law banning former prostitutes from speaking in the Assembly was in force at least as early as 424 BCE.[156] It seems likely that these laws were enacted (not necessarily at the same time) sometime in the mid- to late-fifth century in response to the growing popular anxiety about the institution of homosexual pederasty, particularly as practiced by Athens' political leaders.[157] Of course, by their terms these statutes outlawed prostitution, not pederasty. But we have seen in our literary sources anxiety that some pederastic relationships might cross the line into prostitution, and a particular worry that such relationships could corrupt politicians. Surely the Athenians did not pass these laws because they were worried that ordinary, manifest prostitutes were frequently speaking in the Assembly and taking leadership positions in the city. It seems much more likely that these laws were aimed at curbing what was perceived to be the most harmful aspects of pederasty without going so far as to ban all those who had engaged in this long-standing elite practice from political leadership.

---

[153] Aesch. 1.29; see also Dem. 22.30–32.

[154] Xen., *Symposium* 8.34ff; Fisher 2001:44–53; D. Cohen 1991a:181–201; Dover 1989:103–109; Halperin 1990:95–97; Golden 1984:317–318; Davidson 1998:159–182.

[155] Davidson 1998:159–182; Winkler 1990:56–57.

[156] It is unclear whether this passage refers to the *graphe hetaireseos* (Fisher 2001:144; Dover 1989:33–34) or the *dokimasia ton rhetoron* (Sommerstein 1997: ad loc.).

[157] These laws are often assumed to date from the fifth century BCE. (e.g., Arnaoutoglou 1998:66). The statement in Demosthenes 22.21 that the law is Solonian is widely considered an example of the tendency of orators to falsely attribute laws to Solon to give them added solemnity (MacDowell 2000:21). The *dokimasia ton rhetoron*, which included several grounds in addition to prostitution for disqualifying Athenians from speaking in the Assembly, was probably also motivated by anxiety about the leadership abilities of the "new politicians" of humbler origins who rose to prominence at the end of the fifth century (on which, see generally Connor 1971).

We know of two successful prosecutions[158] and a handful of cases where speakers were threatened with prosecution,[159] but it is impossible to say how frequently these laws were formally enforced. It seems likely that most prosecutions, like the case against Timarchus, were motivated by political, legal, or personal disagreements rather than a public-spirited interest in enforcing the laws related to prostitution.

What are we to make of the Athenian laws that formally permitted prostitution, but excluded those who had been prostitutes and, by implication, *eromenoi*, from taking an active role in the political life of the city? The dominant view among modern scholars is that these laws reflect the Athenians' recognition of a legally unregulated private sphere in which citizens were free, in the words of Pericles' funeral oration, to do as they pleased.[160] Under this view, morals legislation did not exist in Athens as such. Rather, Athenian law only regulated private conduct, including homo-erotic conduct, if it was perceived to directly affect the public life of the city.[161] It is important to note that the recognition of a private sphere free from legal regulation does not mean that there were no checks on behavior perceived to be immoral: as Cohen emphasizes, informal social norms relating to homosexuality could still have a powerful effect on citizens.[162] But the *law* left the prostitute free to do as he wished, so long as he did not endanger the good governance of the city by attempting to hold public office or advise the Assembly or the Council. According to these scholars, the law might deter the relatively small number of elite young men who expected to have active political careers, but would have no effect on the vast majority of private homoerotic conduct.[163]

Halperin, by contrast, focuses not on the direct effects of the prostitution laws but on their symbolic importance.[164] He argues that in a society

---

[158] In addition to the trial of Timarchus, Aristophanes refers to a successful prosecution in the *Knights* (876–879).

[159] Dem. 22.21–24; Aesch. 1.64; And. 1.100.

[160] Thuc. 2.37; D. Cohen 1991a:175, 222–223; Fisher 2001:39; Wallace 1997:151.

[161] Fisher 2001:39, D. Cohen 1991a:229; Wallace 1997:151. According to D. Cohen 1991a:231–236 and Wallace 1997:153–161, this approach was controversial, particularly among the critics of democracy, and some forms of moral legislation, though not legislation dealing with homo-sexuality, were enacted after the city took a conservative turn around 350 BC.E.

[162] D. Cohen 1991a:90, 229.

[163] D. Cohen 1991a:229; Fisher 2001:39; E. Cohen 2007a. Winkler 1990:59 emphasizes the distinc-tion between "rigorous scrutiny [of] the sexual behavior of the politically active.... [and the] laissez-faire [approach for] the private lives of 'private citizens.'"

[164] Halperin 1990.

characterized by radical political equality but severe economic and social inequality it was vital to mark off free citizens from their subordinates. The prostitution laws, under this view, reinforced the image of the free Athenian citizen as masculine and autonomous by declaring the "political and ideological incompatibility of citizenship and prostitution."[165] Although Halperin recognizes the symbolic function of the prostitution laws, he shares the view of most classicists that these laws had little effect on behavior:[166]

> the goal of the democratic legislation was not practical or moral but symbolic: it was designed not to alter the facts of Athenian social life or to reform individual Athenians but to disseminate among the citizens of Athens a new collective self-understanding, an image of themselves as free and autonomous and equal participants in the shared rule of the city precisely insofar as they were all (rich and poor alike) – *in principle*, at least – equally lords over their own bodies.[167]

But the law had not only a symbolic importance to civic identity, but also a more concrete effect on sexual behavior by shaping social norms and influencing the private conduct even of citizens who did not anticipate a political career and were therefore not liable to prosecution under the laws.

The Expressive Effect of the Prostitution Laws

What expressive effect might the Athenian prostitution laws have had? The laws prohibiting those who had engaged in *hetairesis* from political activity signaled that a majority of the Athenian population viewed *hetairesis* as incompatible with honorable citizenship. We have seen that the line between pederasty and prostitution was blurry at best. As a result, an Athenian would likely recognize that the law could be interpreted to include many pederastic relationships, and that even careful *eromenoi* could easily find themselves on the wrong end of public opinion.

---

[165] Halperin 1990:103.

[166] In an interesting study, Lape 2006:139–140 contends that the moral arguments made in law court speeches such as Aeschines 1 may have influenced behavior beyond the elite few who were prosecuted by serving as moral precedents for all citizens. I focus here on the potential expressive effect of the prostitution laws rather than the moral force of arguments made in individual trial speeches; in Chapter 5 I discuss how court arguments, including Aeschines 1, may have shaped norms and behavior.

[167] Halperin 1990:99.

Of course, the laws did not forbid prostitution or pederasty; they merely forbade political participation by anyone who had taken money for sex. But this feature may have given the law more influence over private sexual behavior, rather than less. It is not clear that members of the aristocratic elite who were most commonly involved in traditional pederasty would be influenced by the law's statement of public disapproval about their social activities. We have seen that pederasty was closely connected in literature and vase painting with the aristocratic elite, similar to other leisure activities uniquely associated with the noble and wealthy such as horsemanship and hunting.[168] Moreover, the gymnasium and the symposium – the two primary sites of pederastic activity – were elite preserves, where the well-born were unlikely to mix with ordinary Athenians.[169] Such aristocratic social gatherings may have developed their own set of social norms, impervious to criticism by ordinary Athenians. It has been pointed out, for example, that the symposium in particular operated as a kind of counterculture with distinct social norms.[170] The practice popular among some young aristocratic Athenians who admired Sparta to wear their hair in long, Spartan style – when Athens was at war with Sparta, no less – is an extreme example of elites being impervious to popular disapproval when it came to matters of leisure and style.[171] It seems likely that elites would not be greatly influenced by popular disapproval of activities like pederasty that were uniquely associated with the wealthy and well born and that were well respected within that subculture. A law prohibiting *hetairesis* would therefore likely have little effect on social norms beyond the direct deterrent effect of the law's sanction. But the Athenian prostitution laws were not direct prohibitions. Instead, they banned former prostitutes from holding public office and speaking in the Assembly. These indirect sanctions may have changed the social meaning of *hetairesis* in a way that would affect elite social norms far more than a direct prohibition.

By banning former prostitutes from political participation, the prostitution laws made *hetairesis* incompatible with political honor. In addition

---

[168] E.g., Dem. 61.23; Isoc. 7.45; for discussion see Ober 1989:252–253. On the connection between pederastic activity and other elite activities such as hunting, see Lear and Cantarella 2008:86–105.

[169] Davidson 2007:484–485.

[170] Pellizer 1990.

[171] Lys. 16.18; Todd 2000:178–179.

to attaching a significant sanction to the practice (at least for those who intended to enter public office), the laws changed the social meaning of homosexual pederasty. Rather than conferring honor by indicating one's participation in an elite institution that traditionally produced the city's political leaders, having been an *eromenos* might now detract from a man's status by marking him as potentially unable to assume positions of power and influence in the democracy. To engage in these activities was to admit that one did not have political ambitions. Even youths who were unlikely to have political careers may have been reluctant to lose honor by advertising this fact. In this way, the law's decoupling of pederasty and elite honor may have affected youths who had nothing to fear from the law's legal sanction. Pericles' funeral oration provides the most famous statement of the centrality of political engagement in Athenian culture: "we [the Athenians] are unique in regarding a man who takes no share in politics not as minding his own business, but as useless."[172] Elites may not have responded to the prostitution law's signal of majority disapproval as such, but they could not afford to ignore the proposition that prostitution, and by extension all homosexual pederasty, was a potential basis for exclusion from the most honorable activity in Athenian life.[173]

Ironically, the indirect and less severe sanction may have actually been more effective than a direct prohibition. Of course, it is highly unlikely that the Athenians were expecting this effect when they passed the prostitution laws. The decision to use indirect regulation rather than a direct ban may reflect a sincere reluctance to formally regulate private conduct or simply an attempt to address the perceived danger of permitting a man who had compromised his autonomy to make political decisions. The interesting point for our purposes is that, whatever the original rationale, by changing the social meaning of pederasty the Athenian prostitution laws may have

---

[172] Thuc. 2.40. For discussion of the importance of public engagement in mainstream Athenian society, see Carter 1986:1–27.

[173] McGinn (Forthcoming) points out that the story of the "virgin suicides" of Miletus may offer a parallel. According to Plutarch (*Muoralia.* 11 24B–D) and Aulus Gellius (15.10), when the young women of the city inexplicably began hanging themselves, all efforts to ban the practice failed, but a decree that the naked bodies of the suicides would be paraded in public effectively ended the suicides. Some legal scholars (Schwartz, Baxter, and Ryan 1984; Lessig 1995:968–972) have suggested that a similar mechanism may have been at work in laws that banned individuals who had participated in the aristocratic practice of dueling from holding public office in the American South, though others (e.g., LaCroix 2004) have argued that larger forces explain the demise of dueling.

had an effect well beyond the small number of Athenians who might anticipate being prosecuted under these laws.

We can see evidence of several different reactions among Athenian elites
to the prostitution laws' decoupling of pederasty and political honor. Perhaps
the most powerful effect was to drive some portion of pederastic practices
underground, creating, in effect, an Athenian "closet." The laws may have
made some number of potential *eromenoi* less apt to court publicly and encouraged others to be more careful about their choice of lovers and method of
courtship, and more mindful of how the relationship might be perceived.

We see hints of this effect in several sources. The speaker in the Lysianic
Eroticus in Plato's *Phaedrus* contemplates an *eromenos* who is afraid of public
opinion and would prefer that his lover not publicize their relationship or
be seen in public pursuing him.[174] Pseudo-Demosthenes' *Eroticus* describes
youths who "are annoyed by their lovers' company," considering the entire
institution "shameful" because some *erastai* who care only for sexual grat-
ification have debased an otherwise honorable practice.[175] Aware of the
negative effects of having been an *eromenos* on one's reputation, parents
and guardians tried to keep their charges' activities under wraps. Plutarch
reports a rumor that when Alcibiades was a young man, he ran away from
home to be with one of his lovers. Although his tutor wanted to publicly
announce his disappearance to the heralds, Pericles, his guardian, refused,
saying "If he is dead, the announcement will reveal the fact just one day
sooner, but if he is safe, his reputation will, for the rest of his life, be
beyond repair."[176] Alcibiades' son later put him in a similar position. If
the prosecutor in Lysias' *Against Alcibiades* can be believed, Alcibiades the
Younger used to recline under the same cloak with his lover "with many
people looking on" at drinking parties, leading his father to send for him
"since he was publicly misbehaving."[177]

The prostitution laws may also have significantly altered the norms
surrounding pederastic relationships in some circles. The notion of
"Platonic love" — a chaste, primarily intellectual pederastic relationship
described in Plato's *Symposium*[178] and the *Phaedrus*[179] and praised by other

174 Pl. *Phaedrus* 231e–232b.
175 [Dem.] *Eroticus* 3–4.
176 Plu. *Alcibiades* 3.1.
177 Lys. 14.25–26.
178 Plato, *Symposium* 206C–212C.
179 Plato, *Phaedrus* 238–257. See also Xen. *Memorabilia* 1.3.8.

authors[180] – may represent an attempt by members of the philosophical elite to adapt the norms of pederasty in response to the prostitution laws. In the *Symposium*, Socrates relates the virtues of chaste pederasty as told to him by Diotima. Under this view, lovers should place a higher value on mental than on physical beauty,[181] and should abstain from sex in favor of *logoi* that teach the *eromenos* about the character and behavior of the good man and, eventually, direct him toward true knowledge.[182] Similarly, in the *Phaedrus* Socrates argues that the greatest rewards are reserved to couples who resist physical temptation and engage instead in philosophy.[183] Platonic love thus attempted to maintain pederasty's traditional association with political honor by emphasizing the pedagogical aspects of the practice and by rejecting sex, with its danger of prompting servile and immoderate behavior on the part of both parties.[184] In this way, the new conception not only took chaste pederasty clearly outside the ambit of the prostitution laws, but also addressed the underlying concerns about the loss of independence, dignity, and self-control involved in some pederastic relationships that appear to have motivated the legislation. Of course, "Platonic love" may have been more of an ideal or even a charade than a new set of actual pederastic practices employed by elites.[185] But there is some evidence in both Plato and Xenophon that the historical Socrates, at least, tried to put this ideal into practice.[186] It is possible that some other members of the elite, particularly those who traveled in philosophical circles, did so as well.

The prostitution laws also coincided with the rise of an apolitical subset among the elite, suggesting that these laws may have had far-ranging – and unintended – consequences. Carter has noted that around 430 BCE a distinct subset of elites emerges who appear to have made a conscious decision to reject active engagement in politics in favor of a quiet life of traditional aristocratic pursuits.[187] We learn from Plato's *Meno*, for example,

---

[180] Ar. *Nichomachean Ethics* 8.4.1-2; [Dem.] *Erotic Essay* 3. For discussion, see Hubbard 2003:9; Lear and Cantarella 2008:17–21.

[181] Pl. *Symposium* 210B.

[182] Pl. *Symposium* 209B–C.

[183] Pl. *Phaedrus* 244A–249E.

[184] Pl. *Symposium* 210 C–D; *Phaedrus.* 239A–C; Xen. *Memorabilia* 1.3.11.

[185] Some comic authors clearly thought the notion of Platonic love was a ruse. E.g., Amphis, *Dithyramb* fr. 15 PCG.

[186] Pl. *Symposium* 219b-d; Xen. *Memorabilia* 1.2.29–31.

[187] Carter 1986:52–75.

that the sons of such prominent politicians as Themistocles, Aristeides, Pericles, and Thucydides took no part in public life despite having distinguished themselves in the course of their education.[188] This social group, known as the *apragmones*, shared several traits, including devotion to traditional aristocratic pursuits such as homosexual pederasty.[189]

Young aristocrats who took no interest in public life can be seen in Platonic dialogues from this period which are often set in gymnasia and involve explicit discussion of pederastic courtship or attraction.[190] In one dialogue set in 432 BCE, for example, Charmides, a beautiful young man surrounded by admirers in the gymnasium, converses with Socrates and identifies "minding your own business" (i.e., *apragmosyne*) with *sophrosyne*.[191] In the same dialogue, Critias, known from other sources as an enthusiast of Spartan drinking parties,[192] is similarly depicted, at this point in his life, as interested in intellectual rather than political pursuits.[193]

Aristophanes' *Wasps*, performed in 422 BCE, may offer us another view of this elite set. In the play, the fictional Bdelycleon appears to belong to the *apragmones*: he is stylish[194] and effeminate,[195] socializes in exclusive circles,[196] and disdains democratic institutions, particularly the lawcourts to which his father is so devoted.[197] Before bringing his father to a party, he instructs him in how to walk and move effeminately[198] and to discuss aristocratic pursuits like hunting and athletics.[199] Some of the other guests at the party, such as Antiphon and Lycon, are historical figures who seem to have turned away from politics in this period.[200] Antiphon, a distinguished

---

[188] Pl., *Meno* 71e.
[189] Carter 1986:70–75. Carter notes that this constellation of interests had a reactionary, nostalgic, even pro-Spartan quality to it.
[190] Platonic dialogues set at least in part in the gymnasium include *Charmides and Lysis*.
[191] Plato, *Charmides* 154D, 161B. For discussion of the *Charmides* as evidence for the *apragmones*, see Carter 1986:56–63.
[192] D-K B6, B33.
[193] Plato, *Charmides* 163D, 164D.
[194] Ar. *Wasps* 1130–1159.
[195] Ar. *Wasps* 466 (he is ridiculed as a long-haired Amynias, a reference to a man who was ridiculed in comedy for effeminacy).
[196] Ar. *Wasps* 1301–1302.
[197] Ar. *Wasps* 466, 1196. For discussion of the *Wasps* as evidence for the *apragmones*, see Carter 1986:63–70.
[198] Ar. *Wasps* 1168–1169 (on the interpretation of *diasalakonison/dialukonison/dialakonison* as suggesting effeminacy, see Sommerstein 1983 ad loc.; MacDowell 1988 ad loc.).
[199] Ar. *Wasps* 1191–1204.
[200] Ar. *Wasps* 1301–1302; for discussion, see Carter 1986:65–70.

speechwriter, was famous for his *apragmosyne*. Thucydides states that "he was one of the most capable Athenians of his time ... but he never went before the people or willingly before any other assembly."[201] Lycon is depicted by Xenophon as hosting a symposium in honor of his son (and paid for by the son's wealthy *erastes*) whose guests, including Socrates and Charmides, were picked in part to avoid "generals and cavalry and men eager for public office."[202]

Taken together, these snippets suggest a subculture in the 420s of Athenian elites who avoid active participation in politics and engage in aristocratic leisure activities in which pederasty plays a prominent role. Carter attributes this group's conscious rejection of public life to a general distaste for Athenian politics in this period, in which nonelite demagogues were ascendant and noblemen like themselves occupied a precarious position, at the mercy of the rabble if attacked in the Assembly or the courts by their political opponents. But the prostitution laws may have been an additional, and more direct, cause of this group's exit from public life. We have seen that the prostitution laws were likely passed right around this period, sometime between the mid-fifth century and 424 BCE. The prostitution laws' sanctions may have had a direct deterrent effect: participating in politics now left them open to prosecution by their enemies under these laws. But the prostitution laws may have had an even stronger expressive effect by radicalizing this group. The legislation may have provoked a powerful negative reaction among this social group, who would interpret them as a direct attack on their values and institutions, including pederasty. The laws may have converted a vague and general dissatisfaction with democratic politics into a concrete and specific grievance. The prostitution laws brought into focus just how far removed this social group's mind-set was from that of the demos. Forced to choose between political honor and pederasty and the aristocratic values it represented, some elites chose honor, but the *apragmones* chose pederasty. As Carter has pointed out, the *apragmones'* rejection of democratic politics was of immense significance to Athenian society. Several members of the *apragmones* played an active role in the oligarchic revolutions at the end of the fifth century.[203] Thus the prostitution laws may have not only helped drive some elites out of politics,

---

[201] Thuc. 8.68.
[202] Xen. *Symposium* 1.4.
[203] Carter 1986:70.

they may also have radicalized them and thereby contributed to the rise of the oligarchic movement at the end of the fifth century.

✲✲✲

In this section, I've suggested that the prostitution laws may have changed the norms and practices surrounding homosexual pederasty in several different ways. The expressive effects of the laws may have forced some into the closet, induced others to embrace chaste pederasty, and provoked resistance in still others, radicalizing them and driving them out of democratic politics. It is not surprising that Athenians would exhibit a wide variety of reactions to the laws. A study of the expressive effects of unenforced sodomy laws in modern South Africa found similar – and similarly diverse and wide-ranging – reactions among gays: some were driven into the closet, others became sexually radicalized, and some became generally alienated from the police and mainstream society.[204] Because the Athenian prostitution laws challenged well-entrenched elite norms and practices, these laws did not end the practice of pederasty, but instead had a variety of expressive effects, ranging from driving the practice underground to fostering open resistance.

The Athenian prostitution laws may at first seem like a strange choice for a case study. Unlike the *hubris* law, the prostitution laws did not help reduce violence, ensure economic security, or foster social stability. In fact, the expressive effects of these statutes appear to have been largely unintended and, in some cases, counterproductive. But this examination of the expressive effects of the prostitution laws helps show how formal legal institutions influenced private conduct, belying the widely accepted notion of a "private sphere" in Athens untouched by state interference. The prostitution laws reached far beyond the limited group of active politicians who might anticipate being prosecuted under them. By influencing private norms, these laws did not regulate simply the public sphere of political activity but directly affected private conduct.

The case study of prostitution laws is also helpful because it provides an example of the rare case where it may be possible to isolate some of the expressive effects of a statute. Because law is part of culture, it is often impossible to determine precisely how much an observed change in practice can be attributed to the expressive effect of a specific law as opposed to a more general shift in cultural norms that may have helped produce

---

204 Goodman 2001.

the law. But this difficulty is significantly diminished in cases like ours where the subgroup most affected by law is not likely to respond to general popular disapproval of their behavior, but *is* likely to respond to a statute's manipulation of social meaning. It seems unlikely that the aristocratic elite who primarily practiced pederasty would have been much affected by ordinary Athenians' growing ambivalence toward this elite social practice. It is more likely that it was the prostitution laws that produced the observed changes in elite pederastic norms by making the practice incompatible with honor and political leadership. Moreover, two of the reactions discussed previously appear to be responses to the specific provisions of the laws rather than to a more general disapproval of pederasty. "Platonic love" created a new conception of pederasty, one that fell clearly outside the ambit of the prostitution laws. And the *apragmones'* decision to absent themselves from politics can be seen as a reaction to the dichotomy between pederasty and political leadership created by the prostitution laws.

3.4. Conclusions

The discussion of the expressive effects of the laws relating to *hubris* and prostitution provide two examples of how Athenian laws may have had a much greater impact on behavior than their formal enforcement through the courts might suggest.[205] The message conveyed by these laws and their expressive effects are far from obvious from the face of the statute. I chose these complicated cases in part because they provide some evidence that the law, even when unenforced, helped shape norms and behavior, rather than the other way around. It is hard to explain the Athenians' unusual solicitude toward slaves in terms of a cultural commitment to slaves' well-being unrelated to the *hubris* law. And changes in pederastic behavior can be linked to the prostitution laws because members of elite pederastic circles were likely to be impervious to general popular disapproval of their lifestyle but sensitive to the statutes' decoupling of pederasty and honor.

The communicative message of most Athenian laws – prohibitions on political corruption, lying in the agora, or mistreatment of one's parents, for example – were much more straightforward, and much less controversial

---

[205] For an interesting analysis of the possible expressive effect of Pericles' citizenship law on how Athenians viewed their wives and families, see Osborne 1997.

or likely to provoke resistance than the *hubris* or prostitution laws. In these cases, the laws may have helped to publicize and reinforce existing social norms, and thereby promote compliance, even in situations where the laws were unlikely to be enforced in court. A man who failed to support his elderly parents, for example, might have little reason to fear that a volunteer prosecutor would take it upon himself to sue him in court. But the frequent recitation of the law requiring support of parents in court speeches and in qualification hearings for public office (*dokimasia*)[206] might encourage him to comply, either because he feared that his reputation with his neighbors would suffer, or because he liked to think of himself as an upstanding citizen. And neighbors might feel emboldened to impose social sanctions on such a man because his behavior was not only immoral, but had been determined by the demos to be important enough to pass a law prohibiting it. It is tempting to assume that Athenian statutes are essentially irrelevant to our understanding of the Athenian legal system since the courts did not predictably and reliably enforce statutes. What I have tried to show in this chapter is that these laws must have had a symbolic force that operated as a significant influence on everyday behavior.

---

[206] Support of parents was a qualification of office, and was asked of each potential magistrate in his *dokimasia*.

FOUR

Enforcing Norms in Court

In this chapter we turn to the operation of the Athenian popular courts. Just as in the case of Athenian statutes, court verdicts played a vital role in maintaining order despite the absence of the operation of the rule of law. I argue that the courts may have had a substantial impact on Athenian behavior despite the ad hoc nature and inherent unpredictability and inscrutability of individual court verdicts. While the Athenian courts did not reliably and predictably enforce the laws under which cases were brought, the courts did, in the aggregate, enforce norms. Many of these norms were informal social norms, not subject to explicit legal regulation: norms relating to the treatment of friends and family and private sexual conduct, for example. Other norms enforced by the courts were the subject of statutes, but were unrelated to the charge in the case. I refer to these norms enforced by the courts as "extrastatutory norms," meaning that they were unrelated to the statute at issue in the case in which they were raised, though some of these norms were the subject of other statutes.

The sheer volume of litigation and routine legal proceedings such as citizenship hearings meant that the average Athenian could anticipate being involved in a legal proceeding far more often than someone living in contemporary Western society, and that during this hearing the jury would very likely consider aspects of his character and past behavior unrelated to the dispute. As a result, the court system played a disciplinary role, providing concrete incentives to conform to a host of social norms. Paradoxically, the aspects of Athenian court argument that seem most removed from a rule of law may actually have played the most important role in fostering order.

Athens' unusual approach to norm enforcement adds a new twist to the legal academic literature that examines the relationship between social norms and informal sanctions, on the one hand, and formal legal rules and institutions, on the other.[1] While much of the norms literature focuses on the choice between informal and formal norms and institutions,[2] in Athens informal norms were enforced *through* the formal court system.

This chapter also argues that the Athenian courts' peculiar approach to norm enforcement compensated for apparent weaknesses in the Athenian apparatus of coercion. Courts facilitated the operation of informal sanctions by encouraging litigants to publicize their opponent's norm violations. Moreover, allegations of misbehavior made in court and adverse verdicts served as important shame sanctions in themselves, quite apart from any formal penalties meted out by the jury. The Athenian approach also compensated for difficulties in legal enforcement. As discussed in Chapter 2, the Athenians' reliance on private initiative resulted in systematic underenforcement of laws, particularly "victimless" offenses and offenses committed against victims who lacked the resources to bring suit. By permitting any past norm violation to be used against a litigant at trial, the Athenian approach encouraged litigants to uncover and punish their opponents' past unprosecuted violations. Finally, court enforcement of extrastatutory norms permits a state to regulate behavior while maintaining the fiction that it is not doing so. In the Athenian context, this meant that the Athenians could enforce a variety of norms while maintaining the fictions of voluntary devotion to military and public service[3] and of limited state interference in private conduct. In this way, the formal enforcement

---

[1] E.g., Milgrom, North, and Weingast 1990; Ellickson 1991; Bernstein 1992, 1996, 2001.

[2] Bernstein (1992) describes why the diamond trade opted for private dispute resolution procedures; West (1997) discusses the relative advantages of rules and norms in the context of the governance of sumo wrestling in Japan; Ellickson (1991) argues that the relationship of the parties, the size of the stakes, the complexity of the dispute, and the ability to externalize costs determine whether informal or formal norms are favored. Cooter (1996) has suggested that in some circumstances courts should look to norms that have arisen in specialized business communities in determining fault and liability. And, of course, custom has long been a part of the common law. But Cooter's suggestion and the use of custom are different from the Athenian approach in one crucial respect: rather than using informal norms to give content to the rules and standards provided for by law, Athenian courts enforced extrastatutory norms that were completely unrelated to the legal issue in dispute.

[3] As I explain in more detail subsequently, both military service and liturgies were required by law, but informal norms dictated service beyond the minimum requirements, and law court speakers regularly crow about their exceptional service.

of putatively informal norms veiled some of the highly coercive aspects of Athenian society.

4.1. Norms in Court

There appears to have been no rule setting forth the range and types of information and argument appropriate for popular court speeches.[4] Speakers were limited only by the time limit and their own sense of which arguments were likely to persuade the jury. Arguments based on extrastatutory norms appear again and again in the speeches, indicating that speechwriters believed that jurors would be influenced by such arguments. By "extrastatutory norms" I mean norms that were unrelated to the legal charge in the given case: bringing up an opponent's bribery conviction in an inheritance case, or boasting of one's public services or devotion to family in an assault case, for example. To be sure, Athenian jurors probably perceived discussion of these norms as character evidence relevant to deciding whether the defendant had committed the act charged, or whether he deserved the prescribed or suggested penalty, or both.[5] An Athenian litigant or juror would not perceive statutory and extrastatutory arguments as fundamentally different in character or effect.[6] By labeling these norms "extrastatutory" I am simply highlighting the fact that Athenian verdicts appear to have often turned not on evidence about whether the defendant's behavior had or had not met the criteria for the charge or indictment, but rather on evidence about whether one or other of the litigants had or had not adhered to norms not expressed in the statute. What is important for our purposes is that the norm enforced by a verdict was often not the law under which the case was brought.

To give an idea of the content of the norms enforced by Athenian courts, I would like to briefly review six general categories of extrastatutory norms cited by Athenian litigants with particular frequency: (1) treatment of family and friends; (2) moderation rather than litigiousness in the face

---

4 The *Athenaion Politeia* (67.1) refers to an oath to speak to the point taken by litigants in private cases, but this oath is never mentioned in our surviving popular court speeches and if in fact it existed, it appears to have had no effect. For discussion, see Lanni 2006:113 and n.4.

5 Lanni 2006:59–64.

6 However, the treatment of statutory and extrastatutory arguments in the popular courts was not entirely symmetrical: law court speakers do not explicitly urge the jurors to ignore the law in favor of other considerations; rather, they typically argue that both law and justice support their claim (Lanni 2006:72–73).

of conflict; (3) honesty and fair dealing in business affairs; (4) loyalty and service to the city; (5) adherence to norms of private conduct, particularly sexual mores; and (6) obedience to laws unrelated to the subject of the dispute.[7] Some of these norms were purely informal. Others were subject to legal regulation, but were used by speakers in cases involving unrelated statutes. For example, legal procedures were available against those who violated the law banning desertion from military service. Litigants in suits about completely unrelated matters eagerly exploit any opportunity to argue that their opponents had contravened these norms.

A quick word on methodology is in order before we take a closer look at how the six categories of extrastatutory norms arise in our surviving speeches. Since we rarely know the outcome of an Athenian case, it is impossible to say whether a particular speech was considered persuasive. Even in the few cases where we do know the outcome, the absence of reasons for the jury's verdict makes it difficult to discern which arguments swayed the jury. Kenneth Dover long ago laid out the standard approach for dealing with these difficult rhetorical sources: a litigant who wished to be successful would presumably limit himself to statements and arguments that were likely to be accepted by a jury.[8] Legal arguments may be self-serving, but they generally remain within the realm of plausibility. When particular types of arguments are used many times over by different speechwriters in a wide array of cases, as they are in the case of our extrastatutory norms, we can surmise that these arguments were thought to be persuasive.[9] This chapter focuses on how the courts helped enforce

---

7 Although discussion of these extrastatutory norms were common *topoi*, and their use was influenced to some degree by the requirements of genre and jurors' expectations, speakers did not present generalized "stock" characters and arguments. Instead, they presented highly individualized arguments based on the specific character of the parties (Lanni 2006:46–64).

8 Dover 1994:8–14.

9 There is no reason to think that the (possibly revised) published versions of our speeches are more likely to contain references to extrastatutory norms than the speeches actually delivered in court. Speechwriters published speeches to attract future clients; they may have been tempted to respond to persuasive counterarguments that were raised in court, but they had no incentive to misrepresent the types of argumentation used. A handful of speeches in political cases were written, delivered, and presumably published by famous politicians such as Demosthenes or Aeschines. These authors may have had more of an incentive to expand on references to their good character in the written version to enhance their public reputations, but these texts do not make more use of extrastatutory argumentation than our other surviving court speeches, and in any case they represent a very small proportion of our corpus. Moreover, several sources, both legal and nonlegal, comment on the tendency of Athenian court speakers to resort to extrastatutory arguments (e.g., Ar. *Wasps* 562–570; Pl. *Apology* 35a–b).

a limited set of relatively stable, uncontroversial norms. Of course, many other norms were the subject of disagreement, ambivalence, and change over time. The mechanisms described in Chapters 3 and 5 address how the legal system helped define and reinforce more contested norms.

Treatment of Family and Friends

Perhaps the most well-entrenched norms in Athenian society related to the obligations of *philia* ("friendship"). *Philia* does not correspond to modern ideas of friendship. It encompassed a variety of relationships, including (from strongest to weakest) immediate family, kin, friend, neighbor, demesman (roughly, "fellow villager"), and even fellow-citizen, and included the reciprocal duties and obligations that accompanied each of these relations and differed according to the strength of the relational tie.[10] One was expected to offer assistance in times of emergency or shortage to those with whom one shared a bond of *philia*.[11] A few of these obligations were regulated by statute: for example, it was illegal to mistreat one's parents or grandparents by failing to provide food or housing in their old age, physically abusing them, or failing to provide them with a proper funeral.[12] But most of the norms relating to proper treatment of neighbors, friends, and relatives were purely informal and of a vague and general character.

The surviving court speeches include many discussions of the litigants' treatment of friends, neighbors, and relatives. Discussion of these norms appear in legal disputes of all sorts, from charges of political corruption[13] to inheritance disputes.[14] Litigants commonly describe how they dutifully took care of their female relatives[15] and charge that their adversary mistreated his parents or other close kin.[16] The prosecutor charging the defendant with being a state debtor in *Against Aristogeiton* provides a long list of the defendant's violations of these norms: he charges that Aristogeiton failed to bail his father out of prison, refused to pay for his subsequent burial,

---

[10] Arist. *Nicomachean Ethics* 1165a14–35; Konstan 1997:53–59; Millett 1991:110–114.

[11] Dem. 53.4; Lys. 1.14; Din. 2.9; Ar. *Clouds* 1214, 1322; Xen. *Memorabilia* II.2.12.

[12] Lys. 13.91; Aesch. 1.28; Dem. 24.103; *Ath. Pol.* 56.6.

[13] E.g., Din. 2.8, 11, 14.

[14] E.g., Is 5.39–40. For a list of references to litigants' treatment of kin and parents, see Hunter 1994:118.

[15] E.g., Lys. 16.10; Is. 10.25.

[16] E.g., Dem. 24.107, 201; 25.54–55; Din. 2.8; Lys. 10.1–3; 14.28; 32.9, 11–18; Is. 5.39–40; 8.41; Aesch. 1.102–104; 3.77–78.

physically abused his mother, and even sold his own sister into slavery.[17] Similarly, speakers emphasize their generosity toward friends and neighbors and their opponents' disloyalty.[18] To continue with the example of *Against Aristogeiton*, the prosecutor recounts that Aristogeiton so completely and routinely flouted the norms of friendship, according to the prosecutor, that even his fellow criminals in prison voted to shun him.[19]

Moderation in the Face of Conflict

The second category of informal norms that arises in the speeches is the obligation to act in a moderate and reasonable way when faced with conflict. Speakers charge their opponents with being litigious and emphasize that they are unaccustomed to being involved in legal disputes.[20] Speakers routinely claim that they were reluctant to litigate and would have preferred to settle the dispute amicably or through arbitration, and allege that the suit only reached the trial court because of their opponent's stubbornness or aggressiveness.[21]

Honesty and Fair Dealing in Business Affairs

A third category of extrastatutory norms is honesty and fair dealing in business relationships. Speakers frequently bring up their general reputations for fair dealing and good business practices quite apart from the details of the deal in question with the expectation that this evidence will influence jurors. To cite just one example, the speaker in Demosthenes 37, a case involving a series of mining contracts, expresses fear that his case will be prejudiced by his opponent's arguments that he is a moneylender and therefore presumptively dishonest, and presents witness testimony

---

[17] Dem. 25.53–55.

[18] Ant. 2.2,12; Is. 5.35,40, 43; Lys. 6.23; 12.67; 19.56; Dem. 25.26–28; 37.15; Aesch. 2.22, 55.

[19] Dem. 25.61–62. For further discussion, see Chapter 1.

[20] E.g., Dem. 54.24.

[21] Dem. 21.74; 27.1; 29.58; 30.2; 40.1–2; 41.14–15; 42.11–12; 44.31–32; 47.81; 48.2,40; 54.24; Lyc. 1.16; Lys. 3.3; 9.7; Is. 5.28–30; for discussion see Hunter 1994:57; Dover 1994:187–192. One litigant claims that he was willing to accept a settlement that was less than fair to avoid litigation: "we agreed [to a settlement], gentlemen of the jury, fully aware of our rights under the contract but thinking we should settle for a bit less and reach an agreement that would not make us appear overly litigious" (Dem. 56.14). Demosthenes 47 offers an example of the speaker's contrasting his own restraint in pursuing his claim with his opponent's violent and inappropriate use of self-help (Lanni 2006:49).

"regarding what kind of person I am in my dealings with those who make loans and those who ask for them."[22] The fact that litigants were expected to speak for themselves in court may have provided valuable demeanor evidence to help the jury evaluate all types of character arguments, but particularly those involving honesty and fair dealing.[23]

Loyalty and Service to the City

Litigants' claims of loyalty and public service are perhaps the most interesting for our purposes because they provide the most blatant example of discussion of norms unrelated to the legal charge in the case. The epilogue of many of our forensic speeches includes a list of the speaker's (and his family's) services to the city and criticisms of his opponent for insufficient or deficient public service.[24] As several scholars have pointed out, litigants were sometimes quite forthright about their expectation that the jury will find for them out of gratitude (*charis*) for their public services.[25] Typical is the rhetoric used by a defendant in a public corruption case. He lists various public dramatic competitions that he sponsored and describes his naval exploits during the Peloponnesian War. He then suggests that the evidence of his public-spiritedness should determine the verdict: "having put myself in danger defending you and completed so many services for the city, I am not seeking a reward like other men do, but simply that I not be deprived of my own property [through this suit]."[26]

The norms relating to public service took several forms. Most prominent in the speeches is the importance of performing liturgies, which involved paying for either a festival event, such as a tragic drama, or equipping a navy ship for a year.[27] Performance of liturgies was a legal requirement for wealthy citizens. A man seeking to avoid serving could seek one of several

---

22 Dem. 37.52–54. Other examples: Dem. 35.1, 17–25; 36.55–58; 45.68; 49.1–2; Is. 5.40.

23 In fact, speechwriters attempted to write their speeches in a way that helped the speaker make a positive impression on the jury through the use of *ethos* and dramatic characterization. Carey 1994:34–43.

24 E.g., Ant. 5.74; And. 1.141–149; Lys. 6.46; 7.31; 16.18; 18.2; 20.23; 25.12; Is. 4.27; 5.36; 7.37–41; Dem. 21.161–162; 25.78; 54.44. For a list of references to public services and military service in the speeches, see Hunter 1994:118.

25 Christ 2006:172–181; Johnstone 1999:100–108; Ober 1989:226–230; Whitehead 1983.

26 Lys. 21.11.

27 Christ 2006:146–155; Gabrielsen 1994; Sinclair 1988:54–64.

statutory exemptions,[28] and could even bring a suit arguing that another, wealthier, citizen should perform in his stead.[29] Although liturgies were legally required, there was some flexibility in which liturgies to perform (some were much more expensive than others), how often to participate, and how much money to spend. Informal norms encouraged citizens to go beyond the minimum requirement; litigants listing their public services tend to focus on high-priced liturgies such as the trierarchy, suggest that their service has entailed significant financial sacrifice, and emphasize that they performed liturgies many times, implying that they volunteered to perform extra services.[30] Litigants also attack their opponents for shirking liturgies or the taxes periodically assessed from the rich, or for performing their liturgies in a cheap or shoddy manner.[31]

While the norms surrounding liturgies and taxes applied only to wealthy litigants, all citizens could boast about (or be attacked regarding) their approach to military service.[32] Laws prohibited draft dodging, deserting the ranks, and other forms of cowardice,[33] but these laws were rarely enforced through lawsuits.[34] Extrastatutory norms relating to military service, by contrast, abound in our court cases. Speakers routinely boast of their (and their family's) long-standing and courageous service in the military, and charge their opponents with draft evasion and cowardice.[35]

Loyalty to the democracy was another extrastatutory norm discussed in court cases. Athens suffered two short-lived oligarchic revolutions in 411 and 404 BCE.[36] Following the restoration of the democracy in 403

---

[28] E.g., there were limits on how often a citizen could be called to perform certain liturgies (Dem. 50.9; *Ath. Pol.* 56.3; Is. 7.38); for discussion, see Christ 2006:151–153.

[29] Under the *antidosis* procedure, a man called to perform a liturgy could challenge an allegedly wealthier man to choose between carrying out the liturgy and exchanging his property with the challenger. If the man refused both options, the case would be brought to court to decide who should perform the liturgy (MacDowell 1993:161–164).

[30] E.g., Lys. 21.1–5. 25; Lyc. 1.139–140; Lys. 3.47–48; Is. 4.27–29; 5.41–46; 7.37–41; Lys. 18.21, 24–25; 19.56–57; 19.9; 21.1–5; Dem. 38.26; 50.7. Christ (2006:172–176) provides examples of speakers describing the extra financial burden liturgies had placed on them; Christ also (2006:200–204) discusses how speakers sought to represent themselves as voluntarily performing public services.

[31] Lys. 1.27–28; 6.46, 21.20; 26.21; 36.26; Is. 5.45; Dem. 21.154; 54.44; 42.22; Aesch. 1.101.

[32] Balot 2014:7, 184–185.

[33] Lys. 14.5; Aesch. 3.175–176; Christ 2006:118–124; Hamel 1998.

[34] Christ 2006:63, 133.

[35] Attacks on opponents for draft evasion: Lys. 6.46; 21.26; 30.26; Isoc. 18.47–48; Is. 4.27–29; 5.46; Dem. 54.44; Boasts of hoplite service: Lys. 16.13; Is. 7.41; Aesch. 2.167–169.

[36] Hansen 1999:40–43.

BCE, an amnesty was passed to protect citizens who had participated in the oligarchy.[37] Although the Amnesty prohibited prosecutions based on participation in the oligarchy, a citizen's actions during the city's political upheavals could help or hurt him in lawsuits arising out of unrelated matters. As we explore in detail in Chapter 6, in the years following the revolutions, litigants regularly boast that they actively resisted the oligarchic regime, and suggest that their opponents participated in the oligarchic revolutions.[38]

Norms of Private Conduct

The frequent use of attacks on an opponents' private conduct is another of the more striking aspects of Athenian forensic oratory. We will see subsequently that the legal regulation of sexual activity appears to have been limited to behavior that was perceived to threaten public order. Yet litigants regularly charge their opponents with sexual deviance of all sorts.[39] Litigants also criticize their opponents for everything from extravagance,[40] poor money management,[41] and drunkenness[42] to walking quickly and talking loudly,[43] and cite their own moderation and private virtue.[44] Aeschines' personal attacks on Timarchus when prosecuting him under the law forbidding former male prostitutes from speaking in the Assembly is particularly memorable: he charges that Timarchus squandered his family estate and "was a slave to the most shameful pleasures, fish-eating, extravagant dining, girl-pipers and escort-girls, dicing, and the other activities none of which ought to get the better of any man who is well-born and free."[45] The relevance of "private" conduct in court extended to members of the litigants' household. Litigants occasionally charge the female members of

---

37 *Ath. Pol.* 39; Wolpert 2002:29–47.

38 E.g., Lys. 13.90; 18.10; 24.24; 25.15; 26.5; 28.12; 30.15; for discussion see Wolpert 2002:100–119.

39 E.g., Aesch. 2.151; 3.238; And. 1.100, 124–127; Lys. 13.66; 14.25–26; Is. 6.18–21; 8.44; Dem. 36.45. For a list of references to private conduct and sexual mores in the speeches, see Hunter 1994:118–119.

40 Dem. 21.133–134, 158; 36.45; 38.27; Aesch. 1.95–100; Din. 1.36.

41 Lys. 14.27; Aesch. 1.97–105; Din. 1.36; Is. 5.43.

42 Lys. 3.5–9; 24.25–29; 30.2; Dem. 38.27.

43 Dem. 37. 52.

44 Lys. 5.2; Andoc. 1.144–145; Isoc. 16.22–24; Is. 10.25.

45 Aesch. 1.42. (trans. Fisher 2001). On fish-eating as paradigmatic gluttonous behavior, see Fisher 2001:174–175; Davidson 1998:3–35.

their opponent's *oikos* with violations of extrastatutory norms in an effort to influence the verdict.[46]

Legal Norms Unrelated to the Charge

Legal norms other than the statute under which the case was brought are also frequently discussed by law court speakers. Litigants regularly emphasize their own clean records and describe any prior crimes and/or convictions of their opponents.[47] Discussions of past crimes are not limited to charges similar to the case at hand; any prior violation of the law by a litigant or his ancestors could be used against him. For example, when Alcibiades the Younger, the son of the famous general, was charged with deserting the ranks, his prosecutor provides a long list of his past crimes, including adultery and attempted murder, and recounts the treasonous behavior of his father. He then states, "In response to these acts it is fitting both for you and for future jurors to take vengeance on whomever of these men [i.e., the members of Alcibiades' family] you can get your hands on."[48] A litigant could help his case by exposing any bad acts or crimes committed by his opponent against anyone else in the past, even if the past act was completely unrelated to the current dispute. Similarly, anytime a litigant walked into court, he could wind up defending himself for any act he had committed in the past. The prosecutor in *Against Aristogeiton*, for example, explicitly argues that the jury should convict in part on the basis of the defendant's past crimes, stating that he deserves the death penalty "on the basis of both his whole life and the things he has done now."[49] Interestingly, even bad acts committed against slaves, such as the cases of *hubris* described in the previous chapter, could be used to taint a litigant in court.[50]

What I hope I've shown so far is that the extent to which a litigant had conformed to a wide variety of extrastatutory norms could influence

---

[46] Dem. 25.26 (past crime committed by mother); Is. 6.49–50 (religious morality); Dem. 40.50 (extravagance). Discussion of women is much more common in attempts to raise doubts about an opponent's citizenship status. See, e.g., Aesch. 2.78; for discussion see Hunter 1994:111–115.

[47] E.g., Aesch. 1.59; 2.93; Din. 2.9ff; Lys. 6.21–32; 13.64, 67; 18.14; Is. 4.28; 8.41; Dem. 21.19–23; 25.60–63; 34.36. For a list of references to an opponent's criminal record, see Hunter 1994:119.

[48] Lys. 14.30–31.

[49] Din. 2.11.

[50] Dem. 19.196–198; Aesch. 2.4; Dem. 54.3.

his legal case. In essence, a litigant's conduct over the course of his entire life was deemed relevant to the jurors' decision. I've argued elsewhere that the Athenians' broad approach to relevance in the popular courts reflected a conscious choice to embrace discretionary, individualized justice rather than a rule of law.[51] That is, the prominence of extrastatutory norms in the court speeches reflects a distinctive Athenian notion of procedural and substantive justice. The balance of this chapter attempts to trace how this peculiar Athenian arrangement operated in practice to help maintain order in Athens.

4.2. Enforcing Norms, Not Statutes

What role did extrastatutory norms play in Athenian verdicts? And what, if any, effect did the discussion of these norms in court have on Athenian social life? In this section I argue that the consideration of extrastatutory norms in the courts created powerful incentives to abide by these norms. In this way, the Athenian courts *did* play an important role in fostering order, but not through the traditional mechanism of enforcing statutes.

Unpredictable Outcomes, Predictable Arguments

Chapter 2 described how vague statutes and the absence of binding precedent made trial outcomes uncertain. Did shared norms and values such as those described in this chapter nevertheless make verdicts predictable in many cases? That is, would it be possible to predict how most Athenians would react to a given case, thereby creating consistency and deterrence even in the absence of clear legal rules? Shared norms are insufficient to create predictable verdicts when a vast array of factors are considered relevant to the decision. Multiple statutory and extrastatutory norms were often implicated in an Athenian case. The speaker in one inheritance suit, for example, charges his opponent[52] with violating several extrastatutory norms: he was a reluctant and stingy participant in liturgies, cheated and failed to support his relatives, committed incest with his mother, and failed to repay debts to friends.[53] The speaker, by contrast, boasts of his ancestors'

---

[51] Lanni 2006.
[52] Dicaeogenes is not technically the legal opponent in the case, but is the opponent in interest.
[53] Is. 5.34–40.

public services, including trierarchies and prize-winning choruses, and lists the people in his family who died defending Athens in war.[54] The opposing speech does not survive; doubtless it also appealed to some combination of legal and extrastatutory norms. While it was not hard to anticipate how the jury might have reacted to each of these arguments in isolation, it was much less clear how a jury would weigh the multiple competing norms in any particular case. There was no consensus on a hierarchy of norms in Athenian society. This is most evident in Attic tragedy. Tragic dramas often dramatize a conflict of norms – to name the most famous example, duty to the family versus duty to the state in the *Antigone* – with no clear moral resolution. In the law courts, too, the jury was often presented with conflicting norms and left to decide on a case-by-case basis which arguments to credit.

It is important to distinguish here between predictability of outcomes as opposed to predictability of arguments. While it may have been difficult to anticipate the ultimate verdict in an individual case, there was no question that adherence or nonadherence to particular extrastatutory norms would tend to help or hurt one's case. Ordinary Athenians as well as professional speechwriters were likely to be very familiar with the types of arguments used in the law courts. Not only did citizens serve on juries by the hundreds, but the courts were a form of public entertainment, frequently drawing spectators for ordinary as well as high-profile trials.[55]

Ordinary Athenians were aware that litigants who adhered to these well-known extrastatutory norms or whose opponent flouted them would be in a position to argue that these considerations should weigh in their favor in any dispute. To cite just one example, a litigant states: "I have before now seen defendants who were convicted by the facts themselves, and who were not able to show that they were not guilty, who were able to escape on account of their moderate and respectable lifestyles, others on account of the good deeds and liturgies of their ancestors, and other such things, leading the jurors to pity and compassion."[56] Since extrastatutory norms could become an issue in any suit, regardless of its subject matter, Athenian court verdicts, in the aggregate, had the effect of enforcing these extrastatutory norms.

---

54 Is. 5.40–44.
55 Lanni 1997.
56 Dem. 25.76.

Creating Incentives to Conform to Extrastatutory Norms

A decision based on a litigant's conformity to informal norms had effects that reached beyond the case at hand. We have seen that the uncertainties surrounding the prosecution, interpretation, and enforcement of any particular statute reduced the incentive to comply with the law. Incentives to comply with extrastatutory norms, by contrast, were much stronger because compliance could be used to one's advantage in any future legal proceeding, regardless of the underlying charge. The high likelihood that an Athenian might find himself involved in a legal proceeding in the future meant that the legal system created incentives to conform to extrastatutory norms for later use in court. Despite being ad hoc and unpredictable, court verdicts thus may have had a profound influence on Athenian social life. Athenian courts may have played a disciplinary role, enforcing not the statutes under which cases were brought, but a host of well-known extrastatutory norms.

The prospect of being involved in some form of legal action where one's past adherence to social norms might be of assistance was substantial. There was a great deal of litigation in Athens. The courts were in session about 200 days a year, and were capable of hearing anywhere from four to as many as forty cases a day, depending on the type of case.[57] Thucydides tells us that foreigners called the Athenians *philodikoi* ("lovers of litigation"),[58] and Athenian litigiousness is a common joke in Aristophanes' comedies.[59] The high frequency of Athenian litigation provides the premise for two of Aristophanes' plays: the characters in the *Birds* establish a new city in the sky in large part to avoid the excessive litigation of Athens; and the protagonist of the *Wasps* is an old man addicted to jury service. The fact that private cases were suspended at various times in the fourth century due to lack of funds to pay juries also suggests a large caseload.[60]

Classicists disagree about whether ordinary Athenians were regular law court speakers or whether the courts were dominated by an elite "litigating

---

57 Hansen 1999:186–187 estimates that the court met between 175 and 225 days a year; that *dikai* worth less than 1,000 drachma could be completed in under an hour; and that up to four courts might be in session on any given day. Of course, the courts likely did not hear cases at their full capacity every day they were in session.

58 1.77.

59 Ar. *Peace*, 505; *Clouds*, 206–208; *Wasps* passim; *Birds*. 35–45.

60 Dem. 39.17; 45.4.

class."[61] Certainty on this point is impossible. But in my view Victor Bers has convincingly argued that ordinary Athenians did litigate with some regularity.[62] The poor greatly outnumbered the wealthy in Athens.[63] It is hard to account for the high caseload if litigation was limited to members of the elite.[64] If we assume that the courts typically heard an average of only ten cases per court day, one-fourth of their capacity, then roughly 4,000 litigants, drawn mostly from the citizen body of 30,000, would appear in court in an average year.[65] Despite the elite bias of our surviving speeches, two speeches appear to have been delivered by poor men.[66] Moreover, discussions of litigation in the comedies of Aristophanes seem to suggest that litigation was not limited to the wealthy.[67]

But even if it is true that only a small proportion of Athenians wound up litigating *dikai* or *graphai* to trial, the average Athenian still faced a high likelihood of being involved in some form of legal proceeding in which extrastatutory norms might play a role. Very small claims – roughly equivalent to four to ten days' wages for a laborer – were heard and adjudicated by magistrates.[68] These magistrates were not legal experts. Like most Athenian officials, they were chosen by lot for one-year terms. There is no reason to think that arguments based on extrastatutory norms would have any less influence in small claims adjudication than they did in the courts. In the fourth century, in an attempt to take some of the burden off the courts, private claims above the small claims limit were sent to mandatory but nonbinding public arbitration prior to trial.[69] All men were required to become

---

[61] Bers (2009:7–24) is particularly persuasive on this point; see also Rhodes 1998:145. For the argument that the elite dominated litigation, see Christ 1998a:32–33.

[62] Bers 2009:7–24.

[63] Davies 1981:35.

[64] Bers 2009:7–24.

[65] Hansen 1999:186–187. Ten cases per day for 200 court days per year and two litigants per case yields 4,000 litigants.

[66] Isoc. 20.19; Lys. 24.1. Some have questioned the authenticity of Lysias 24. For discussion, see Todd 2000b:253–254. While it is true that prosecutors may have had little to gain financially by bringing private cases against poor men, many Athenian litigants appear to have been motivated by interests other than money, such as revenge, and of course in most public cases any fines collected went to the state in any case. On the motivation of Athenian litigants, see Chapter 2 of this book; Christ 1998a:34–36, 118–159.

[67] To give just one example, there is a reference in the *Wasps* (1205–1207) to Philocleon, the poor juror, having brought lawsuits in the past.

[68] Todd 1993:128.

[69] Todd 1993:187.

public arbitrators once they retired from military service,[70] which suggests that the number of suits that reached at least this preliminary stage was very high. Extrastatutory norms presumably played a role in these arbitrations just as in the courts. In fact, Aristotle in the *Rhetoric* suggests that arbitrators were *less* bound by the law and *more* influenced by notions of fairness than jurors in the courts.[71]

In addition to lawsuits arising from disputes, every male citizen was subject to an examination before a public body at which their character might become an issue. At the age of eighteen each boy was presented to his deme (roughly, "village") assembly for a vote on whether to register him as a citizen.[72] Periodically, worries that aliens had infiltrated the rolls led the city to order the demes to requalify each citizen by vote.[73] Presumably many of these votes were pro forma, but personal enemies of a candidate or his family could make trouble.[74] A candidate who was denied or stripped of citizenship had the option of appealing to a court for a final decision.[75] The formal criteria for citizenship were age and parentage,[76] neither of which was easy to prove definitively in an age without detailed record-keeping.[77] Moreover, our one surviving case involving disputed citizenship indicates that at both the deme and court level adherence to extrastatutory norms could influence one's case: the speaker recounts how he was voted honors while serving as a demarch, lists ancestors who had died fighting for the city, and suggests that his opponent's business practices were notorious.[78]

All magistrates also faced a public scrutiny before taking office (*dokimasia*) and an accounting when leaving office (*euthyna*).[79] The *dokimasia* procedure for the various magistrates differed somewhat. It seems that archons (the most powerful magistrates) faced a double scrutiny, first in the Council and then by a popular court, while Council members faced a

---

70 *Ath. Pol.* 53.5.
71 Ar. *Rhetoric* 1374b. Scafuro 1997:137 points out that arbitrations, unlike court speeches, had no time limit, and notes that "we are not likely to insist that arbitral procedures required a stricter adherence to lawful criteria than cases presented before a dikasterion."
72 Todd 1993:179–181.
73 Todd 1993:180.
74 E.g., Dem. 57. For discussion, see E. Cohen 2000a:69–78.
75 Todd 1993:180–181; Harrison 1998:207–208.
76 Todd 1993:180–181.
77 Scafuro 1994.
78 Dem. 57.11, 33, 36–38, 63–65.
79 Todd 1993:126, 285–289; Harrison 1998:200–210.

scrutiny by the Council with the possibility of appeal to a court, and all other magistrates were subject simply to a public hearing in court.[80] The requirements of the *dokimasia* invited discussion of the candidate's adherence to extrastatutory norms: according to the *Constitution of the Athenians*, a candidate was expected to put on evidence showing not only that he was a citizen, but also that he treated his parents well, paid his taxes, and had performed military service.[81] As has often been pointed out, our surviving *dokimasia* speeches indicate that these procedures typically went far beyond establishing the formal requirements of office.[82] For example, the defendant in a *dokimasia* states that he intends "to render an account of [his] whole life," and proceeds to describe his generosity with his siblings, his disdain for dice and drinking, the fact that he had never been named in a lawsuit, and his bravery in military service on several campaigns.[83] All magistrates were also subject to a public accounting as they left office. As part of this procedure, any citizen could present a written complaint to an official about a departing magistrate's conduct in office; if the official thought that the charge was legitimate, the case was referred to court.[84]

The high likelihood that an Athenian would find himself involved in a public hearing where his adherence to extrastatutory norms might matter becomes clear when we realize that most citizens held public office at some point in their lives. There was in the range of 1,200 officials,[85] out of a total adult male citizen population of perhaps 30,000,[86] many of whom were chosen by lot for only one-year terms. Hansen has estimated that with respect to service on the Council alone, "over a third of all citizens over eighteen, and about two thirds of all citizens over forty, became councillors, some of them twice."[87] The speaker in *Against Euboulides*, the citizenship case mentioned earlier, illustrates how often a seemingly ordinary Athenian might find his character the subject of public scrutiny: in addition to his registration as a citizen at eighteen, he also faced a deme

---

80 *Ath. Pol.* 45.3; 55.2–4; Rhodes 1993:615–617; Harrison 1998:200–203.
81 *Ath. Pol.* 55.3. Like the citizenship enrollment procedure, most of these hearings were probably routine.
82 Rhodes 1981:472; MacDowell 1993:168; Hunter 1994:106–109.
83 Lys. 16.9–21.
84 MacDowell 1993:171.
85 Hansen 1999:341.
86 Hansen 1999:90–93.
87 Hansen 1999:249.

and court hearing about his citizenship when his deme revised its rolls, and a *dokimasia* when he was chosen by lot for a priestly office.[88]

It therefore seems fair to say that the average Athenian could anticipate that he might find himself involved in legal proceedings during which his character might become an issue, whether they took the form of trials in a private or public lawsuit or other legal procedures such as small claims hearings, arbitrations, citizenship registration, or public scrutiny and accounting of magistrates. As a result, he had strong incentives to adhere (and to ensure that members of his *oikos* adhered) to well-known social norms so that he could point to these facts to help support his case. Similarly, any opponent or accuser in these proceedings could use his failure to abide by these and other norms against him. It is important to emphasize that the incentives to conform were all the greater because litigants were not limited to violations of extrastatutory norms that were related in some way to the subject matter of the suit or that were committed against the opposing party. Any bad act against any party, however unrelated, could be used against a man in any future case. And a litigant could call upon any good act to help bail him out of any sort of legal trouble.

Did this system simply create incentives for litigants to lie about their opponents' and their own character and past record in court without actually affecting behavior? To be sure, there must have been some false accusations. It would be easier to invent norm violations against a single victim than to allege more public transgressions, like failure to report to military service. Nevertheless, there were several mechanisms to limit these types of misrepresentations in court. Witnesses who affirmed a litigant's statements could be prosecuted for providing false testimony; a third such conviction led to loss of citizenship.[89] A litigant who wanted to advance baseless claims would have to find witnesses who were willing to put themselves at serious risk to help his case. Moreover, juries numbered in the hundreds, increasing the chances that someone on the jury or among the spectators would be familiar with the litigants' reputations and past actions. One litigant, for example, assumes that at least some of the jurors and spectators will be familiar with his opponent's previous conviction: "these facts are widely acknowledged, as those who served as jurors at that time and many

---

[88] Dem. 57.62.
[89] MacDowell 1993:244–245.

of the spectators know well."[90] Litigants regularly ask jurors and spectators to interrupt their opponents by shouting out when they made controversial claims; in fact, the Athenians had a term for this phenomenon, *thorubos*.[91] Aeschines recounts an incident where his opponent in a treason case tried to falsely accuse him of having committed *hubris* against a woman, but the jury shouted him down on account of his good reputation. He adds, "I think that this is my reward for the decent life I have lived."[92] One speaker suggests that the potential for mischaracterization and exaggeration by opponents may have provided an even greater incentive to lead a life beyond reproach: "For the decent man's life should be so clean that it does not even allow the suspicion of blameworthy conduct."[93]

One might also wonder why there was so much litigation in Athens if the accumulation of incentives I describe led to a well-ordered society. The Athenians appear to have been an extremely litigious people by modern standards. Bringing a lawsuit could enhance one's public reputation and jump-start a political career. Even for non-elites the courts provided a forum for status-competition; some prosecutions may have been motivated as much by these concerns as by a feeling that a serious breach of the peace or injury had occurred.[94] It is also true that litigation was, in comparison to modern standards, extraordinarily cheap and easy. We see a similar pattern of extreme litigiousness in many societies where the right and practical access to legal process, particularly legal process against one's social and economic superiors, is relatively new.[95] But this litigiousness does not necessarily reflect a lack of social order: a high level of both litigation and order characterized the New England colonies, for example.[96] A pessimistic interpretation might be that the members of these societies had not yet figured out how rarely litigation results in true satisfaction.

At first blush it might seem far-fetched to think that Athenians would alter their behavior in anticipation that it might sway a future court in their favor. But at least with respect to the performance of public services such as liturgies, litigants could be quite explicit that they were motivated

---

90 Dem. 30.32; for discussion of knowledgeable spectators watching trials see Lanni 1997:188.
91 Lanni 1997; Bers 1985.
92 Aesch. 2.4–5.
93 Aesch. 1.48.
94 Like Christ (1998a:34–36), I believe that prestige was an important, but not the only, motivation for litigation.
95 Mann 1987; Stern 1993; Taylor 1979; Borah 1983.
96 Mann 1987:19; Zuckerman 1970:48–50; Nelson 1975:1–10.

to perform services in part because they thought it might help them in future lawsuits. In fact, the notion that one performs public service with the expectation of receiving *charis* ("gratitude") from the jurors is a common topos in our surviving court speeches.[97] One speaker, for example, lists his public services (four trierarchies, service in four naval battles, and contributions to several war levies) and then baldly states that he performed public service for use in later court cases: "I spent more than was required by the city in order that I might be thought better of by you, so that if I happened to suffer any misfortune I would be in a better position to defend myself in court."[98] Litigants don't make similar statements about their adherence to the other categories of social norms, but that is not surprising. While a litigant might admit without too much shame his hope that generosity to the state would be repaid down the line, a litigant would have to be more circumspect in recasting his honesty or his fidelity to friends in terms of ulterior motives, because in such instances the ulterior motive was antithetical to the norm.

Of course, there is only anecdotal evidence that this mechanism of enforcing extrastatutory norms though the legal system influenced behavior. We can no more prove that Athenians obeyed extrastatutory norms in part because of their enforcement through the legal system than we can say, in the absence of hard data, that any modern statute's sanctions actually cause compliance. We simply don't have enough data to say for certain whether any compliance with these extrastatutory norms should be attributed to the mechanism of norm enforcement described here as opposed to social sanctions, internalized value systems, or, for those norms that were also the subject of legal regulation, direct legal sanctions. It is likely that all these mechanisms played an important role in compliance. But, as noted in Chapter 2, the reliance on private initiative to enforce the laws may have made formal legal sanctions less certain, and therefore less effective, than they are in many other societies. And we saw in Chapter 1 that social sanctions and internalized norms are unlikely to have accounted entirely for Athens' high level of order.

Moreover, there may have been some situations where social norms were likely to be enforced through the court, but not through informal

---

97 Christ 2006:172–181; Johnstone 1999:100–108; Ober 1989:226–230; Whitehead 1983.

98 Lys. 25.13. Another example: the speaker in Lysias, *For Polystratus* explains his motivation for public service: "the reason we treated you well was not to receive money, but so that if we were ever in trouble, you would grant our request for acquittal as a fitting reward" (Lys. 20.31).

Law and Order in Ancient Athens

sanctions. The possibility of finding oneself in serious legal trouble might provide incentives to avoid minor norm violations even though the potential social sanction was low. Athenians appear to have thought that it was worth a lot to be able to claim in court that they had an unblemished record.[99] Litigants also appear to have feared the impression created by a slew of minor infractions, none of which individually was sufficient to incur serious social sanctions.[100] It is impossible to quantify what percentage of compliance with extrastatutory norms can be traced to court practice. But the added incentives generated by court enforcement of norms taken together with litigants' statements that they performed public service in order to improve their chances in court suggest that court enforcement of extrastatutory norms may well have had a significant impact on behavior. It therefore seems plausible to suppose that the Athenian courts played a disciplinary role not by enforcing formal legal rules, but by enforcing extrastatutory norms.

Norm Enforcement, Ancient and Modern

Does anything akin to Athenian-style norm enforcement occur in modern American courts? All but the most hard-liners of legal formalists would admit that modern courts do at times enforce extrastatutory norms, in the sense that these norms play a role in the resolution of some cases, particularly cases heard by juries.[101] But when modern courts enforce extrastatutory norms this process does not, for the most part, affect behavior in the same way that Athenian law seems to have done. Few modern individuals would alter their behavior toward their family for their entire adult lives in the hope that it would help them in any legal dispute over an

99 Litigants regularly make a point of noting that they have never wronged anyone or been prosecuted. E.g., Lys. 5.3; 12.4; 16.10; 21.19; 24.24–26; And. 1.147; Dem. 36.57; 37.56; 54.16.
100 As several of the examples described previously demonstrate, litigants commonly list a long slew of norm violations committed by their opponent (e.g., Dem. 25.53–55; Aesch. 1.42). The impression these passages create is that the speaker hopes to paint a general negative picture of his opponent with multiple charges. This strategy is consistent with Aristotle's discussion in the *Rhetoric* (1.15) of the use of *ethos* in court speeches.
101 E.g., Burns 1999:20–30; Frug 1988. But for the most part in modern courts extrastatutory norms can only trump legal ones surreptitiously while the Athenians openly recognized extrastatutory norms as legitimate factors in court verdicts (Burns 1999:36). In a few limited cases, such as sentencing, and particularly capital sentencing, modern courts do explicitly permit consideration of a party's adherence or nonadherence to a wide range of norms as part of the legal framework for deciding the case.

138

inheritance that might arise in the future. With the exception of some classes of repeat litigants or individuals who can anticipate or are in the midst of litigation,[102] the likelihood of being involved in litigation in the future is not high enough to justify changing behavior based on extrastatutory norms that might or might not affect litigation. This is all the more true because, unlike in Athens, adherence to extrastatutory norms that are perceived to be completely unrelated to the dispute are less likely to play a role. Being involved in a local charity, for example, might help in a criminal sentencing hearing but would likely be much less helpful for a litigant in a family inheritance dispute.

If modern court decisions enforcing extrastatutory norms affect behavior prospectively, they do so primarily through the expressive function of law, a more indirect mechanism than the Athenian approach. Modern courts rarely give individuals concrete incentives to alter their behavior with regard to extrastatutory norms in direct anticipation of litigation. Rather, when a modern court enforces extrastatutory norms in a high-profile case the decision communicates a message about community norms that may then filter down through the culture to affect behavior. For example, a highly publicized unsuccessful rape prosecution may communicate a message that the community believes that provocatively dressed women "deserve" to be raped, and this message may indirectly alter how women dress.[103]

Athenian courts also served an expressive function.[104] Court speakers regularly discuss examples of what they consider to be proper and improper behavior.[105] And the Athenian jury was permitted through its

---

[102] E.g., high-profile, large corporations who routinely find themselves the subject of lawsuits might find it worthwhile to enhance the company's public image for fear of bias in court. Similarly, individuals under investigation for white collar crimes might attempt to improve their image in anticipation of criminal litigation and sentencing. Michael Milken, e.g., touted his charitable work in connection with sentencing on SEC-related criminal charges. In addition, individuals who are likely to be subject to a court's power for a prolonged period of time, e.g., individuals in bankruptcy, those subject to a court-ordered shared custody arrangement, and those whose children have been removed from their homes by social services, have incentives to conform to extralegal norms to win favor with the court.

[103] Kennedy 1993:136–138, 162–175.

[104] In a related vein, the choice to publicly display lists of certain types of convicted offenders – notably traitors – was intended, if we can rely on Lycurgus' interpretation, to leave a "lasting example of the Athenians' attitude toward traitors" (Lyc. 1.117–119). For discussion, see Ober 2008a:186–190.

[105] As we will explore in Chapter 5, court speeches also have served an important role in creating, shaping, and disseminating community norms through persuasion.

verdict to make a public statement about whether the litigants had abided by the community's values, regardless of the result suggested by a strict reading of the statute, will, or contract at issue. But because a jury's verdict could turn on any of a number of specific legal or extrastatutory factors raised in the case, the jury's ability to express a clear and precise moral statement was limited. The trial of Socrates is a good example. Although the jury's overall condemnation of Socrates was well known, his precise crime and exactly what the jury thought of him is unclear (and seems to have been unclear even at the time).[106] As we will see in the next chapter, courts fostered the articulation of norms less through the expressive effect of their verdicts than by providing a forum for court arguments that both reinforced and contested existing standards of behavior.

4.3. The Advantages of Athenian-Style Norm Enforcement

The approach of enforcing extrastatutory norms through formal court processes was particularly well suited to the Athenian context: that is, court enforcement of extrastatutory norms helped Athenian society function more smoothly, and more in keeping with Athenian values, than might have been the case if these norms had been reduced to statutes that were strictly enforced. This is not a normative argument. I make no claims with respect to whether the Athenian system helped to produce "efficient" norms. And, of course, from a modern perspective the conflict between the Athenian approach and contemporary rule-of-law values is hardly attractive. When I say that the Athenian approach was "effective," I mean simply that it was likely to produce incentives for Athenians to comply with the norms that the Athenians sought to enforce. The Athenian approach of enforcing extrastatutory norms in court compensated for deficiencies in the operation of both informal social control and formal legal enforcement. Athenian trials facilitated informal enforcement of norms by publicizing norm violations and by serving as shaming ceremonies. The Athenian approach also compensated for problems in law enforcement stemming from a private prosecution system. A third advantage was that by permitting courts to enforce norms while appearing not to do so, the system bolstered the democratic ideal of a limited state.

106 Millett 2005.

It may bear repeating that that by noting the advantages of the Athenian approach to norm enforcement I am not providing a functionalist analysis.[107] Nor am I arguing that the Athenians consciously adopted this approach. The enforcement of extrastatutory norms through the courts was in my view the natural by-product of a legal system that permitted and encouraged consideration of facts and arguments unrelated to the specific requirements of the statute under which the suit was brought. My argument here is that the Athenian mode of norm enforcement, though rooted in democratic cultural values, had several advantageous effects.

Given the Athenian cultural context, enforcing extrastatutory norms through the courts was preferable to using formal rules to enforce these norms in court. The Athenian approach was preferable to a conventional rule-of-law approach because it promoted order and compliance with norms while preserving the Athenian attachment to discretionary and popular justice. In the context of a private prosecution system with sporadic enforcement, the Athenian approach may even have been more effective at fostering compliance with norms than if the Athenians had attempted to enforce these norms through formal rules.

Facilitating Informal Sanctions

What was the relationship between the phenomenon of norm enforcement I am describing and the conventional mechanism of informal norm enforcement – social sanctions? The courts complemented, rather than supplanted, social sanctions. As discussed in Chapter 1, Athens was not a face-to-face society; the urban center was a bustling metropolis, and even members of the smallest rural demes would be forced to interact with men they didn't know on frequent trips to the city.[108] Information about norm violations would not always become known to potential business partners or the small group of neighbors and fellow demesmen who were in a position to enforce social sanctions. The courts may have assisted informal norm enforcement by improving information flow.[109] Court

---

107 For further discussion, see the Introduction.

108 Osborne 1985b; E. Harris 2002:72–74; Ober 2008b:74. Theophrastus' *agroikos* ("country man"), e.g., goes to the city to shop and get his hair cut. Hansen 1999 also discusses evidence that Athenians regularly walked long distances from the countryside to attend the assembly, choruses, festivals, and so on.

109 Cf. Milgrom, North, and Weingast (1990), who argue that medieval institutions played a role in facilitating information flow about merchants' trustworthiness.

arguments based on violations of extrastatutory norms resulted not only in formal sanctions for norm violations through court verdicts. The courts gave litigants incentives to ferret out their opponents' norm violations, and court speeches publicized these violations, making it more likely that other citizens in small village communities would impose informal social sanctions.[110]

The Athenian courts were the ideal institution for publicizing allegations and findings of wrongdoing. Not only were hundreds of jurors present at every case, but court cases were a major form of public entertainment.[111] Litigants regularly assume that the community at large will be aware of court verdicts.[112] It seems likely that news of allegations made during a court case would find its way back to a litigant's deme community, potentially resulting in informal sanctions. In this respect, allegations of misconduct made in court could affect the reputation of the victorious litigant as well as his less fortunate opponent. Aeschines states, for example, that even if he wins his suit he will consider his life not worth living if anyone in the jury is convinced by his opponent's extrastatutory accusation that he had committed *hubris* against a woman.[113]

The Athenian trial was also in some sense a form of shaming ceremony. Litigants typically represented themselves in court,[114] personally presenting their case (and their character) to the assembled jurors. The experience of having one's character publicly attacked or losing a vote of hundreds of one's fellow citizens must have been extremely humbling for seasoned orators, let alone ordinary Athenians. The announcement of the verdict would ensure that the losing party suffered some punishment for his violation of legal and extrastatutory norms, whether or not the victorious litigant managed to collect on the judgment rendered by the court. Indeed, even the very fact of an accusation was thought to bring shame: Demosthenes alleges that his enemy Meidias convinced someone to bring charges against Demosthenes for military desertion even though he had no evidence and had no intention of proceeding to trial, because the notice of the charge in the agora would hurt Demosthenes' reputation.[115]

---

110 Hunter 1994:117.
111 Lanni 1997; 2012; see also Chapter 5.
112 And. 1.105; Din. 1.22; Lys. 1.36.
113 Aesch. 2.5.
114 They could also use cospeakers (*sunegoroi*). For discussion, see Rubinstein 2000.
115 Dem. 21.103.

The collateral shame sanctions that accompanied being charged and convicted in an Athenian court supplemented any formal legal sanctions meted out by the jury.

Compensating for Underenforcement of Statutes

The second advantage of the Athenian approach arises from its peculiar quality that permitted a litigant to raise any norm violations his opponent had committed in the past against any person, however unrelated to the subject of the suit at hand. The Athenian approach compensated for difficulties of enforcement stemming from a private prosecution system by encouraging litigants to uncover and sanction their opponents' past violations.

As described in Chapter 2, the legal system's reliance on private initiative appears to have resulted in systematic underenforcement of Athenian statutes through suits brought under those statutes. And the prosecutions that did occur may have been irregular and unpredictable, stemming from factors like political or personal rivalries that were not related to the seriousness or visibility of the infraction. The Athenian approach of enforcing extrastatutory norms in court helped compensate for the underenforcement of the laws. A litigant could attack his opponent for any norm violation committed against anyone in the past, no matter how unrelated to the issue in dispute. This system gave litigants incentives to investigate their opponents and uncover any past violations of statutory or extrastatutory norms.[116] For this reason, Athenians could not blithely commit victimless crimes or injure those who might be powerless to sue them; these offenses could come back to haunt them if they ever found themselves in a court or other public hearing in the future. The prevalence of discussion of extrastatutory norms related to military service and other public services in our speeches may have been particularly important in enforcing these norms since such victimless offenses rarely became the subject of a formal legal charge.

Demosthenes 47 offers an example of how the use of extrastatutory norms could offer retribution for crimes committed against those who were effectively unprotected by law. The speaker attacks his opponent for

---

[116] Demosthenes (21.23) tells us, e.g., that in preparing for his prosecution of Meidias he collected examples of Meidias' wrongful acts against others for use in his suit.

collecting on a judgment by violently seizing his property when he was not home rather than going with the speaker to the bank to get the money.[117] He offers an extended, poignant account of how his opponent violently pried a cup from the hands of his faithful, elderly former nurse, beating her so badly that she died from her wounds.[118] He describes how he sought legal advice and learned that because the nurse was neither his relative nor a slave (she had been freed but returned to his household in her old age) he did not have standing to bring homicide charges.[119] But the prominence of this incident in the case suggests that although the defendant could not formally be punished for homicide the allegations regarding treatment of the nurse would be incorporated in the jury's judgment.[120]

The surviving speeches offer other examples. One litigant states that his father is afraid to come into court to support him because the father is afraid that if he does someone will confront him with allegations of past wrongs he may have committed against them during his public life.[121] Demosthenes is quite explicit about how consideration of unrelated crimes can compensate for problems of underenforcement in the Athenian system. He lists the many people Meidias has wronged in the past, noting that most of them did not bring suit because they lacked the money, or the speaking ability, or were intimidated by Meidias.[122] He then urges the jury to punish Meidias for these unprosecuted crimes: "for if a man is so powerful that he can commit acts of this sort and deprive each one of you of exacting justice from him, now that he is securely in our power, he should be punished in common by all of us as an enemy of the state."[123] The speaker in Lysias 30 expresses a similar sentiment: "since [the defendant] has not paid the penalty for his crimes individually, you must exact satisfaction now for all of them collectively."[124]

It is of course true that the Athenian approach also decreased the incentives to obey statutory law because even clear-cut violations of law might result in acquittals on extrastatutory grounds. It is impossible to quantify

[117] Dem. 47.52ff.
[118] Dem. 47.52–61.
[119] Dem. 47.68–70.
[120] For a discussion of the central place of the death of the nurse in the argumentation of this speech, see Wohl 2010:98–114.
[121] Dem. 39.3.
[122] Dem. 21.141.
[123] Dem. 21.142.
[124] Lys. 30.6.

the gains and losses in compliance that would result from choosing either the Athenian or a rule-of-law system. But given the problems of underenforcement produced by the private prosecution system, particularly in the case of victimless offenses and offenses committed against victims who lacked the resources to sue, it seems likely that making any bad act fair game in any case would increase the chances of punishment (and thus the incentives to comply) more than a conventional rule-of-law approach. In any case, from the Athenian perspective their approach had the distinct advantage of fostering compliance while also promoting the Athenian commitment to individualized and popular justice.[125]

So much for cases where the legal or extrastatutory norm violation had not been raised in a previous lawsuit. But the Athenian system also created redundancy in the system. In essence, litigants could be sanctioned again and again for the same legal or extrastatutory norm violation in every future lawsuit. Did this approach lead to overenforcement? Not necessarily, because evidence of an individual norm violation did not mean that the litigant automatically lost his case. The jury considered the violation as part of a broader evaluation of the litigant's conduct over his entire life; each past violation continued to be relevant to this exercise in every subsequent evaluation of the litigant's character. For the same reason, with the exception of particularly heinous crimes, the system did not undermine itself by creating a class of outlaws who had little incentive to comply once they had developed a reputation as a norm violator that might be used against them in court. Because any particular norm violation was just one factor among many considered by the jury, Athenians with prior records had incentives to rehabilitate themselves by demonstrating adherence to statutory and extrastatutory norms.[126] In this way, the enforcement of extrastatutory norms in Athenian courts was much more nuanced than those informal social sanctioning systems that rely on the relatively crude measure of temporary or permanent exclusion from the group for all violations.[127]

Perhaps most important, the Athenian approach did not set up a system whereby those with good character and public service had no incentives

---

[125] Lanni 2006.

[126] E.g., Lys. 31.24.

[127] E.g., Bernstein (1996) and Milgrom, North, and Weingast (1990) describe systems using the informal sanction of exclusion. But many informal systems do use a gradation of sanctions (Ellickson 1991:213–219).

to obey the law. As I've described in detail elsewhere,[128] jurors considered extrastatutory argumentation as part of their evaluation of what was a just and fair result, given the particular circumstances of the case and the character of the parties. In other words, the jury was not simply trying to determine and reward the litigant with the better character. Rather, jurors considered issues such as character and past acts as a way to help determine what the litigants deserved in the context of the dispute before them.[129] The litigants' character was extremely important, but having good character references would be unlikely to save a litigant from conviction in a dispute where he had clearly acted unfairly, and evidence of one piece of misconduct would be unlikely to doom the case of a litigant who was clearly in the right. We have several references to successful prosecutions brought against prominent citizens who had performed public services.[130] Given the stark economic differences between the liturgical class and the average juror, jurors were probably particularly sensitive to making sure that wealthy citizens could not place themselves above the law by virtue of their public services.

Maintaining the Fiction of a Limited State

The Athenian approach to norm enforcement also promoted compliance with norms relating to private conduct and public service while maintaining the fiction of a limited state. By enforcing extrastatutory norms rather than formal statutes relating to personal conduct and public service, the Athenians were able to maintain the fictions of an unregulated private sphere and of a city and military supported by patriotism and volunteerism rather than coercion.

Athenian democratic ideology included the notion that the state did not interfere with private conduct that did not impinge on the state's interests.[131] Scholars have interpreted such statements, along with Athenian legal practice, as evidence of a "private sphere" of conduct free from legal regulation.[132] These scholars have pointed out that in Athens there was no

---

[128] Lanni 2006:41–74.
[129] Lanni 2006:59–64.
[130] E.g., Dem. 34.50, 59.72–86; Din. 1.13; 3.17.
[131] D. Cohen 1991a:229 provides examples, including Thuc. 2.39; Dem. 22.51; Lys. 25.33; Ar. *Pol.* 1320a30; see also Hansen 2010.
[132] D. Cohen 1991a; Wallace 1997.

morals legislation as such; legislation was limited to activity that harmed a specific victim or affected the state's interest.[133] Thus there was no provision to prosecute an adulterer in the courts because Athenian law "did not aim at regulating adultery as a form of sexual misconduct."[134] Rather, the law sought to regulate adultery "as a source of public violence and disorder" by addressing only a limited situation: what options were available to a man who caught an adulterer in the act.[135] Similarly, the law generally permitted homosexuality and prostitution. In fact, prostitution was subject to state taxes and the state condoned the practice by treating contracts for sexual services just like any other enforceable contract.[136] But several laws protected young boys from homosexual advances by older men.[137] And we have seen that a citizen who had been a prostitute was not permitted to speak in the Assembly, apparently on the theory that such a man was morally unworthy of democratic leadership.[138] For the Athenians, limited state interference in private conduct was one of the primary characteristics of a democracy.[139]

We have seen that the state, through the law courts, *did* play a role in enforcing norms relating to private conduct. The courts played a disciplinary role, providing incentives for Athenians to comply with sexual and other norms of private conduct. But the fact that these norms were not expressed in statutes and were not the formal basis for lawsuits permitted the Athenians to maintain the fiction, central to their democratic ideology, that they enjoyed freedom in their private lives. At the same time, the legal system did in practice help to foster adherence to norms of private conduct by creating incentives to comply beyond those provided through traditional informal sanctioning mechanisms.

Another central tenet of Athenian democratic ideology was that its citizens served the state out of patriotism rather than coercion. The Athenian

---

[133] D. Cohen 1991a; Wallace 1997.

[134] D. Cohen 1991a:124.

[135] D. Cohen 1991a:124.

[136] Aesch. 1.119, 160–161; Lys. 3.22–26; Aesch. 1.160–161; E. Cohen 2000b, 2007.

[137] If a relative or guardian hired out a boy as a prostitute, both the relative/guardian and the customer could be prosecuted under a *graphe* (Aesch. 1.13–14). A separate law provided that acting as a pimp for a free boy was punishable by death (Aesch. 1.14). For a discussion of this topic, see D. Cohen 1991a:176.

[138] Aesch. 1.19–20, 28–32; Dover 1989:19–31; MacDowell 2000; Cohen 1991a:175–186; Fisher 2001:36–52.

[139] Thuc. 2.39; Dem. 25.25. Arist. *Politics* 1310a30; Pl. *Republic* 557b, 560–561, 565b, *Laws* 700a; D. Cohen 1991a:124; Hansen 2010.

victory over the much more numerous Persians was often put down to the superiority of free men fighting for their homeland over a force made up, in Euripides' words, of "all slaves but one."[140] The Athenians also compared their approach of exhorting citizens to virtue through education to that of the Spartans, who attempted to force its citizens to be brave and public-spirited through strict regulations, only to find them "running away from the law as boys from a father, because they have not been educated by persuasion but by force."[141] Christ has detailed the Athenian "preference for persuasion over compulsion" in promoting good citizenship.[142] He notes that although legal procedures existed for prosecuting draft-dodging and avoidance of liturgies and taxes, such prosecutions were relatively rare.[143] Athens did not actively try to encourage these prosecutions by, for example, providing for a state prosecutor[144] or relaxing the risks borne by volunteer prosecutors because "compulsion to serve the city was potentially in conflict with ideals of personal freedom ... [;] Athenians were apparently uncomfortable with the rigid exercise of public authority against private individuals."[145]

Just as in the case of norms of private conduct, the courts did enforce norms relating to military and public service. But because these norms were extrastatutory and rarely served as the legal basis for lawsuits, the Athenians could tell themselves that discussion of these norms in court may have served to persuade and educate citizens, but did not constitute coercion. The Athenian approach of enforcing extrastatutory norms through the courts created state sanctions for violations of public service norms, while permitting the Athenians to maintain the fiction that Athenians fought for and served the state out of patriotism.

Did the Athenians really buy into this fiction, given that it was well known that juries might be influenced by appeals to extrastatutory norms? We cannot know for sure, but two examples suggest that the Athenians may have thought the distinction between direct enforcement through a statute rather than through extrastatutory norms was significant. We will

---

140 Eur. *Helen* 276.
141 Pl. *Republic* 548a–b (trans. Christ 2006); for discussion see Christ 2006:42–43.
142 Christ 2006:42–43, 62–64.
143 Christ 2006:40–45, 62–64.
144 For the exceptions to this rule, principally high profile political cases and *euthunai*, see the discussion in Chapter 4.
145 Christ 2006:62–63.

see in Chapter 5 that the Athenians rejected Lycurgus' attempt to prosecute for treason a private citizen who fled Athens during a crisis precisely
because, according to one prominent theory, such a direct prosecution
against a private citizen for private conduct was novel. Presumably dis-
paragement of the defendant's actions in an unrelated lawsuit would not
have raised any eyebrows. And as we will see in Chapter 6, the Athenians
celebrated their restraint and moderation embodied in the amnesty that
prohibited direct prosecution of oligarchic collaborators during the reign
of the Thirty tyrants, even as litigants' behavior during the oligarchy continued to be raised as character evidence in unrelated lawsuits after the war.

***

It is fashionable among historians and legal scholars to emphasize the limits of courts' and law's ability to influence behavior. An Athenian court
appears at first glance to have been an even weaker player in its milieu than
its modern counterpart – highly unpredictable and prey to distracting stories about the litigants' morality and "private" lives. But this system must
have been capable of producing anxiety about the potential consequences
of any violation of the community's norms. This state of affairs is fright-
ening to anyone brought up in a Western culture of individual rights and
the rule of law. But it must have been central to the operation of a society
(and, for a time, an empire) that depended to a large degree on voluntary compliance with onerous norms of personal conduct – the norms of
courage, sacrifice, public service, participation in self-governance, and obedience to law celebrated in Thucydides' presentation of Pericles' funeral
oration.[146]

---

[146] Thuc. 2.37–40.

FIVE

Court Argument and the Shaping of Norms

The mechanism for fostering order that I described in the previous chapter — enforcing extralegal norms through formal court processes — focused on norms that were relatively stable and uncontroversial. But what about norms that were unclear or in flux? Arguments in Athenian courts not only reinforced existing norms but also helped shape them. This chapter explores how the courts promoted order by providing a public forum for collective norm contestation and definition. After a general discussion of the features that made the Athenian courts particularly favorable sites for shaping norms, I turn to a number of short case studies in which court speakers debate controversial norms relating to pederasty, interpersonal violence, self-help, and the military and civic responsibilities of private citizens.

5.1. The Courts as Sites for Debating and Shaping Norms

In the absence of a formal education system or a religion with moral content, it is unsurprising that the city's political and legal institutions played a central role in shaping as well as reinforcing shared norms of conduct.[1] Several aspects of the Athenian court system made it a particularly effective forum to elaborate public norms. Some of these features — such as publicity and the opportunity for dialogue — also existed in the Assembly, the other formal legal institution that helped shape norms in Athens. While legislative debate in the Assembly produced a more focused discussion and

---

[1] For discussion of potential other fora for shaping norms, see Chapter 1.

decision regarding a particular norm, we will see that the courts' ad hoc and incremental approach may have actually given it some advantages over the Assembly as a forum for the elaboration of norms.

Perhaps most important is the sheer volume of debates over norms that took place in the courts. While the Assembly normally met forty times a year,[2] the courts were in session approximately 200 days a year.[3] Moreover, controversies over the norms most critical for maintaining order — those relating to interpersonal relations, violence, business transactions, and the duties of citizenship — were likely to come up more often in the context of the courts than in political assemblies. To take one example, in Chapter 1 we examined the statutes governing the use of violent self-help. It appears that only a handful of laws were passed on this topic, and several of them seem quite old, some even predating the democracy. By contrast, if our surviving speeches are any indication, court disputes often raised questions about the proper limits of self-help.[4] Discussion of the proper and improper use of violence was not limited to cases arising out of a violent incident, but could also occur as part of the discussion of the parties' conduct in the course of litigation[5] or a party's prior unrelated conduct.[6]

In fact, the Athenians' flexible approach to evidence and laws made the Athenian courts a far more receptive forum for debate over norms than modern courts. Because Athenian litigants were not limited to discussion of the official charge, court speeches could serve as a vehicle to debate broader issues, from the moral status of homosexual pederasty[7] to the level of forgiveness to be accorded those who had collaborated with the Thirty Tyrants.[8] The vagueness of many Athenian laws invited litigants to debate the definition, purpose, and merits of the norm expressed in the law, rather than simply the application of the law to the facts of the particular case. For example, Conover has shown how the broad laws against

---

[2] Hansen 1999:133–134. At different periods it is possible that the standard number of meetings was ten or thirty; additional meetings may also have been called in some periods for political trials held in the Assembly.

[3] Hansen 1999:186–187.

[4] On which, see the subsequent text.

[5] E.g., the speaker in Demosthenes 47 contrasts his opponent's use of violence while seizing property for a debt to his own respectful and peaceful attempt to collect on a debt. For discussion, see Christ 1998b.

[6] E.g., Dem. 25.55, 57, 61; see generally Lanni 2006:59–64.

[7] See the following text and Chapter 3.

[8] See Chapter 6.

bribery (*dorodokia*) opened up a space for the Athenians to contest and articulate what constituted legitimate (and illegitimate) political practice as they shifted over time.[9] Moreover, because jurors were not bound to apply the law strictly or to follow precedent,[10] even where the law was clear, litigants could question the normative underpinnings of a particular law and jurors had discretion to change the law or its application to bring it into line with popular sentiment.

To be sure, there was a key limit to the Athenian courts' ability to foster deliberation and articulation of norms: the absence of written, reasoned decisions prevented Athenian juries from expressing a clear statement of community norms. Debate in the Assembly centered on a specific policy question and the vote revealed a clear statement of the majority's position. Court cases, by contrast, typically involved multiple normative questions, often bound up with factual disputes. Because so many legal, factual, and extralegal norms might be in play in any given case, it could be difficult to know which argument had swayed the jury, or even whether there was a consensus among the jurors who had voted for the same verdict.

Yet in some respects the very lack of clarity in court verdicts may have made the courts a more receptive venue for debating norms than the Assembly. As is well known, the Athenians were very conservative when it came to their laws.[11] Older laws, particularly those attributed to Solon, garnered the most respect. Under the fifth-century *graphe paranomon* procedure, anyone who proposed a law that was *paranomos* ("unconstitutional" or "contrary to law") could be prosecuted and punished within a year of making the proposal, even if the Assembly had approved the law. In the fourth century the Athenians' resistance to legal change was enshrined in

---

9 Conover 2010:243–257. Conover (2010:185–186) emphasizes the educative function of judicial outcomes (i.e., verdicts), but we will see subsequently that the "message" of a verdict was not always so clear, and that losing arguments and arguments that play a minor role in a case could also shape public norms. In a similar vein, Lape (2006:140) describes how jury verdicts served as "social precedents" by clarifying both the meaning of the law and the values endorsed by the law. Riess (2012:17–18, 140–157) views the courts as a venue for ritual reenactment of permissible and impermissible violence that helped to instill the prevalent values regarding violence into the citizens. While I agree with Riess that court cases provided a forum for debating the proper limits of permissible violence, I do not agree with his general assessment of the courts as serving a ritual function akin to magic and unrelated to deciding who was right and wrong (Riess 2012:145).

10 On the lack of binding precedent, see Lanni 2004; on the discretion of Athenian jurors, see Lanni 2006:41–74.

11 See, e.g., Boegehold 1996; Thomas 1996.

the *nomothesia* procedure, the multistep process for changing or introducing new laws of general application (*nomoi*), which would include laws regulating violence, business transactions, litigation procedure, and the like.

Court cases provided an opportunity to challenge the normative underpinnings of a law as applied in a particular situation without challenging the law.[12] The incremental nature of court cases made it easier for litigants and jurors to critically examine norms that might be in flux, and to slowly change the law case by case without actually overturning any statute. In the modern context, scholars have shown that "norm entrepreneurs" — that is, actors seeking to shift society's thinking about a particular norm — are more successful when they proceed slowly, using "gentle nudges" in the desired direction rather than risking a backlash by getting too far ahead of popular sentiment.[13] Athenians may have been more receptive to attempts to change norms, if, for example, they came in the form of an argument that a particular litigant had crossed the line in using self-help in a specific situation, rather than an argument that the Athenians should adopt a new rule limiting the use of self-help more generally.

Moreover, norms could be questioned and tentatively challenged in the context of a court case, beginning a public debate on an issue without eliciting a direct vote on the question. In this way, even arguments raised by a losing litigant might begin to shift public opinion, while fledgling changes raised in the Assembly might be squelched by the clear statement of public disapproval generated by a negative vote.[14] The case studies in the next part offer concrete examples of how the incrementalism of the courts contributed to their role as a forum for norm contestation and elaboration.

In addition, the normative debate initiated by individual court cases may have been richer than the discussion over more general laws in the Assembly. As already mentioned, Athenian laws were notoriously vague, and often did not define the criteria for the offense, let alone applicable defenses or exceptions.[15] The courts may have been an even more influential forum for norm elaboration than the Assembly precisely because court

---

12 In fact, litigants do not directly argue that the law is wrong or that the jurors should ignore the law in favor of justice; rather, they tend to argue that both the law and justice/equity are on their side. For discussion, see Carey 1996:41; Christ 1998a:195; Lanni 2006:73.

13 See, e.g., Kahan 2000.

14 On the tendency for disapproval by one decision maker of a proposed norm change to result in "self-reinforcing resistance" to the change, see Kahan 2000:608.

15 On the vagueness of Athenian laws, see Lanni 2006:67–68.

cases invited the speakers, jurors, and spectators to contemplate what constituted proper behavior in the context of a specific situation, with all its complexities and confounding features.

Hyperides' *Against Athenogenes* may offer an example. Recall that the prosecutor, Epicrates, fell in love with a slave boy and offered to buy the freedom of the boy as well as his brother and father from their owner, the defendant Athenogenes. When they met to conclude the deal, Athenogenes proposed that Epicrates buy the slaves instead, along with the perfume shop they managed. This would mean that Epicrates would become liable for any debts they owed, but Athenogenes assured him that the stock in the shop was worth far more than any debts. Epicrates admits that Athenogenes read out the contract, but he claimed that he was too distracted and eager to get access to the boy to listen carefully. Soon after concluding the deal he learned that the boy's father had considerable debts and that the contract included a provision that Epicrates would assume responsibility for any debts owed by the slave to anyone else.

The applicable law stated simply that any voluntary agreement made between two parties was binding.[16] One can imagine that the Assembly debate[17] over such a general and seemingly uncontroversial law likely would not generate significant discussion about norms in business transactions, since the lawmakers made no effort to anticipate and provide for circumstances where jurors might consider making an exception to the rule. Epicrates' case, by contrast, invites debate about how to assess the conduct of each party and how the state should react. Certainly Athenogenes does not come off well, at least in Epicrates' telling. But Epicrates is not without fault either: he walked into a deal intending to buy some slaves' freedom and walked out the owner of a perfume shop without doing any due diligence, and he admits that he barely listened to the reading of the contract terms before signing the agreement. Should the court punish the

---

[16] Hyp. 3.13; cf. Dem. 42.12; 47.77; 56.2. Epicrates suggests that the law provides that the agreement must be just, but since this provision is not cited in other cases discussing the law it is unclear whether this was part of the law or an interpretive gloss provided by Epicrates. For a convincing argument that the general contract law did not include limitations, see Phillips 2009:89–106. In any case, the point that debate over such a general and seemingly unobjectionable rule in the Assembly would be much less likely to generate productive debate than a case like this one holds true even if the law included a clause requiring that the agreement be just.

[17] We do not know the date of the general contract law; Gernet (1955:220) posits the end of the fifth century; Phillips (2009:106–107) suggests that the law may be Solonian.

unscrupulous seller even though the contract was in order, or should it take the position that the careless and gullible buyer got what he deserved? One can imagine jurors and court spectators discussing this case, and the broader question of what is and isn't acceptable business behavior, in barbershops and with their neighbors;[18] it is harder to imagine that the passage of the general contract law would have generated as much discussion and debate about business norms.

Finally, debates about norms in court were likely to have a broad impact because of the publicity surrounding trials. In addition to the hundreds of jurors in attendance, trials regularly attracted spectators.[19] Trials involving prominent politicians appear to have been particularly popular,[20] but we also hear of Athenians stopping to watch ordinary trials they came across in the agora as they went about their business.[21] The Athenian courts enjoyed a monopoly of cultural space unparalleled in the modern world, in which myriad sources of information and entertainment vie for citizens' attention. For the Athenians, the primary sources of entertainment and activity were festivals, Assembly meetings, and trials. For the two-hundred odd days a year that the courts were in session, trials were the only game in town. It is important to note that jurors and members of the audience were not merely passive spectators; the common practice of audience clamor (*thorubos*) provided immediate feedback about the public's reaction to particular controversial arguments.[22]

This public dialogue continued long after the conclusion of the case. Speakers regularly assume that information about court proceedings will reach beyond the immediate courtroom audience. Typical is Aeschines' admonition to the jurors that their fellow citizens will hear about their decision: "And so you should cast your vote not as a man giving judgment, but as men under observation, with an eye to your defense before those citizens who are not here but will ask you about your verdict."[23] Discussion of court cases and the norms they implicated was not limited to citizen men. The speaker in Lysias' *Against the Grain Dealers*, declares that traders,

---

[18] On discussion of court cases outside of court, see the following text.

[19] See Lanni 1997.

[20] Just more than half of the references to bystanders in our court cases come from speeches delivered by famous politicians (Lanni 1997).

[21] See, e.g., Eubulus fr. 74 K-A; for discussion, see Lanni 1997.

[22] On *thorubos*, see Bers 1985.

[23] Aesch. 3.247; see also Din. 1.22; 2.19; Dem. 20.165.

presumably many of them noncitizens, are watching the case closely.[24] The speaker in Demosthenes' *Against Neaira* contemplates a juror being challenged by the female members of his family who disagree with his verdict.[25] Vlassopoulos has examined the noninstitutional sites for public debate, including the agora, barbershops, taverns, triremes, and houses, which might permit women, noncitizens, and slaves to participate in the dialogue about norms raised by particular court cases.[26] In this way, discourse in the courts may have played a role in reinforcing and shaping norms even among women and noncitizens who could not participate as jurors.

5.2. Case Studies

We turn now to a series of case studies that illustrate in more detail how the courts helped shape and define norms by offering speakers an opportunity to articulate a case for acceptance or rejection of a new norm. We will see that in some cases, the norm at issue in the case had already gained significant traction in society but was not yet enshrined in law (Lysias 1); in others the norm was disputed (Demosthenes 21 and 54); and in still others the speaker used the court to float a relatively innovative position (Lycurgus 1). Of course we cannot quantify the extent to which a particular court argument contributed to a norm shift, independent of other societal factors. But these cases illustrate how Athenian litigants could range beyond the details of the case before them to advance, in the presence of hundreds of jurors and spectators, a particular viewpoint about a new or controversial norm.

Aeschines, Against Timarchus: *Testing the Limits of Noble Pederasty*

Aeschines' prosecution of Timarchus for speaking in the Assembly after having been a prostitute[27] offers a vivid illustration of how court speeches could foster debate over controversial norms. As discussed in Chapter 3, the trial took place against a backdrop of popular anxiety and ambivalence about homosexual pederasty, particularly as practiced by the

---

24 Lys. 22.18–22.
25 Dem. 59.109.
26 Vlassopoulos 2007.
27 Timarchus was also accused of having squandered his estate. For detailed discussion of the case, see Chapter 3.

city's political leaders. This famous speech has been the subject of many studies,[28] and I will not examine every aspect of Aeschines' rhetorical strategy and how it may have been received by the audience. Rather, the focus will be on how Aeschines took advantage of the flexibility and incrementalism of the Athenian courts not only to secure Timarchus' conviction, but also to advance a moral argument about the boundaries of acceptable sexual behavior.

Of course, Aeschines' primary aim in prosecuting Timarchus was revenge against a political opponent, not a moral crusade. But Aeschines seized on the moral anxiety of the time[29] to frame the prosecution as an opportunity for the jurors "to make a new discipline in the city" by encouraging the young toward models of virtue and deterring shameful conduct like that of Timarchus.[30] As Fisher points out, Demosthenes' later description of how Aeschines presented the case as an attempt to save the city's youth from moral turpitude[31] suggests that many members of the jury may also have viewed the case in these terms.[32] In fact, this interpretation offers one plausible explanation for the jury's vote to convict Timarchus despite the paucity of hard evidence of actual prostitution.

The Athenians' flexible approach to law and evidence made it possible for Aeschines to range far beyond the specific charge against Timarchus to debate the contours of acceptable sexual behavior. First, a significant portion of the speech is devoted to discussion of the various laws designed to ensure sexual morality of boys and young men and to protect the integrity of the democratic process from sexually corrupt influences.[33] Second, we have seen that the law did not define *hetairesis*, and that the line between noble pederasty and prostitution was blurry and shifting. As a result, Aeschines focuses not on applying the terms of the law to

---

[28] Of the many discussions of Aeschines' rhetorical strategy, Fisher (2001:53–66) and Lape (2006) are most helpful here. Lape (2006) in particular focuses on how Aeschines, in the course of vilifying Timarchus' behavior, articulates a contrasting set of democratic moral values for the jurors.

[29] Fisher (2001:6–67) describes additional factors unrelated to ambivalence about pederasty that may have fostered a sense of moral crisis at the time, including the threat from Macedon, widespread worries about bribery and corruption of public officials, and worry about corruption in the citizens' rolls.

[30] Aesch. 1.191–192.

[31] Dem. 19.285–287.

[32] Fisher 2001:54. Lape (2006:140) argues that although the law and the case involved a public figure, the verdict was seen as exemplary for all citizens.

[33] Aesch. 1.6–36.

Timarchus, but on showing more generally that his behavior was shameful and rendered him unfit to serve as a political leader.[34] Aeschines' narrative of Timarchus' youthful debauchery criticizes the defendant's behavior on a number of grounds: promiscuity,[35] subservience and/or dependence,[36] lack of self-control,[37] and submission to anal penetration.[38] This approach invited debate about proper sexual mores both within and beyond the context of the trial, and opened up the possibility that sexual norms and the understanding of *hetairesis* might shift over time even as the statute remained unchanged.

It is important to emphasize Aeschines' achievement in gaining a conviction in this case: he convinced the jurors to disenfranchise an active politician for acts taken as a youth, basing his case not on any evidence that he was paid for sex, but on transgressions against the subtle and ill-defined norms of noble pederasty.[39] The incrementalism of the Athenian courts may have lightened Aeschines' burden and increased the chances of conviction: there was no need for the jury to officially adopt stricter norms regarding pederasty,[40] or even to pinpoint what it was about Timarchus' behavior that brought him within the ambit of the statute. It was enough that the jurors agreed that Timarchus' behavior, taken as a whole, had crossed the line. Although the jury's verdict applied only to the specific circumstances of this case, it is hard to imagine that Athenians would not view Timarchus' conviction, years after the fact, as a signal that the norms around pederasty were tightening. In fact, the very lack of clarity in the verdict may have created even more momentum for shifting norms in this case: as discussed in Chapter 3, the blurriness of the line between honorable pederasty and prostitution may have induced some to avoid any activity that could be misconstrued and leave them open to prosecution.[41] The absence of a clear message regarding the boundaries of acceptable

---

34 Aesch. 1.39–70.
35 Aesch. 1.40; 51–52.
36 Aesch. 1.41–42
37 Aesch. 1.42.
38 Aesch. 1.41, 45–46, 55.
39 Fisher 2001:53–54.
40 In fact, Aeschines is careful to suggest that some subset of pederastic relationships were noble (Aesch. 1. 131–141); for discussion, see Fisher 2001:59.
41 For discussion of how minor uncertainty in the breadth of a legal standard may lead to over-compliance, see Hadfield 1994 and discussion in Chapter 2.

behavior in the court's verdict may have also helped fuel public discussion about the case and the moral issues it raised.

In sum, we see in Aeschines 1 how a litigant whose primary interest was simply to win his case might find himself enlisting the jurors in a broader debate over sexual norms. Both Aeschines' arguments and the jury's verdict may have subtly shifted the public's view of these issues. Perhaps most important, the salacious details of Timarchus' case were bound to generate discussion and debate outside the courtroom.

Demosthenes' Against Meidias *and* Against Conon: *Debating Interpersonal Violence*

Demosthenes' *Against Meidias* and *Against Conon* illustrate the important role played by the courts in Athens' gradual and incomplete transition from tribal norms of violent retaliation to cooperative norms of physical restraint. These two cases, which both involve long-standing personal enmity that erupted into violence, have been used to validate opposing views of Athens as either an honor-bound feuding society or a model of non-retaliation and communal feeling.[42] These speeches can be interpreted in such radically different ways because they reveal that the norms surrounding interpersonal insults and violence were controversial. In both speeches, the speaker argues for an ethic of physical restraint in the face of personal insults while acknowledging the existence of contrary views. We will see that court argument in cases such as these may have helped shift popular norms away from resolving interpersonal conflicts with violence and self-help and toward physical restraint and litigation.

In Demosthenes 54, Ariston prosecutes Conon for battery (*aikeia*) for brutally attacking him in the agora one evening. Ariston and Conon had been enemies for some time before the attack. According to Ariston, Conon's son saw him walking at night in the agora and ran off to summon Conon and several friends from a party. The drunken posse not only viciously beat Ariston, but also humiliated him by stripping him of his clothing and crowing like a victorious cock over his prone body.[43]

---

[42] Compare D. Cohen 1995:90–101; 119–142 with Herman 2006:156–159; 167–176; 190–215; see also Fisher 1998; Riess 2012:131–140.

[43] Dem. 54.7–9.

In describing the long-standing enmity between the parties, Ariston contrasts his own restraint with Conon's actions, which he characterizes repeatedly as *hubris*. Ariston describes how Conon attacked his slaves, emptied a chamber pot over them, and urinated on them when they were on garrison duty together. Ariston's reaction was not to retaliate, but to first approach Conon, and, when that failed, to report the behavior to the general in command.[44] Conon, far from being chastened, attacked Ariston in his tent in retaliation as soon as it was dark, resulting in a brawl that had to be broken up by other soldiers. Ariston reports that despite continuing animosity when they returned to Athens, he chose not to bring suit or retaliate but simply to avoid Conon.[45] After the severe beating in the agora, Ariston consulted his friends and relatives about what to do. Ariston describes discussion of which legal procedure would be most appropriate, but nowhere mentions revenge as a potential course of action.[46]

Ariston's self-presentation conforms to what appears to be the dominant ideal of self-restraint from violent retaliation or escalation. As modern commentators have observed, in several cases litigants pointedly boast that they have endured multiple insults and violent injuries from their opponents without retaliating.[47] At the same time, Ariston is careful to acknowledge the existence of an opposing viewpoint likely to be espoused by Conon, namely that the use of nonlethal physical violence in disputes over prostitutes or in response to personal insults was trivial, particularly when it involved young men and drinking.[48]

The flexibility of Athenian law permitted Ariston to argue not only that Conon's attack was far too serious to fit into anyone's conception of tolerable youthful antics,[49] but also to advance a full-throated defense of a

---

44 Dem. 54.4–5.

45 Dem. 54.5–6.

46 Dem. 54.1–2.

47 E.g., Lys. 3.9. For discussion, see Herman 2006:159–175, 190–202, 402–414; Gagarin 2005; Fisher 1998; Riess 2012:96–98. Herman characterizes this as an ethic of complete non-retaliation, "tit for two tats," while Fisher, I think more plausibly, emphasizes the importance of seeking revenge in court rather than through immediate retaliation or escalation or later extralegal revenge. Of course, this ideal may not have always been followed in practice; as discussed in Chapter 1, some minor interpersonal violence, particularly when youths and/or drinking was involved, was probably tolerated as inevitable. For the view that nonlethal violence may have been common despite an ideology of moderation see Riess 2012:49, 137.

48 Dem. 54.14. On drink and youth as (mostly) mitigating factors in the use of violence, see Riess 2012:69–72.

49 Dem. 54.20–23.

no-tolerance policy toward interpersonal violence. He explains how retaliation for minor insults can easily escalate into serious violence, and argues that for this reason it is vital that offended parties be forced to seek legal satisfaction rather than taking private revenge:

> There is provision [in the law] for the least important of these crimes, verbal abuse, to avoid the final and worst, homicide, from happening and to prevent the escalation by small steps from verbal abuse to blows, and from blows to wounds, and from wounds to death; instead, the laws provide a legal action for each of these, instead of letting these actions be decided by the individual's anger or desire.[50]

In this way, Ariston's speech does much more than simply present an argument that Conon violated the battery statute.[51] The trial invites jurors and spectators to evaluate competing normative views regarding interpersonal violence. Ariston makes a strong case for cooperative values by favorably contrasting his behavior with Conon's and by offering a policy rationale for enforcing restraint.

Demosthenes' prosecution speech *Against Meidias* similarly provokes examination of the proper response to personal insults.[52] We hear that the animosity between Demosthenes and Meidias arose more than a decade before the events in question.[53] Their enmity came to a head when Demosthenes was serving as a chorus producer (*choregus*) at the Dionysia. Meidias allegedly tried to sabotage Demosthenes' chorus in various ways, including challenging his choristers' exemption from military service, attempting to bribe the chorus director, and even breaking into a shop to try to destroy the chorus' crowns and costumes.[54] During the festival, Meidias strode up to Demosthenes and punched him in the face in front of the entire audience. Demosthenes did not offer immediate retaliation but instead charged him with misconduct during the festival. The normal procedure for this charge (*probole*) involved a nonbinding vote by

---

50 Dem. 54.18–19.
51 In this sense, the courts' role was more expansive than proposed by Riess: trials provided not only dramatized illustrations of prevalent notions of the boundaries between acceptable and unacceptable violence (Riess 2012:18), but also offered moral and policy arguments for particular norms, thereby defending/challenging/shaping, as well as reflecting, dominant norms.
52 Wohl (2010:186–187) points out that Demosthenes invites the jurors to imagine themselves in Demosthenes' situation and contemplate what they would do in response to Meidias by not describing the punch in his narrative.
53 Dem. 21.77–101.
54 Dem. 21.15–17.

the Assembly in an initial hearing, followed by trial in a popular court. We know that the Assembly condemned Meidias at this initial hearing. Demosthenes, perhaps feeling sufficiently vindicated by the Assembly's endorsement, did not immediately proceed to a trial, and there is some uncertainty about whether the case ever reached a jury.[55]

Like Ariston, Demosthenes recognizes that some Athenians condone some nonlethal interpersonal violence, but nevertheless argues that the jurors should endorse an ethic of self-restraint. He describes examples of other men who were engaged in fierce personal or political enmity and competition, none of whom stooped to using physical violence.[56] He then offers a complicated analysis of two previous situations in which men insulted at a drinking party retaliated immediately with lethal force.[57] It is unclear whether the first homicide, which occurred at Samos, was ever prosecuted; in the second case, Demosthenes tells us that the man who took revenge (Euaion) was convicted by only one vote. He expresses sympathy with Euaion and anyone "who has been the victim of *hubris* and has come to his own rescue,"[58] and conjectures that those who narrowly voted to convict Euaion did so not because he retaliated, but because killing his opponent was disproportionate to the insult.

Although Demosthenes presents these cases of private retaliation as understandable, he makes it clear that he believes the proper response is not to retaliate. He notes that Euaion would have been praised by his friends if he had managed to restrain himself,[59] and describes himself as self-controlled (*sophronos*) for not responding when punched by Meidias.[60] In fact, the entire premise behind describing these cases is to boast that he had exercised restraint despite having suffered a greater affront than those who had lost their heads and retaliated.[61] For Demosthenes, the ideal response when insulted is to refrain from private violence and seek justice in court. Recognizing that this norm is not universally held, he urges the jurors to set an example (*paradeigma*) through their verdict: "this case should serve as an example that one should not strike back in the heat of anger at

---

[55] There is some debate about whether this speech was ever delivered in court. See Aesch. 3.51–52, with discussion by MacDowell (1990:23–26).

[56] Dem. 21.58–69.

[57] Dem. 21.71–76.

[58] Dem. 21.74.

[59] Dem. 21.73.

[60] Dem. 21.74.

[61] Dem. 21.73–75.

all men who commit outrage and are abusive, but bring them before you because you are the men who maintain and preserve the protections for victims provided by the laws."[62]

Both Ariston and Demosthenes, then, attempt to persuade the jury that the code of restraint is superior to the tribal code that was no longer dominant, but still endured. Of course, in the defense speeches (which do not survive), Conon and Meidias no doubt attempted to downplay the seriousness of the incidents at issue, and perhaps defended the use of limited violence in some situations. But it would be difficult for them to offer a broad endorsement of the tribal code in the same way that the prosecutors presented a broad argument in favor of restraint: it would be unwise and insulting to suggest that the jury has no business evaluating these sorts of disputes since they should be handled through private self-help rather than brought to court. In this way, arguments in court cases that involved interpersonal violence had a natural tilt against self-help. The party bringing the suit would naturally support recourse to legal procedure over private violence and, once in court, the defendant could hardly offer an expansive defense of the tribal code that eschewed the use of courts in most cases. Thus, cases like *Against Conon* and *Against Meidias* not only provoked public debate about the controversial norms surrounding interpersonal disputes; they also by their very existence may have helped make private violence and revenge seem primitive and outdated.

Lysias' On the Death of Eratosthenes*: Updating the Law on Self-Help*

Lysias 1, *On the Death of Eratosthenes*, offers another example of the Athenian courts' role in shaping norms. Euphiletus defends himself from a charge of homicide by arguing that the killing was legal because he caught his victim in the act of committing adultery with his wife. By the time of this case, social practice regarding the treatment of adulterers had deviated substantially from the law on the books. As we have seen,[63] although the justifiable homicide law attributed to Draco permitted killing the adulterer caught in the act, by the fourth century the Athenians favored nonlethal forms of self-help including physical humiliation and collecting compensation. Trials like Euphiletus' offered an opportunity for speakers and jurors to

---

62 Dem. 21.76.
63 For discussion, see Chapter 1.

articulate evolving norms regarding the use of lethal self-help without formally overturning the law.

Euphiletus tells us that he learned of his wife's adultery from a slave. When the slave alerted him one evening that his wife's lover was in the house, he quickly gathered a group of neighbors and they returned to his house en masse, bursting in on Eratosthenes, still in bed with his wife.[64] According to Euphiletus, he tied Eratosthenes up and elicited a confession from him. He then rejected Eratosthenes' plea that he accept compensation, declaring, "it is not I that kill you, but the law of the city."[65] Then he killed him on the spot.

Euphiletus finds himself in a tough spot in court: although the justifiable homicide statute seems to permit his actions, the jurors were likely to view his use of lethal self-help as excessive under the circumstances. Perhaps for this reason, he misrepresents the statute in question to eliminate the possibility of discretion on his part, arguing that the law required him to kill Eratosthenes.[66] At the end of his speech, Euphiletus betrays worry that the verdict will be guided not by the statute but by the newer norms of conduct. He urges the jurors to "hold fast to the same opinion" expressed in the law, stating that it would be better for the Athenians "to erase the existing laws and enact others" than to deviate from the statute law in their verdict.[67] He expresses exasperation at the possibility of being "trapped by the laws: for the laws instruct the man who catches an adulterer to treat him in any way he pleases, whereas the court turns out to be far more dangerous to the victims than to the men who break the law and dishonor other people's wives."[68]

Although Euphiletus, by necessity, argues for a norm that adulterers be killed on the spot,[69] he attempts to depict the killing as compatible with the newer cooperative values rather than as an act of private self-help. As has often been pointed out, the scene in the bedroom is reminiscent of a trial: he does not simply kill Eratosthenes, but secures his confession and

[64] Lys. 1.24.
[65] Lys. 1.25–26.
[66] Lys. 1.34.
[67] Lys. 1.47–48.
[68] Lys. 1.49.
[69] He argues that the justifiable homicide statute reflects a universal norm, pointing to similar laws in both democracies and oligarchies (Lys. 1.1.). He also offers a consequentialist reason for the norm: if adulterers could not be killed, thieves in the night would have incentives to claim to be adulterers to avoid death (Lys. 1.36).

then delivers sentence before the assembled neighbors. With the statement that it is not Euphiletus but the law of the city who will kill Eratosthenes, Euphiletus seeks to reinterpret the death as an example of legitimate private enforcement of public law sanctioned by the legal system rather than an act of private vengeance. He reiterates this theme at the close of the speech, stating "I do not accept that this penalty was exacted privately on my own behalf. Instead it was for the sake of the whole city."[70]

The prosecution speech does not survive, but Lysias' speech provides some clues to what Eratosthenes' relatives may have argued. The prosecution apparently argued that the statutory requirements of having been caught in the act were not met, either because the slave girl lured Eratosthenes to come to the home when Euphiletus was waiting for him, or perhaps even that he was snatched from the street and not found in the act of adultery at all.[71] But the prosecution speech appears to also have included the argument that killing in this circumstance was no longer acceptable. Indeed, the fact that Euphiletus responds to these concerns in both his opening and closing suggest that he may have viewed the argument that Athenians no longer sanctioned lethal self-help as the most dangerous for his case. We have already described Euphiletus' closing plea that the jurors not let him be "trapped by the laws" by enforcing a different set of non-statutory norms. Similarly, Euphiletus' opening defensively proclaiming that everyone agrees that adulterers deserve harsh penalties[72] suggests that the prosecution may have portrayed killing an adulterer to be excessive and wrong.

We do not know what the jury decided in this case. The flexibility of Athenian law and lack of reasoned verdicts meant that jurors who believed that lethal revenge in this sort of situation was wrong could convict without having to directly confront the conflict with the terms of the justifiable homicide statute. Spectators couldn't know for certain whether the verdict reflected changed norms or a finding that the facts in this particular case did not satisfy the requirements of the statute, but it seems likely that a high-profile conviction in spite of the statute might make a man in a similar situation think twice before exacting revenge. Even if Euphiletus was acquitted, it would be hard not to conclude from the speeches that lethal

70 Lys. 1.47.
71 Lys. 1.27, 37–42.
72 Lys. 1.1–3.

private revenge was not the favored response to adultery, even if the jury in this case ultimately concluded that this response was not punishable as homicide. We have seen that even Euphiletus is at pains to portray himself as enforcing the city's laws rather than taking private revenge, and that he seems to concede in his closing that the law may deviate from current norms of behavior. The prosecution likely offered a much more direct defense of moderation. Perhaps just as important, a compelling case like this one was likely to spark conversations outside of court about what Euphiletus should or should not have done, thereby helping to elaborate and reinforce norms.

Lycurgus the Norm Entrepreneur

In the cases we have studied so far, litigants often raise broader questions of proper behavior and values in the course of advancing their cases. But Lycurgus, the leading Athenian politician from approximately 336 to 324 BCE, seems to have brought public prosecutions as part of a calculated program of public moral education. The *eisangelia* procedure was traditionally used to charge generals and politicians with treason, subverting the democracy, or misleading the people.[73] Lycurgus was involved in several prosecutions that attempted to extend *eisangelia* to cover cases in which ordinary citizens failed to live up to the highest standards of patriotism and morality. In 338 BCE, Lycurgus successfully prosecuted a member of the Areopagus who sent his wife and children away from Attica to keep them safe in the harrowing days after the Athenians were defeated at the Battle of Chaeronea.[74] He was, presumably, executed, the standard penalty for treason under this procedure.[75] *Against Leocrates*, our only surviving speech by Lycurgus, involves a private citizen[76] who also left Athens during the crisis following Chaeronea. After living as a metic trader in Megara for several years, he returned to Athens and was prosecuted for treason, but acquitted by just one vote.[77] We also hear of Lycurgus' involvement in other prosecutions against ordinary citizens for offenses quite removed from traditional

---

73 Hyp. 4.7–8. For discussion, see, e.g., MacDowell 1993:183–186; Hansen 1975:12–20.
74 Lyc. fr. iii; 1.53. For discussion see, Hansen 1975:104.
75 Lyc. 1.8.
76 He apparently had no military responsibility (Lyc. 1.59).
77 Aesch. 3.252.

eisangeliai.[78] In one case, Lycophron was prosecuted under the *eisangelia* procedure based on having committed adultery with a married woman. A fragment from Lycurgus' prosecution speech suggests that he argued that Lycophron's acts of adultery constituted subversion of the democracy under the *eisangelia* statute.[79] If the surviving speech against Leocrates is any indication, these suits provided Lycurgus with an opportunity to publicly advocate for a more robust notion of civic duty and morality. Even more important, by bringing treason prosecutions against ordinary citizens for moral failures, Lycurgus sought to persuade the jurors to alter the traditional understanding of public and private spheres in Athens.[80]

As the manager of public revenue from approximately 336 to 324 BCE,[81] Lycurgus enacted a series of reforms that restored Athens' financial position and permitted an extensive public building program. He also took an active role in supporting and administering traditional Athenian religious cults.[82] Perhaps most relevant for our purposes, in this period the *ephebeia*, the two-year military training program for young men, was comprehensively redesigned.[83] Besides introducing more formalized military training, eleven civilian officials were selected to take the *ephebes* on a tour of Athens' shrines and instill patriotic and moral virtues.[84] In this way, the Lycurgan *ephebeia* took on aspects of a public education system in which the state actively attempted to foster the moral, military, and civic virtues necessary for active citizenship.

Lycurgus' prosecution of Leocrates for fleeing Athens in a time of military crisis offered another opportunity to advance his moral agenda and attempt to establish official civic norms. After being soundly defeated by Philip in 338 BCE at the Battle of Chaeronea, the Athenians frantically tried to prepare for a possible attack: they ordered the women and children from the countryside into the city for protection and empowered the generals to order anyone in the city to take up guard duty as they saw fit.[85]

---

78 Hyp. 1, 4.

79 Lyc. fr. X-XI; cf. Hyp 1.12.

80 Several scholars have made this point, e.g., Phillips 2006:390–394; Allen 2000b; Humphreys 1985:217–219; Faraguna 1992:280–285. My analysis in this section is particularly indebted to Azoulay's (2011) interpretation of *Against Leocrates* in the context of the Lycurgan program. For an interpretation of the speech that focuses on legal argumentation, see E. Harris 2000:67–75.

81 Faraguna 1992:197–205.

82 Wallace 1989:195–196; E. Harris 2001:157; Parker 1996:242–255.

83 Faraguna 1992:274–280; Steinbock 2011:294–306.

84 *Ath. Pol.* 42; for discussion, see Steinbock 2011:295; Parker 1996:252–255.

85 Lyc. 1.16.

Lycurgus reports that in their desperation they called upon men more than fifty to defend the city, and even the elderly and infirm went about dressed to fight if necessary.[86] At the height of the panic, Leocrates took his mistress and sailed away. It seems clear that Leocrates had not abandoned any military assignment[87] or contravened any specific law when he left Athens.[88] Nevertheless, when he returned to Athens in 331 BCE after spending several years as a metic in Megara, Lycurgus charged him with treason (*prodosia*) under the *eisangelia* procedure.

Remarkably, Lycurgus admits that Leocrates' behavior is not covered by the treason statute, and he instructs the jurors to act not only as judges but lawgivers (*nomothetai*): "The penalty for such an offense was omitted from our laws not through any oversight of the lawgiver but because no such crime occurred in earlier times, and no one at the time expected it would happen in the future. As a result, gentlemen, you must act not only as judges in this case but also as legislators."[89] Although he acknowledges that he is advocating for an extension of the statute, he cleverly attempts to reframe the issue in terms of stable and uncontroversial norms of citizenship. He quotes from the Ephebic Oath and recounts stories of military bravery and sacrifice from the heroic and recent past to portray Leocrates' actions as defying traditional Athenian values.[90] Lycurgus emphasizes that the importance of the case lies not in punishing the individual defendant, but in educating the citizenry: "your vote for conviction not only will punish this man today but will inspire all our younger men to lead a life of virtue."[91]

Lycurgus is more direct about the potential of court oratory to shape norms in part because he perceives his role as quite different from most Athenian prosecutors. As has often been pointed out, while most volunteer prosecutors emphasize their personal motives for bringing suit, Lycurgus portrays himself as a disinterested public servant motivated only by a desire to punish those who have wronged the city.[92] His apparent conception of

---

[86] Lyc. 1.3–40.

[87] Lyc. 1.59.

[88] An emergency decree did forbid flight after Chaeronea (Lyc. 1.16, 53–54), but as Whitehead (2006:144) points out, Leocrates must have departed before the passage of this decree.

[89] Lyc. 1.9.

[90] For discussion, see, e.g., Steinbock 2011.

[91] Lyc. 1.10.

[92] Lyc. 1.5–6; Allen 2000b. While Lycurgus' denial of personal interest is unusual, particularly for a suit that did not involve a team of appointed prosecutors, it is not unprecedented. For

his *eisangeliai* prosecutions as a tool of moral reform may also partly explain the extremely long and highly unusual excursus on patriotism, complete with extended quotations of poetry.[93] For Lycurgus, the opportunity to hold forth on the requirements of civic virtue before hundreds of jurors and spectators may have had its own value, quite apart from any contribution this discussion may have made to the argument in the case.

Lycurgus' prosecution of Leocrates thus sought to shift norms on several levels. He attempted to redefine treason to include the failure of private citizens to exhibit patriotism in the face of danger. Moreover, his position as a personally disinterested, but politically powerful, prosecutor meant that norms of citizenship and public service would no longer be enforced indirectly, if at all, against ordinary citizens.[94] The leading politician of the day could now take it upon himself to directly prosecute lapses in patriotism by ordinary individuals. Prosecutions of cases involving even less serious charges, like the alleged adultery by Lycophron, suggest an even more ambitious program to use the *eisangelia* procedure against private citizens for what one scholar has termed "un-Athenian activities."[95] If the prosecution of Leocrates is any guide, these prosecutions also offered an opportunity to discuss and advocate for traditional religious, civic, and moral values.

The case against Leocrates appears to have provided a public forum for the Athenians to consider this highly controversial shift in the extent and form of public intrusions on private conduct.[96] The very close final verdict — we are told that Leocrates was acquitted by one vote — reveals that what was at stake in the case was not the presumably uncontroversial question of whether a good Athenian should have stayed to defend the city under the circumstances. What was at stake was a much bigger question about the extent and reach of the community into private activity. The prosecution must have sparked public debate and discussion about both the responsibilities of citizenship and the proper role of the state in defining and enforcing norms of private behavior. *Against Leocrates* illustrates how

---

discussion, see Kucharski 2012; cf. Kurihara 2003. Whitehead (2006) suggests that Lycurgus' impersonal, sermon-like approach may partially explain the speech's failure to win over the jury.

93 Lyc. 1.72–132.
94 See Chapter 4.
95 Phillips 2006:390–394.
96 For discussion, see Azoulay 2011; Wallace 1993, 1997.

the incrementalism of the courts could facilitate norm shifts. If Leocrates had proposed to change the law of *eisangelia*, he undoubtedly would have lost, and the negative signal from the Assembly vote might have killed his agenda. But a series of prosecutions created an opportunity to gradually build support for a major norm change.

***

In these case studies it is possible to glimpse Athenian society undergoing profound changes. Feuds, violence, and self-help were gradually being replaced by restraint and litigation; sexual mores may have been tightening, as Timarchus discovered; and in the latter half of the fourth century the city (or at least certain leaders like Lycurgus) may have been demanding more patriotism, conformity, and sacrifice in times of crisis. These changes left hardly a trace in the statutes that supposedly governed Athens. These were literally etched in stone and remained largely unchanged. There was no need: popular juries were so powerful, and Athenians so comfortable with this power, that a democratic society could be radically revised with little or no legislative action, and without any sense of an overt break from the ways of their forefathers. The popular courts were essential in this process, not merely the place where we find evidence of a change occurring elsewhere, but instead a vitally important forum where the Athenians tried out ideas and very self-consciously told ordinary Athenian jurors to change rules in ways that would have been difficult to accomplish through lawmaking. Speech by speech, case by case, the Athenian world became quite different in any number of concrete ways, yet the changes were so gradual that there was hardly anything to complain or fight about at the time.

SIX

Transitional Justice in Athens

Law, Courts, and Norms

Thucydides famously describes how Corcyra and other Greek cities were convulsed by civil wars between oligarchic and democratic factions during the Peloponnesian War, leading to a complete breakdown of civil society. Violence and mistrust spiraled out of control with no end in sight:

> Revenge was dearer than self-preservation.... An attitude of suspicious antagonism prevailed; for there was no word binding enough, no oath terrible enough to reconcile enemies. Each man had concluded that it was hopeless to expect a permanent settlement....[1]

Toward the end of the war, Athens experienced a civil war marked by horrific violence: in an eight-month period at the end of the fifth century, an oligarchic coup resulted in the killings of between 5 and 10 percent of the citizenry and the expulsion, by some accounts, of more than half its population.[2] But unlike other Greek states, Athens pulled itself back from the brink. When the oligarchy was overthrown, an amnesty was instituted for all but the top officials in the former regime, and the restored democracy endured without significant internal threat until Athens was conquered by Philip of Macedon in 338 BCE. The Athenian reconciliation was admired

---

[1] Thuc. 3.82–83 (translation adapted from Jowett).
[2] Approximately fifteen hundred Athenians were killed (Isoc. 7.67; Aesch. 3.235; *Ath. Pol.* 35.4). Strauss (1986:70–86) provides the lowest estimate of the male citizen population at 14,000–16,250; Hansen (1985) suggests 25,000; Ober (1989:127) estimates that the population range throughout the fourth century was 20,000–30,000. As for the expulsion, Diodorus 14.5.7 states that more than half the population was driven out; Isocrates 7.67 states that more than 5,000 were expelled.

throughout Greece for its success in avoiding the cycle of revolution and counterrevolution that afflicted other cities.

This chapter describes how Athens' legal institutions helped restore order after the civil war. The civil war, the reconciliation agreement, and the rhetorical echoes of these events in Attic oratory have been extensively studied.[3] The goal of this chapter is not to provide a comprehensive account of why the reconciliation succeeded. Rather, I want to present the Athenian reconciliation as a single episode that illustrates the various ways in which the courts maintained order in the absence of a rule of law that we have been exploring in the previous chapters. That is, the Athenian response to civil war demonstrates how Athenian courts fostered order and a peaceful transition, though not through the familiar Austinian mechanism of imposing sanctions for violating statutes.

To a modern, this may not seem surprising. Modern transitional justice mechanisms typically take the form of special war crimes tribunals, truth and reconciliation commissions, and administrative justice procedures that disqualify those involved in the former regime from public office or employment. To varying degrees, all these procedures forfeit full criminal accountability for all crimes committed during the prior regime in return for a peaceful transition. Many transitional justice procedures, particularly truth commissions and war crimes tribunals, consciously pursue a variety of goals besides determining the guilt of individuals, including providing an outlet for victims to tell their stories, understanding the larger pattern of complicity in atrocities, and promoting reconciliation. In this way, modern transitional justice mechanisms tend to operate apart from the ordinary legal system, and their procedures and goals are often in some tension with the rule of law. But because of Athens' unique legal culture, we will see that its ordinary popular courts were able to accommodate the broader goals of transitional justice, from creating a shared understanding of the civil war to promoting trust between neighbors on opposite sides of the conflict. The Athenian popular courts routinely performed functions that moderns tend to associate only with extraordinary legal responses to conflict.[4]

---

3 E.g., Ostwald 1986:460–524; Krentz 1982; Loening 1987; Elster 2004:3–23; Carawan 2002, 2006, 2013; Quillin 2002; Dorjahn 1946; Loraux 2002. I should mention in particular Wolpert 2002 and D. Cohen 2001, both of whom address the way in which court speakers portray the reign of the Thirty and the Amnesty, a topic that I discuss subsequently.

4 On the extraordinary nature of modern transitional justice, see, e.g., Teitel 2000:4–9. For an argument that modern transitional justice is not different in kind from ordinary domestic law, see Posner and Vermeule 2004.

I first describe the mass violence committed during the reign of the Thirty Tyrants and the collaboration by various portions of the population. I then discuss the terms of the reconciliation agreement and its success in achieving peace and encouraging those on opposite sides of the conflict to cooperate and govern together, if not quite to forgive each other. The remainder of the chapter traces the role of Athenian legal institutions in the reconciliation. I argue that Athens' unique legal culture permitted the Amnesty to be implemented in a way that promoted unity while avoiding a sense of impunity at the local level. Court rhetoric helped construct a unifying collective memory of the tyranny. At the same time, indirect legal sanctions for collaboration in unrelated lawsuits and examinations of incoming magistrates minimized resentment at the local level by providing some limited accountability. And Athens' civic institutions, including courts, helped repair individual social relationships by forcing former oligarchs and democratic rebels to work together productively.

6.1. The Terror

Between September 404 and May 403 the Thirty Tyrants executed approximately 1,500 Athenians,[5] drove out of the city and confiscated the property of thousands more,[6] and terrorized the resident alien population.[7] According to one contemporary historian, more Athenians were killed by the Thirty in less than a year than were killed in ten years during the Peloponnesian War.[8] What follows is a basic account of the violence, with a particular emphasis on what we can discern about the level of complicity of various elements of the population. Although there are discrepancies in the sources and many facts about the oligarchic period are still contested by historians,[9] particularly the chronology of events, these debates are not relevant to our story and I will largely avoid them.

Accession of the Thirty and Judicial Murder

The Athenian Assembly had little choice in the initial appointment of the Thirty. The Athenians had been soundly defeated by the Spartans and

5 Isoc. 7.67; Aesch. 3.235; *Ath. Pol.* 35.4.
6 Isoc. 7.67; Diod. 14.5.7.
7 Lys. 12.4.
8 Xen. *Hellenica* 2.4.21.
9 See, e.g., Wolpert 2002:3–28; Ostwald 1986:460–490; Loening 1987; Carawan 2006, 2013.

were literally starving because of a Spartan blockade when they agreed to surrender, tear down their walls, and hand over most of their fleet. Under pressure from the Spartan commander,[10] the Assembly acceded to the local oligarchic faction and appointed thirty men to draft a constitution in accordance with the ancestral laws (*patrioi nomoi*).[11] Once in power, the Thirty ignored the order to draft a constitution and instead appointed magistrates and a new Council of 500 from among their supporters.[12] Even more ominous, they hired 300 "whip-bearing servants" to carry out their orders and intimidate the populace.[13] While it is not clear whether the Assembly decree appointing the Thirty authorized them to govern Athens temporarily until the new constitution was drafted,[14] there is no question that by refusing to issue a constitution and taking complete and indefinite control over the government the Thirty crossed the line into illegal rule.

A major element in the Thirty's reign of terror was judicial murder. The jury courts had been suspended during the war and were not revived by the Thirty. Instead, they tried opponents before the Council of 500. Our sources generally do not specify the charges, but death appears to have been the only possible penalty. From the beginning, the trials appear to have been a farce. One description of a trial held soon after the Thirty rose to power against men who had opposed the peace treaty with Sparta recounts the intimidating atmosphere, as the secret ballot was dispensed with and members of the Council cast their votes in front of the Thirty:

> The Thirty were seated on the dais. Two tables were set out in front of them, and one had to cast one's vote not into voting urns but openly on these tables, with the vote to convict going on the further table: so how could any of them [i.e., the defendants] be rescued? In a word, the death penalty was passed on all who went to the Council-chamber to face trial.[15]

At first, the Thirty executed only a small number of political opponents and sycophants (men known for bringing frivolous prosecutions).

---

10 Lys. 12.71–75; Diod. 14.3.2–7.
11 Xen. *Hellenica* 2.3.11.
12 *Ath. Pol.* 35.1; Xen. *Hellenica* 2.3.11.
13 *Ath. Pol.* 35.1.
14 The subject of *politeusousi* in Xenophon's (*Hellenica* 2.3.2) description of the Assembly decree is unclear, but may refer to the Thirty. For discussion, see Ostwald 1986:477–478 and n.70; Krentz 1982:50.
15 Lys. 13.36.

Despite the procedural irregularity of these trials, both Xenophon and the Aristotle's *Constitution of the Athenians* report that these actions were widely popular.[16] Over time, the executions multiplied, and, with them, opposition to the regime: Xenophon describes the "great numbers continually – and unjustly – put to death," causing "many to band together and wonder what the state was coming to."[17]

The Creation of the 3,000 and Widespread Extrajudicial Killings

Theramenes, one of the Thirty, opposed the prosecutions, arguing that the terror tactics were alienating potential supporters and weakening the regime. In response, the Thirty agreed to widen their base of support slightly by drawing up a list of 3,000 citizens who were to share in the government, disenfranchising the remaining three-quarters of the population.[18] To the extent we can discern the motivations of the Thirty, they appear to have wanted to establish a society along the Spartan model, in which a narrow group of elite *homoioi* would exercise citizenship rights, relegating the rest of the population to a second-class status analogous to the Spartan *perioikoi* who conducted commerce and served in the army but were denied the vote.[19] The 3,000 appear to have been handpicked by the Thirty.[20] In practice, the 3,000 did not play an active role in the government; we know of only one meeting of the full 3,000 and another involving all hoplites and cavalry on the list, both of which were held after the democratic opposition had gained the upper hand and the Thirty were on the defensive.[21]

The consequences of exclusion from the list of 3,000 went beyond the humiliation of formal disenfranchisement. The Thirty announced that anyone not in the 3,000 could be killed by the Thirty without trial, while members of the 3,000 had a right to a trial before the Council.[22] Not long

---

[16] Xen. *Hellenica* 2.3.12; *Ath. Pol.* 35.3.
[17] Xen. *Hellenica* 2.3.20–22.
[18] Xen. *Hellenica* 2.3.18–22; *Ath. Pol.* 36.1–2.
[19] Krentz 1982:64–67; Whitehead 1982–1983:106–130; Ostwald 1986:485–487.
[20] There does not seem to have been a transparent standard such as a property qualification; we are told that the Thirty kept the list secret for a long time and altered the status of several individuals before it was finally published. *Ath. Pol.* 36.2.
[21] Xen. *Hellenica* 2.4.9, 23; *Ath. Pol.* 38.1.
[22] Xen. *Hellenica* 2.3.18; *Ath. Pol.* 36.1. But the Thirty did not let even this minimal protection for the 3,000 stand in the way of their attempts to rid themselves of opposition; when it became

after the list of 3,000 was published, the Thirty collected the arms of the disenfranchised and began a brutal killing spree.[23] Xenophon suggests that many of the murders were motivated by personal enmity or a desire to confiscate property rather than political opposition.[24] At one point the Thirty decided to kill a number of metics (resident aliens), perhaps out of xenophobia, perhaps because they supported the opposition, or perhaps simply to confiscate their property.[25] Isocrates claims that over three months the Thirty executed more people without trial than the number of subjects the Athenians put on trial during the entire period of its empire.[26]

Informers and Citizens' Arrests

In addition to acquiescence to the senseless violence, ordinary citizens sometimes served as informers or assisted in arrests. However rigged they might be, trials before the Council required some evidence, which could be provided by willing or unwilling informers. The trial of one such informer after the restoration of the democracy survives.[27] Predictably, it seems that the defendant asserted that he testified only under duress, while the prosecution argues that he informed willingly, pointing out that he had a chance to escape by fleeing Athens but did not take it.[28] Interestingly, the prosecutor's narrative reveals that informers were often subject to considerable pressure. He recounts how another man, Menestratus, turned informer only after he was arrested on a capital charge in order to gain immunity; he praises the heroism of one Aristophanes who refused to inform on others and was executed as a result; and his case is predicated on the notion that the defendant would have to go into voluntary exile to avoid serving as an informer.[29]

The guilt of citizens who actually carried out the arrests and handed them over to the Thirty is murkier. In Plato's *Apology*, Socrates recounts

clear that the Council would not vote to condemn Theramenes, the Thirty ended the trial before the vote, struck him from the list of 3,000, and put him to death. Xen. *Hellenica* 2.3.50-51.

23 *Ath. Pol.* 37.2; Xen. *Hellenica* 2.4.1.

24 Xen. *Hellenica* 2.3.20–21.

25 Xenophon (2.3.20–22) and Lysias (12.4) attribute the Thirty's actions to greed; for an argument that political opposition was the true motive, see Krentz 1982:80–82; on possible xenophobia, see Ostwald 1986:487.

26 Isoc. 4.113.

27 Lys. 13.

28 Lys. 13.31, 52.

29 Lys. 13.52–61.

how the Thirty ordered him and four others to arrest Leon of Salamis so that he could be put to death. He states that the Thirty "issued such orders to many men, since they wanted to implicate as many as they could in their crimes."[30] While the four others arrested Leon, Socrates simply went home, refusing either to take part in the arrest or to try to save or warn Leon. Socrates was not punished for his disobedience. Perhaps, as Socrates claims, the Thirty would have killed him in retaliation if the regime had not been close to collapse. Perhaps Socrates' special stature and association with Critias saved him. Or perhaps failure to carry out an arrest was less likely to provoke retaliation. One source suggests that during the killing spree some citizens took revenge on personal enemies by initiating summary arrests.[31] Law court speakers after the restoration of the democracy at times declare their clean record during the oligarchy by stating not only that they were not members of the Council or officers under the Thirty, but also that they carried out no arrests,[32] which suggests either that citizen arrests were common or were regarded as particularly blameworthy, or both. It is interesting that speakers do not generally state that they did not serve as informers; while having been an informer may have been considered morally blameworthy, informers do not appear to have been considered part of the oligarchy in the same way that those who carried out arrests were. It seems that while it was understood that many informers testified under true threat of death, there was a suspicion that at least some citizens who carried out arrests initiated the action or could have avoided carrying out the Thirty's orders.

Involuntary Exile, Massacre at Eleusis, and the Rise of the Democratic Opposition

At some point after the extrajudicial murders of those excluded from the 3,000, the Thirty took the further step of banning everyone not in the 3,000 from the city (*astu*) and confiscating their property.[33] Most settled in the Piraeus, the port and commercial center of Athens; some may have gone into exile. Some sources suggest that they were settled involuntarily in the Piraeus, which would make sense given the Thirty's apparent ambition

---

30 Pl. *Apology* 32c–d.
31 Lys. fr. 9.
32 Lys. fr. 9; 25.15.
33 Lys. 25.22; Xen. *Hellenica* 2.4.1.

to give them a position similar to the *perioikoi*; another source suggests that they were simply excluded from the city and that many voluntarily moved to the Piraeus.[34]

By this point an opposition force made up of a small number of citizens and a larger group of mercenaries and metics had formed.[35] When the resistance won some victories, the Thirty became nervous and decided to take the village of Eleusis, a town within Athens' territory, as a possible refuge. Xenophon describes in detail how the Thirty murdered the male inhabitants in order to take control over the town.[36] The cavalry ordered the male Eleusinians to register, pretending that they were trying to determine how large a garrison to leave in the town. After each man registered, he was ordered to walk out the city gate, where each was arrested and brought to Athens. Xenophon continues:

> The next day they summoned the registered hoplites and the cavalry too. Critias rose and said: "Gentlemen, we are creating this government no less for your sake as for ourselves. Consequently, just as you will share in our honors, so too you will share in our dangers. You must convict the men from Eleusis who have been arrested in order that you take heart and feel fear in tandem with us."[37]

Those present were then instructed to vote in the open, in the presence of both the Thirty and armed Spartan guards who had been requested to help the oligarchy keep control of Athens.[38] As a result, nearly the entire male population of Eleusis was executed. The Thirty also massacred the inhabitants of Salamis, though our sources do not report how the murders were carried out or whether a similar vote was arranged.[39]

When the opposition forces approached the Piraeus, many of the citizens excluded from the city, as well as metics, foreigners, and even slaves joined the fight.[40] The rebels routed the Thirty in Piraeus, killing two of their leaders, including Critias. Following this defeat, the 3,000 met in

---

34 Compare Diod. 14.32.4 and Justin, *Epitome* 5.9.12 to Xen. *Hellenica* 2.4.1.

35 Krentz 1982:83–84.

36 Xen. *Hellenica* 2.4.8–10.

37 Xen. *Hellenica* 2.4.9.

38 Xenophon and the *Ath. Pol.* offer very different accounts of when the Spartan garrison was called in: according to Xenophon (*Hellenica* 2.3.14) they were called in very early in the reign of the Thirty, while the *Ath. Pol.* (37.2) states that they did not arrive until much later, after the Thirty were seriously threatened.

39 Lys. 12.52; 13.44; Diod. 14.32.4.

40 *Ath. Pol.* 38.3; 40.2; Diod. 14.33.4; Xen. *Hellenica* 2.4.25.

Athens and voted to replace the Thirty with a board of ten; the deposed members of the Thirty settled in Eleusis.[41] As the opposition grew in strength and threatened to attack the city, the oligarchic leaders in the city asked Sparta to send reinforcements.[42] The Spartans at first blockaded the Piraeus, but then changed strategy and the Spartan commander Pausanias negotiated a reconciliation agreement between the two parties.[43]

Forms of Collaboration

Before turning to the details of the reconciliation agreement, it may be helpful to briefly summarize the complicity of various segments of the population in the violence committed during the oligarchy. Of course, members of the Thirty, the Eleven (the officials charged with carrying out executions), and the other public officials bore the most responsibility. Members of the Council sent countless innocents to death. Some citizens gave testimony that led to executions, often in order to save their own lives. Other citizens arrested men and handed them over to the Eleven to be killed without trial, some under threat of death and some on their own initiative. The cavalry arrested the men of Eleusis, and the entire armed forces voted to condemn them. And much of the population stayed in the city and did not object during the unjust judicial murders and massacres of hundreds of citizens without trial. As already noted, the Thirty seem to have tried to implicate as many people as possible in their crimes.[44] The overall picture that emerges is one of widespread collaboration, or at least acquiescence, among the citizenry in the mass violence orchestrated by a small but highly intimidating, repressive leadership.

6.2. "Reconciliation"

The Athenians remembered the reconciliation agreement as a complete success,[45] an act of generosity and unity that set Athens apart from other city-states.[46] One orator told the Athenian jury, "the whole of Greece regards

---

41 Xen. *Hellenica* 2.4.23–24; *Ath. Pol.* 38.1.
42 Xen. *Hellenica* 2.4.28.
43 Xen. *Hellenica* 2.4.28–43.
44 Pl. *Apology* 32c; Xen. *Hellenica* 2.4.9.
45 *Ath. Pol.* 40.2; Xen. *Hellenica* 2.4.43; And. 1.140; Isoc. 18.31–32.
46 And. 1.140; Isoc. 18.31–32.

you as very generous and sensible men, because you didn't devote yourselves to revenge for the past, but to the preservation of the city and the unity of its citizens."[47] The reconciliation agreement *was* successful in the sense that Athens avoided the widespread bloodshed that often accompanied civil wars in other Greek states and established a stable democracy that endured for the remainder of Athens' history as an independent state. But while Athenians on opposite sides of the conflict found a way to live and govern together in the restored democracy, our sources reveal that private, human resentment over actions taken during the oligarchy remained strong for decades after end of the civil war.

The Terms of the Reconciliation Agreement

The terms of the reconciliation agreement were less a product of generosity than military necessity. Although the democrats had gained the upper hand at the time of the settlement, the arrival of Spartan forces to bolster the oligarchs threatened the democrats' success.[48] Pausanias, the Spartan commander, presided over an agreement that guaranteed the restoration of the democracy but also treated the oligarchs and their supporters with relative leniency.

The highest officials of the oligarchy – the Thirty, the Ten who succeeded the Thirty, the Eleven who carried out executions, and the governors of the Piraeus – were given the option of forfeiting their Athenian citizenship to live autonomously in the village of Eleusis with any of their supporters who wished to join them.[49] Remarkably, the agreement not only gave the former oligarchs control over the village whose men they had massacred; it also forced current inhabitants of Eleusis to sell their land if one of the settlers wished to buy it.[50] This experiment in splitting Athens into two autonomous settlements was short-lived; when the Athenians learned two years later that the former oligarchs were hiring mercenaries, the Athenians killed the opposing generals and reintegrated Eleusis into the Athenian state.[51]

---

47 And. 1.140.
48 Xen. *Hellenica* 2.4.30–35.
49 *Ath. Pol.* 39. The émigrés were originally given ten days to register and twenty days to move to Eleusis, but apparently Archinus cut the emigration period short to keep more citizens in Athens. *Ath. Pol.* 40.1.
50 *Ath. Pol.* 39.3.
51 Xen. *Hellenica* 2.4.43.

Under the reconciliation agreement the top oligarchic officials who did not want to relocate to Eleusis could remain in Athens provided they underwent an *euthyna*, a trial-like accounting of their conduct in office, and accepted any punishment meted out by the court.[52] The *euthyna* was not an extraordinary transitional justice institution but the standard procedure faced by all outgoing officials under the democracy both before and after the revolution. The only adjustment made to the procedure was that the oligarchs were to be judged not by a jury drawn from all adult male citizens but from citizens with taxable property,[53] a form, as one scholar has put it, of "loser's justice."[54] The procedure appears to have been as evenhanded in practice as advertised: at least one member of the Thirty appears to have consented to, and passed, an *euthuna*,[55] and the *Constitution of the Athenians* tells us that several of members of the Board of Ten who ruled at the end of the oligarchy passed their accounting.[56]

Everyone except the top officials under the Thirty who refused to undergo an accounting was granted amnesty under the agreement.[57] The Assembly swore an oath *me mnesikakein*, which is sometimes translated "not to remember past wrongs," but is more accurately translated "not to bear a grudge" or "to cancel past grievances."[58] The Amnesty banned physical retaliation and lawsuits against those who committed crimes during the oligarchy. Each year, the Council swore not to accept summary arrests that violated the Amnesty, and jurors similarly swore to uphold the law and not to bear a grudge for events under the Thirty.[59] The Amnesty had one exception: charges of homicide and wounding for actions taken during the oligarchy could proceed provided that the defendant killed or wounded

---

52 *Ath. Pol.* 39.6.

53 *Ath. Pol.* 39.6.

54 Elster 2004:22.

55 Lys. 10.31 states that someone brought a homicide charge against one or more members of the Thirty in 399/398, which suggests that at least one oligarch passed his accounting and remained in Athens. The prosecution speech at the accounting of another member of the Thirty, Eratosthenes, survives (Lys. 12); the outcome is unknown. One scholar has argued that passages in this speech suggest that there was more than one defendant at this accounting, but as Krentz (1982:122) points out, "the plural references can be understood as Lysias' attempt to condemn by association."

56 *Ath. Pol.* 38.4.

57 *Ath. Pol.* 39.5; And. 1.90.

58 Carawan (1998:129–131; 2002:3; 2006:6) examines the use of the phrase in other Greek treaties and agreements. See also D. Cohen 2001:339; compare Loraux 2002:85–91, who translates it as "not to recall past misfortunes," and emphasizes that the Amnesty was a form of amnesia.

59 And. 1.90–91.

"with his own hand" (*autocheir*).[60] But this exception, probably included for religious reasons, had little practical effect. Nearly all of those responsible for criminal violence committed during the civil war were shielded by the Amnesty because the actual executions were committed by the Board of Eleven, who were excluded from the Amnesty and who presumably all fled to Eleusis or into exile after the reconciliation. After the reintegration of Eleusis in 401/400, the Amnesty was reaffirmed[61] to make clear that the terms of the Amnesty extended to those who had relocated to Eleusis.[62]

Implementation and Resistance

Aside from returning the land that had been confiscated,[63] the reconciliation agreement offered little to those who had been victimized by the Thirty. Not surprisingly, some Athenians resisted complying with the Amnesty. We are told of at least one former informer who, though covered by the Amnesty, opted to go into exile because of fear of retaliation.[64] And we hear of one man who immediately violated the Amnesty, probably by taking physical vengeance,[65] prompting one of Athens' leaders to make an example of him by having the Council execute him without trial.[66] Aristotle suggests that this measure successfully deterred those intent on private vengeance.[67] Attempts to bring private suits in violation of the

---

60 *Ath. Pol.* 39.5–6.
61 Xen. *Hellenica* 2.4.43. There is some debate about whether the Amnesty was part of the reconciliation of 403/2 and reaffirmed after the fall of Eleusis, which would accord with the account given in the *Ath. Pol* (39.6) and Andocides (1.90–91), or whether the Amnesty was only instituted after the fall of Eleusis, which is how Xenophon's (*Hellenica* 2.4.43) narrative presents it. For discussion, see Loening 1987:26–28; Carawan 2006.
62 Presumably those in Eleusis who were excluded from the Amnesty, such as the Thirty and the Eleven, went into voluntary exile to escape punishment. We are not aware of any member of the Thirty or the Eleven returning to Athens after the fall of Eleusis. See Loening 1987:116–117; Krentz 1982:122.
63 All real property that had been confiscated was to be returned, as were movables if they had not been resold (Lys. Fr. 7). In the case of real property that had been sold, it is possible that the victims would have to pay some compensation to the buyer, but our text is too fragmentary to determine for certain. For discussion, see Todd 2000:368; Loening 1987:51–52.
64 Lys. 6.45. Todd (2000:74 n.34) points out that one of Lysias' lost speeches is entitled "On the Death of Batrachus," which, if it refers to the same man, may suggest that he was tracked down and killed by his enemies in Athens.
65 Carawan 1998:130–131.
66 *Ath. Pol.* 40.2. Nepos (*Thrasybulus* 3.3.) also states that Thrasybulus stopped some of the returning democrats from killing their enemies.
67 *Ath. Pol.* 40.3.

Amnesty prompted the Athenians to create a new procedure, the *paragraphe*, which allowed a defendant to challenge the legality of a prosecution as contrary to the Amnesty and imposed a financial penalty on the prosecutor if the case was thrown out.[68] And we know of a few attempts, at least one of which appears to have been successful,[69] to use creative legal arguments to get around the Amnesty and hold informers responsible for judicial murders committed under the Thirty.[70] But despite some resistance, it appears that the Amnesty was generally honored in the sense that very few prosecutions were brought for the thousands of confiscations, murders, and other crimes committed under the Thirty.[71]

Although the Amnesty shielded most wrongdoers from direct prosecution, the peculiar features of the Athenian court system left room for indirect accountability. In the generation after the civil war, litigants often attacked their opponents' conduct under the Thirty as a form of character evidence in unrelated cases. Similarly, one's allegiance and behavior during the oligarchy became an important part of the judicial examination of incoming public officials (*dokimasia*). It appears that neither tactic was deemed to violate the terms of the Amnesty, though they were obviously at odds with the spirit of the reconciliation agreement.[72] As much as sixteen years after the end of the civil war, one candidate for the archonship was rejected and the alternate candidate vigorously challenged based on their conduct during the oligarchy.[73] Clearly, the reconciliation agreement did not elicit total forgiveness from victims or completely erase resentment toward citizens who had participated in or collaborated with the oligarchy. Nevertheless, the settlement did succeed in quelling violence, limiting lawsuits, and restoring a functioning democracy.

---

68 Isoc. 18.2–3. There is some question about whether the *paragraphe* procedure was introduced soon after the reconciliation or only after the fall of Eleusis. For discussion of the dating and application of the *paragraphe* procedure, see Ostwald 1986:510; MacDowell 1971; Carawan 2006:75; Loening 1987:99–102; Harrison 1998:106–124.

69 Lys. 13.55–57 argues that the informer Menestratus was tried and condemned.

70 Lys. 13.55–57; Lysias 13.

71 Xen. *Hellenica* 2.4.43 states that the demos abided by its oaths; the speaker in Isocrates 18 (22–23) cites a case in which the defendant presented no defense other than immunity based on the Amnesty and was acquitted, and describes how two powerful individuals refrained from bringing suit to recover money lost during the oligarchy because of the Amnesty; and Andocides 1.94 states matter-of-factly that Meletus has immunity for his arrest of Leon of Salamis due to the reconciliation.

72 Dorjahn 1946:32.

73 Lys. 26.13–15. For discussion, see Todd 2000:271–273.

6.3. The Role of Legal Institutions in Reconciliation

In comparison to the experience of other Greek states, Athens' recovery from civil war stands out as a shining success. In this section, I explore how Athenian legal institutions helped foster reconciliation and a peaceful transition to democracy. I argue that Athens' unique legal and political culture permitted the terms of the reconciliation agreement to be implemented in a way that promoted unity and social solidarity while recognizing the need to avoid a sense of impunity for collaborators at the local or private level.[74] First, in the generation following the war, speeches in the Athenian courts helped cultivate reconciliation by creating a collective memory of the "misfortunes"[75] that downplayed the extent of collaboration and lionized Athens for the generosity embodied in the Amnesty.[76] Second, through the use of character evidence in unrelated cases and challenges to incoming officials at the *dokimasia* hearings, the Athenian courts provided some measure of individualized accountability at the private level, while also encouraging former collaborators to publicly pledge their allegiance to the democracy. Finally, the highly participatory nature of Athenian civic institutions – not just courts, but also polis-wide and local deliberative assemblies – helped repair local relationships by forcing individuals on opposite sides of the conflict to work closely together.[77]

Before discussing these three mechanisms of reconciliation in more detail, I would like to emphasize one broader point, which is that the Athenian legal system was able to perform these functions without any significant change in its culture or design – a continuity that gave it a distinct

---

74 In this way, Athenian transitional justice mechanisms were not epiphenomena but causal factors in the success of the reconciliation. For a similar argument in the modern context, see Posner and Vermeule 2004:770; Teitel 2000:4–9. Gowder (2015) offers a different account of how Athens' transitional justice mechanisms played a causal role in the success of the reconciliation: he argues that the Athenian juries' adherence to the Amnesty following the civil war signaled the Athenians' commitment to the rule of law, thus discouraging future oligarchic threats.

75 And. 1.140.

76 Excellent discussions of how Athenian court rhetoric constructed a collective memory of the civil war include Wolpert (2002:75–99) and D. Cohen (2001). For a discussion of how court rhetoric addressing the civil war and Amnesty influenced the Athenians' notions of law, see Wohl 2010:201–242.

77 For a discussion of possible lessons for modern transitions that can be drawn from the Athenian experience, see Lanni 2010.

advantage over modern institutions charged with dispensing "transitional justice." The broad notion of relevance and contextualized approach to adjudication characteristic of Athenian courts[78] made them a more effective forum for the creation of collective memory than modern war crimes tribunals. In modern tribunals, the desire of prosecutors or judges to use the trial to create a shared understanding of the etiology of administrative massacres is inevitably constrained by the law's narrow focus on the conduct and responsibility of the individual defendants.[79] Athenian court procedures, by contrast, could comfortably accommodate these nontraditional goals. Moreover, in the modern context, the creation of special transitional justice procedures — whether courts, truth commissions, or procedures for administrative penalties — inevitably raises questions of legitimacy for two reasons. First, they are often perceived to be politicized because they are ad hoc institutions designed to address a specific political crisis.[80] Second, modern transitional justice institutions subject individuals to procedures and, sometimes, substantive legal standards that did not exist at the time of conduct that is later challenged.[81] By contrast, Athens' legal response to the atrocities of the Thirty utilized only preexisting democratic legal procedures, precisely because these procedures could accommodate transitional justice goals. In this way, "transitional justice" in Athens was not a departure from but rather an integral part of the restored democratic order.

Was Athenian legal culture the most important element in the success of the reconciliation? Definitive proof is impossible, but it is worth pointing out that the other obvious potential factors cannot completely explain Athens' peaceful transition. Political scientists in the realist tradition often argue that transitional justice measures are epiphenomenal, and that successful reconciliations can be traced to an equilibrium between well-balanced opposing forces. This explanation does not work for the Athenian case. While the initial settlement did emerge from a stalemate between the rebels and the Spartan-backed oligarchs, once the settlement had been made the Spartans quickly exited the picture. There was no balance of power: the democrats were firmly in control and in a position to exact harsh retribution on the former oligarchs if they had chosen to do so. Moreover, the picture that emerges of postwar Athens is not of two

78 On which, see generally Lanni 2006.
79 E.g., Koskenniemi 2002:13; Minow 1998:46–47.
80 Minow 1998:30–31.
81 On the problem of retroactivity, see Minow 1998:30–31; Teitel 2000:11–26.

opposing factions in equipoise but rather of a united restored democracy in which a fair number of former oligarchs played an active role. Second, it is true that after the loss of the empire Athens faced dire economic and military danger, and that it could not afford continued internal strife.[82] And yet Thucydides provides examples of other cities in the grip of civil war who failed to act rationally, for whom, in his words, "revenge was more important than self-preservation."[83] Finally, some scholars argue that the constitutional reforms at the end of the fifth century removed the basis for oligarchic discontent.[84] The significance of the reforms has divided classicists.[85] While my view that the reforms did not meaningfully reduce popular sovereignty is open to debate, there is no question that at least in intellectual circles – Plato is the most prominent example – many remained discontented with the democracy and attracted to oligarchic forms of government. While we cannot determine precisely how much of Athens' success can be attributed to the discourse in the courts, we will see that the courts clearly played an important role in unifying the Athenians and fostering cooperation and reconciliation at the city, local, and even individual level.

Courts and Collective Memory

Legal procedures following administrative massacres can influence the society's "collective memory" of the events, that is, the community's shared understanding of the extent and reprehensibility of the atrocities and the relative culpability of different actors.[86] Trials can serve as legal rituals, which, in the words of David Garland, "provide a kind of didactic theatre through which the onlooker is *taught* what to feel, how to react, what sentiments are called for."[87] While there is no blueprint for designing transitional justice institutions that will positively influence collective memory, the twentieth century offers some success stories.[88] In Western

---

[82] Ober 1989:98–100.

[83] Thuc. 3.82.

[84] E.g., Elster 2004:14–15.

[85] Compare, e.g., Ober 1989:95–103 with Ostwald 1986.

[86] E.g., Teitel 2000:8, 50; Koskenniemi 2002:11; Osiel 1997:2–18.

[87] Garland 1990:67 (quoted in Osiel 1997:38). See also Osiel 1997:24–58 for more discussion of the process through which collective memory is shaped.

[88] On the difficulties facing conscious attempts to construct collective memory, see Osiel 1997:59–292.

Europe, for example, it has been found that the collective memory of the Holocaust (judged from opinion surveys and textbooks) is weakest and least accurate in those countries that conducted few or no postwar trials of collaborators.[89] It is important to note that a society's collective memory need not be historically "accurate" to generate social solidarity; the siege of Masada and the denial of extensive French collaboration during World War II are examples of shared historical fictions that are thought to have fostered solidarity.[90] Similarly, we will see that the shared memory of the reign of the Thirty Tyrants constructed in Athenian court discourse helped foster unity by denying the true extent of collaboration and by depicting the Amnesty as a gesture of pure benevolence rather than a deal struck between evenly matched forces.

Despite the Amnesty, the reign of the Thirty was discussed frequently in Athenian courts in the generation after the civil war. At least one member of the Thirty, and several members of the Ten, underwent accountings (*euthunai*) in court; the prosecution speech against Eratosthenes, a member of the Thirty, survives.[91] Allegations of wrongdoing during the oligarchy arose frequently in examinations of incoming public officials (*dokimasia*); we have portions of two prosecution speeches and three defense speeches at these hearings.[92] We also have speeches involving two prosecutions that appear to have violated the Amnesty: the prosecution of an informer for homicide, and the *paragraphe* speech challenging as illegal under the Amnesty a private suit attempting to recoup money confiscated during the oligarchy.[93] In addition to trials that centered on events during the civil war, several court speeches in unrelated cases discuss the reign of the Thirty, the Amnesty, or the litigants' conduct during the oligarchy.[94]

Of course, the courts were not the only forum for constructing collective memory. War memorials erected after the restoration of the democracy and the funeral orations honoring the war dead (and praising Athens' superior character and form of government) that were delivered annually when Athens was at war also contributed to Athens' shared understanding

---

89 Osiel 1997:229. The countries with the weakest collective memories are Austria, Poland, Italy, and the Netherlands.

90 Osiel 1997:234–235 (Masada); 159–161 (France).

91 Lys. 12.

92 Prosecution speeches: Lys. 26; 31; Defense speeches: Lys.16; 31; fr. 9 *For Eryximachus*.

93 Lys. 13; Isoc. 18.

94 E.g., Pl. *Apology* 32 c–d; Lys. 18.10; 24.24; 25.15; 28.12; 30.12; And. 1.140.

of the tyranny and the Amnesty.[95] Despite the importance of drama and
the arts in many modern postconflict societies, Athenian drama was likely
less significant in postwar Athens.[96] From early on, tragedies were almost
always set outside Athens, and often concerned mythological themes.
When Athenian tragedy does address contemporary politics, it does so
only obliquely and ambiguously. And while comedies in the fifth century often parodied issues of the day, by the fourth century – the age of
"middle comedy" – comic subjects had turned from political commentary
to domestic life. In any case, no forum could rival the courts as a medium
of collective discourse regarding the civil war: these courts met approximately 200 times a year;[97] the importance of character evidence made
discussion of the civil war likely in cases tried in the postwar period;[98] and
hundreds of jurors were present at each case.

The discourse in the courts fostered reconciliation in three ways, which
I will discuss in turn: (1) discrediting the oligarchy by depicting the horrors
of the tyranny; (2) constructing unity by downplaying the extent of collaboration and focusing blame on the Thirty; and (3) praising the Amnesty
as characteristic of the Athenians' unusual wisdom and benevolence.[99]

Courts and Collective Memory: Discrediting the Oligarchy

Athenian trials publicized the crimes committed by the Thirty, thereby
discrediting the former regime. The broad notion of evidence in Athenian
courts permitted prosecutors to range beyond the specific charges against
the defendant to describe the larger pattern of tyranny. The prosecution of
an informant whose testimony led to a judicial murder early in the Thirty's
reign, for example, includes discussion of atrocities that did not involve
the defendant and were committed after the events in question, including

95 For discussion of memorials, see Wolpert 2002:87–90. The only surviving epitaphios from the
    immediate postwar period is Lysias 2, which does praise the Athenians' decision to forgo pun-
    ishment in favor of unity (Lys. 2.60–65). For a brilliant study of how funeral orations helped
    construct a semiofficial (and misleading) history of Athens, see Loraux 1986.
96 For further discussion of the limits of Athenian drama as a site of norm definition, see
    Chapter 1.
97 Hansen 1999:186.
98 On the importance of character evidence, see Lanni 2006:41–74.
99 I am indebted to two excellent discussions of the court speaker's rhetorical strategies when
    discussing the civil war: D. Cohen 2001 and Wolpert 2002.

the massacres of Salamis and Eleusis, the unjust arrests and executions, the confiscations of property, and the expulsion of all but the 3,000 from the city.[100] The trial at Eratosthenes' accounting provides another example. The prosecution speech includes a detailed and poignant description of the murder of the speaker's brother in the massacre of the metics that emphasizes the outrageousness of the Thirty, who had the audacity to rip the earrings directly from the ears of the victim's wife and refused to let the family have one of the victim's cloaks to give him a proper burial.[101] But the speech also includes a detailed account of how the oligarchy came to power[102] and a recitation of the collective crimes of the Thirty.[103] While the speaker opines that many prosecutors would be required to describe all the crimes of the Thirty,[104] the speech does manage to provide a broad-ranging account of the crimes committed under the oligarchy and an assessment of where the primary responsibility should lie.

These public airings in court of the horrific crimes of the oligarchy helped to discredit not only the former regime, but also oligarchic opposition to the democracy more generally.[105] The repressive rule of the Thirty, with its rigged trials and extrajudicial murders, made it easy for democrats to associate oligarchy with lawless tyranny. Although oligarchic sympathies survived and even thrived in elite intellectual circles in the fourth century,[106] oligarchy became a political nonstarter after the civil war. As Cohen points out, decades later even those too young to have been involved in the Thirty could be tarred with accusations of having oligarchic tendencies.[107] The prosecutor in an assault case derides his opponent, "Even if he is younger than those who held power then [i.e., under the oligarchy], he has the character of that government. These were the natures that betrayed our empire to the enemy, razed the walls of our homeland, and executed fifteen hundred of our citizens without trial."[108]

---

100 Lys. 13.43–47.
101 Lys. 12.17–19.
102 Lys. 12.70ff.
103 Lys. 12. 95–96.
104 Lys. 12.99.
105 For discussion, see D. Cohen 2001:347–349.
106 Isocrates, Plato, and Aristotle are prominent examples.
107 D. Cohen 2001:347–349.
108 Isoc. 20.11; for discussion see D. Cohen 2001:349.

Courts and Collective Memory: Constructing Unity

Like many modern transitional justice legal procedures, then, Athenian trials helped to instill a shared sense of condemnation of the crimes committed by the former regime. But while many modern tribunals or truth commissions seek in part to encourage the broader public to engage in self-scrutiny and confront their own complicity,[109] Athenian court speakers did nothing of the kind. In the decades after the civil war, litigants who discussed the violence under the oligarchy took pains to focus blame narrowly on the Thirty while downplaying the extent of collaboration. This understanding of events was quite explicit in the speeches. To cite one stark example: in discussing the massacre of the metics (resident aliens) at the accounting of Eratosthenes, the prosecutor states, "the rest of the Athenians [i.e. those not in the Thirty], it seems to me, could have a plausible excuse for what happened by laying the blame on the Thirty."[110] Both defendants and prosecutors in suits involving participation in the crimes of the oligarchy take this approach, depicting the entire citizenry as opponents and victims of the Thirty.[111] Undoubtedly the speakers (and their speechwriters) chose this tack because they thought that it would be well received by the jurors. But the effect of this rhetorical strategy was to help construct a misleading collective memory of a unified populace victimized by the tyrannical Thirty.

Lysias' depiction in the accounting trial of Eratosthenes of the process by which the Thirty came to power provides an example. His narrative places blame squarely on Theramenes, a member of the Thirty, and minimizes the role of the Athenians who did, after all, vote the Thirty into office.[112] Lysias' account of the Assembly meeting minimizes the citizens' responsibility as much as possible: he states that many in the Assembly initially opposed the proposal, and even after the Spartan general threatened to destroy the Athenians if they did not acquiesce, some Athenians got up

---

[109] The trial of the Auschwitz guards seems to have had this effect (Osiel 1997:192–193). The 1983 junta trial in Argentina also seems to have been premised on this idea, but was less successful (Osiel 1997:194–195).

[110] Lys. 12.28.

[111] Prosecutors: Lys. 26.2, 16; Lys. 12.30; defendants: Isoc. 18.2 (the speaker is the plaintiff in the *paragraphe*, but the defendant in the sense that he is being charged with wrongdoing under the oligarchy).

[112] Lys. 12.70–75.

and left the Assembly, others stayed but remained silent, and only a "few evil-minded scoundrels voted the proposal through."[113]

Perhaps most striking is the historical fiction, employed in several speeches, that every member of the jury was a member of the resistance in the Piraeus and/or a direct victim of the Thirty. As several scholars have pointed out, although most jury panels must have included members of the 3,000 and other types of collaborators, speakers regularly speak to the jury as former men of the Piraeus, discussing how the jurors, addressed as "you," were driven out of the city, had their property confiscated, houses invaded and family members taken, took part in freeing the city, and returned from the Piraeus.[114]

A rare exception is a passage in Lysias' prosecution of Eratosthenes at his accounting, in which he briefly addresses "those from the city (*astu*)" and "those from the Piraeus" separately. But even this passage has a unifying message. Lysias depicts the men who remained in the city as innocent victims forced to fight against their own kin: "you who are from the city should realize that the defendants ruled you so badly that you were compelled to fight a war against your brothers, your sons, and your fellow citizens...."[115] The prosecutor goes on to emphasize that the former men of the city have gone from being slaves of the oligarchy and their Spartan garrison to participating in governing the polis and joining with the democrats to protect it from external threats:

> Realize that you were ruled by the defendants, who were the worst of men; realize too that you now share the government with good men, you are fighting against external enemies, and you are taking counsel for the city; and remember the mercenaries [i.e., the Spartan garrison employed by the Thirty] that the defendants established on the Acropolis as guardians of their power and of your slavery.[116]

One speaker goes so far as to state that the men who did not actively participate in the killings but remained in the city can claim credit for the overthrow of the oligarchy, suggesting, contrary to our historical evidence, that victory was secured by widespread political opposition within

---

[113] Lys. 12.75.

[114] E.g., Lys. 12.30, 57; 13.47; 26.2; And. 1.81; Isoc. 18.2. For discussion, see Wolpert 2002:xv, 90–94; D. Cohen 2001:341.

[115] Lys. 12.92. In a similar vein, the speaker in Isocrates 18.17 emphasizes that while some citizens participated in arrests and property confiscations they did so only out of compulsion.

[116] Lys. 12.94.

the city.[117] To be sure, the use of these rhetorical topoi in court did not erase individual victims' resentment against specific collaborators who had done them harm. But the collective memory of the oligarchy constructed in the courts may have made victims more willing to trust men whose level of active collaboration was minimal or unknown to them. For those who had remained in the city, the discourse in the courts offered a rationalization for past collaboration and provided comfort that there was a place for them in the restored democracy.

Courts and Collective Memory: Praising the Amnesty

Finally, court speeches in the years after the civil war helped create a myth of refounding in which the Amnesty, and the forgiveness that it implied, exemplified the Athenians' superior character. To be sure, defendants accused of collaboration often defend the Amnesty on pragmatic grounds, arguing that taking retribution would endanger the democracy by alienating former oligarchs.[118] But speakers also praise the Amnesty in a way that made a powerful appeal to the Athenians' honor. In these passages, the Amnesty is transformed from a concession made out of military necessity to an act of will that defines the Athenian democratic spirit.[119] Speakers argue that the Athenians' willingness to reject revenge earned them a reputation throughout Greece for extraordinary generosity, reasonableness, and wisdom.[120] Under this reimagining, the Amnesty is not a reminder of the darkest period in Athenian history, but rather one of the high points worthy of celebration: the speaker in Isocrates 18 states:

> while our ancestors accomplished many noble things, the city has won renown not least from these settlements. You can find many cities that have fought nobly in war, but no one could point to a city better advised with regard to civil strife. Moreover, of those activities that carry risk, one might ascribe the greatest part to luck, but no one would attribute credit for our moderation to anything other than our intelligence.[121]

[117] Lys. 26.18–19.
[118] E.g., Lys. 25.3–28; Isoc. 18.44; And. 1.105. Quillin (2002) applies a model based on decision theory to argue that Athenian jurors rarely punished collaboration because of fear of a resurgence of oligarchic sentiment.
[119] Isoc. 18.2, 31–32; And. 1.140; Aesch. 2.176. D. Cohen 2001:354–355 notes that the participation of Sparta in the reconciliation agreements is conspicuously absent from these passages.
[120] And. 1.140; Aesch. 2.176.
[121] Isoc. 18.31–32.

We can see evidence that this identification of the democracy with moderation took root: in the fourth century authors refer to the Athenians' characteristic mildness or forbearance in contexts unrelated to the civil war.[122] Again, it is difficult to imagine that these encomia of the Amnesty could induce victims to forgive individuals directly responsible for the murder of their kin.[123] Nevertheless, the Amnesty – which was reaffirmed by collective oath each year by jurors and members of the Council and was widely praised in court speeches – may have had some expressive effect,[124] encouraging the Athenians to live up to their myths and take a more conciliatory attitude toward former collaborators who did not personally cause them harm.

Courts and Accountability

A recurring theme in studies of modern transitions is that many victims seem to get more satisfaction from punishment of or acknowledgment of guilt by local perpetrators than from broad-ranging investigations of wrongdoing or trials of high-level war criminals.[125] A common complaint among modern victims is repeatedly seeing neighbors, co-workers, and fellow villagers who collaborated in atrocities going about their lives as if nothing had happened.[126] Because Athenian victims could indirectly sanction collaborators for their conduct during the oligarchy, the Athenians were able to minimize this "impunity gap" at the local level, while still maintaining the unifying collective narrative of rejecting vengeance for Amnesty. In this way, the courts fostered reconciliation by offering some limited accountability as a safety valve for local resentments based on crimes committed during the reign of the Thirty.

---

[122] E.g., *Ath. Pol.* 22.4; Lys. 6.34. For discussion, see Debrunner Hall 1996.

[123] On the differing ability of law to have an expressive effect on behavior based on the relative importance and centrality of the issue to the subject's identity, see Chapter 3.

[124] For discussion of the expressive effect of law, see Chapter 3.

[125] See, e.g., Isaacs 2009:136–139; Stover 2004:107. This insight is also part of the impetus behind the gacaca courts in Rwanda. For discussion, see Karakezi et al. 2004.

[126] Sotiropoulos (2007:121) tells the story of a former member of the resistance who had been imprisoned under military rule passing the judge who convicted him sitting in a coffee shop every morning as he walked to work, and of another resistance member who had been tortured learning that his torturer had become the chief of police. For similar stories, see Rosenberg 1996:320 (Stasi informants); Isaacs 2009:136 (victims in Guatemala living near informants or executioners).

Collaboration could be raised in court, without violating the terms of the Amnesty, in two forms: (1) as character evidence in an unrelated public or private lawsuit;[127] and (2) in the *dokimasia*, the examination of incoming magistrates. Where collaboration was introduced in an unrelated lawsuit, it was up to the individual jury to determine how much weight to accord this character evidence in reaching its verdict. At the *dokimasia*, anyone who wished could challenge a candidate for any reason, including collaboration; if rejected by the jury, the only penalty was disqualification for office. The *dokimasia* procedure shares some similarities with modern forms of administrative justice, such as denazification in Germany and lustration in post-Communist Europe, whereby those who were affiliated with or participated in the former regime could be barred from public office and/or public employment.[128]

Athens' indirect accountability mechanisms reduced victims' worries about impunity, but did not go so far as to alienate former collaborators with severe sanctions. Most collaborators were likely to be selected by lot for office or to face litigation at some point in their lives,[129] leaving them vulnerable to attacks based on their conduct during the oligarchy. But this mechanism was self-limiting in that collaboration only became an issue in court if a victim or an enemy brought it up; victims who needed to air their grievances against a particular collaborator were given the opportunity to do so, but there was no attempt to systematically stigmatize or exclude from office all those who participated in the oligarchy.

The uncertainty over whether and when former collaborators in one's village would face punishment through these indirect mechanisms was much less troubling for those seeking retribution in the context of a society that believed in divine sanctions. Divine sanctions were uncertain and unpredictable, and could occur years or even generations after a violation.[130] Even the awareness that those who had participated in the oligarchy *might* face indirect sanctions in court at some later time may have tempered victims' perception of impunity.[131]

---

127 See Chapter 4.

128 Such vetting procedures can take a variety of forms. For discussion, see Mayer-Reich and DeGreiff 2007; Teitel 2000:149–190.

129 For discussion, see Chapter 4.

130 For discussion, see Lanni 2008:475.

131 Of course, the lack of apology or recognition of guilt on the part of the perpetrators might diminish victims' satisfaction. But it is interesting to note that at least in the case of Stasi

At the same time, these potential indirect sanctions were not so severe that they risked permanently alienating all former collaborators. For one thing, the only penalty that attached to being rejected at one's *dokimasia* was disqualification from office; men who were disqualified in this way could still participate fully in the Assembly and the law courts. Moreover, participation under the Thirty did not doom a litigant or prospective magistrate; this evidence was merely one factor in the jury's consideration.[132] One man who was challenged at his *dokimasia* because he was a member of the Council and the cavalry under the Thirty nevertheless appears to have been confirmed as archon, one of the highest offices of the democracy.[133] Another court speaker suggests that many cavalry members under the oligarchy went on to serve in the Council and even as generals.[134] Perhaps most importantly, wide-ranging examination of litigants' and prospective magistrates' character was routine in Athenian courts. Defendants would not experience discussion of their conduct under the oligarchy in court, and any resulting indirect sanctions, as a specific attack aimed at former collaborators but as standard operating procedure. In fact, one defendant in a *dokimasia* claims that he is glad to have the opportunity to refute widespread accusations that he served in the cavalry under the Thirty:

> The people who force those who are unjustly accused to undergo an investigation of their life's record are in my view responsible for great benefits. I am so utterly confident in myself that I expect even someone badly disposed toward me to change his mind when he hears me speak about what happened and to think much better of me in the future.[135]

informants, even when perpetrators do admit the facts of collaboration, they often do not accept full responsibility in a manner satisfying to the victims (Rosenberg 1996). The limited sense of accountability provided by the Athenian procedures was also more acceptable to victims because the oligarchic sympathizers who were most likely to draw retaliation probably opted to resettle in Eleusis. As Elster (2004:22–23) points out, by the time some of those settlers returned to Athens after the fall of Eleusis in 401, retributive emotions had some time to diminish.

132 Of course, accusation alone could serve as a shame sanction and facilitate informal social sanctions. For discussion, see Chapter 4.

133 Lys. 26. For discussion, see Todd 2000:270–273.

134 Lys. 16.8.

135 Lys. 16.2–3. Of course, litigants were vulnerable to completely fabricated accusations of collaboration, just as they could face false accusations of all sorts of violations of legal and social norms in court. This problem was at least reduced by the availability of suits for false witness and the likelihood that someone among the hundreds of jurors or spectators might have knowledge of the facts and shout down the speaker.

Like many modern vetting procedures, such as lustration, the examination of an individual's conduct under the previous regime in the *dokimasia* was both backward- and forward-looking.[136] Disqualification from office was both a sanction for past wrongdoing and a safeguard to prevent those who committed crimes or who had oligarchic sympathies from exercising power in the restored democracy. A passage from the prosecution speech in Evander's examination for the archonship encapsulates the dual purposes of the *dokimasia*. He imagines the public reaction if Evander is confirmed:

> How do you think the rest of the citizens will feel, when they see that a person who ought to be paying a penalty for his crimes has instead been approved by you for this type of office? Or that the man who ought himself to be on trial before the Areopagus [i.e., for homicide] is instead judging homicide cases? Do you not believe that they will be angry, and hold you responsible, when they think back to those times when many of them were summarily dragged off to prison, were executed by these people without trial, were forced to flee their country.... What is Evander's attitude toward the city? For how many crimes has he been responsible?[137]

Unlike most modern vetting procedures, the *dokimasia* was as concerned with a candidate's current political commitments and view of the Thirty as with his past conduct under the former regime. Wolpert points out that the *dokimasia* served in part as a ritual in which former collaborators publicly pledged their allegiance to the democratic constitution.[138] This does not mean that former collaborators expressed remorse or even admitted participation in the oligarchy; in our surviving speeches litigants and prospective magistrates accused of collaboration vehemently deny that they held offices under the Thirty or were in any way involved in the crimes committed by the regime.[139] Because very few magistrates exercised significant individual power, the importance of the *dokimasia* to the security of the democracy lay less in accurately ferreting out and excluding from office those with oligarchic sympathies and more in the symbolism of these hearings. Having passed a *dokimasia*, a former collaborator might gain a sense

---

136 Mayer-Reich and DeGreiff 2007; Teitel 2000:149–190. As Wilke (2007:349) points out, even when the stated purpose of modern vetting procedures is a forward-looking one, such as in East Germany, the social understanding of these procedures is often as a backward-looking sanction.

137 Lys. 26.12–13.

138 Lys. 16.3; for discussion see Wolpert 2002:115–116.

139 E.g., Lys. 16.8; Lys. 25.15–16; fr. 9.110; Pl. *Apology* 32 c–d; Wolpert 2002:115–116.

of membership and belonging under the new regime, and resentment at a collaborators' holding office might be eased by his public repudiation of the oligarchy. Conversely, rejecting a candidate allowed the demos to make a statement about the sort of collaboration that it deemed incompatible with full citizenship.

In sum, the indirect sanctions for collaboration we have looked at in this section, made possible by the Athens' distinctive legal culture, ranged far wider than any direct trials of collaborators could possibly have done. These mechanisms encouraged reconciliation by minimizing the resentment created by the sense that local collaborators enjoyed impunity and by offering a procedure whereby those with questionable pasts could be publicly reintegrated into the community.

Participation and Social Repair

Those who have studied and designed transitional justice systems have recently focused on rebuilding trust and social relationships between those on opposite sides of the conflict at a local and even an individual level.[140] Relying on the "contact hypothesis," the assumption that "tension and hostility between groups will be reduced when these groups are brought in systematic contact with each other,"[141] initiatives in several postconflict societies seek to increase interaction between opposing groups through joint participation in activities such as sports teams, art and music programs, business ventures, schools, and other forms of educational programs.[142] Initial signs indicate that these coexistence programs can help build trust and cooperation between individual members of opposing groups, particularly when groups are not simply brought into contact with one another (e.g., by taking a class or watching a film together) but are required to work together, for example through shared decision making or productive activity.[143] Athens' highly participatory civic institutions functioned like a model coexistence initiative, encouraging members on opposite sides of the civil war to work together in a variety of contexts.

---

140 See, e.g., Chayes and Minow 2003; Stover and Weinstein 2004; Quinn 2009.
141 Donnelly and Hughes 2009:150.
142 See, e.g., Chayes and Minow 2003:xx.
143 Chigas and Ganson 2003:68–75; Babbitt 2003:107.

Jury service in the courts was just one of the many opportunities for men of the city and men of the Piraeus to interact productively together after the civil war. Other venues for joint decision making included the Assembly, the Council, and the deme (village) assemblies. Service on the Council of 500 involved particularly intense interaction. The Council met about 275 days a year, and during the one-tenth of the year that each member served on the fifty-person executive committee, he was expected to live and work in the Council chamber with the rest of the committee.[144] Participation in several civic institutions – Council service, military service, and performance of the dithyrambic chorus at the Festival of Dionysus, for example – was organized by tribe, which meant that one was more likely to participate alongside members of one's local deme (village). Repeated productive interactions in these various contexts between collaborators and the men of the Piraeus may have helped to rebuild trust and foster cooperation after the restoration of democracy.

***

In sum, Athenian legal institutions helped promote peace and reconciliation after the civil war, but not through the straightforward mechanism of meting out sanctions for violations of law. The Amnesty's importance may have lain chiefly in its expressive and persuasive effect, as court speakers constructed a (misleading) collective memory of the tyranny and reconciliation that promoted unity and social solidarity. Indirect legal sanctions for collaboration may have done more to dispel local resentments and promote reconciliation than the formal trials of members of the Thirty. And repeated interactions in participatory institutions like the courts may have helped build trust and cooperation between those on opposite sides of the conflict.

The peculiar features of the Athenian legal system enabled an especially successful approach to transitional justice by leveraging various institutional advantages that for the most part are not available in modern contexts. First, the courts had a larger market share of cultural/communicative space in Athens[145] than modern transitional justice mechanisms can hope to achieve. The desire for a higher profile in the country undergoing transition is one of the driving forces behind the recent creation of "hybrid" international courts that operate locally but combine domestic and

[144] Hansen 1999:251, 254.
[145] On the courts as a form of public entertainment, see Lanni 1997.

international rules and personnel,[146] but even these efforts pale in comparison to the cultural monopoly enjoyed by the Athenian courts. And the broad participatory opportunities created by the Athenian courts fostered a widespread sense of participation in and ownership over the reconciliation rarely attempted in modern contexts.[147]

Moreover, the flexibility of the Athenian legal system mitigated the tension between ordinary, rule-of-law justice and expedient political settlement. The Athenian popular courts could accommodate the broader transitional justice functions generally reserved in the modern world for special tribunals. Athenian legal culture also created the possibility of piecemeal retributive justice without forcing the all-or-nothing choice that a comprehensive, top-down system invites. Finally, the Athenian approach permitted the transitional process to extend over a longer time frame and to proceed gradually and organically rather than attempting the type of once-and-for-all settlement that is commonly seen in the modern context.

Unlike most modern transitional justice schemes, Athenian courts were traditional in form and unimpeachable in composition – to quarrel with a jury verdict was to quarrel with democracy. They did not stir up grievances unnecessarily, since there was no public prosecutor and no detailed understanding of what constituted collaboration. But they also allowed the airing of any wrong, no matter how old or unconnected to the subject of the suit. Moreover, they were inscrutable in their adjudications – no one knew why the jurors decided as they did, and no rule was established. Did the jury believe that an allegation of collaboration was untrue, or did it find that the allegation, even if true, was outweighed by other factors? No one knew. But clarity in the wake of civil war is not necessarily a virtue. People told their story and got their verdict; they believed what they wanted to believe about what it meant. The system moved on to the next case, and slowly everyone got on with their lives.

---

146 On which, see Dickenson 2003.
147 Rwanda's gacaca courts may be an exception. On the Rwanda experience, see Karekezi et al. 2004.

Conclusion

Several years ago I argued that the Athenian courts did an excellent job of resolving disputes fairly and quickly, not despite, but because of the absence of procedural and evidentiary rules.[1] What I have tried to show here is that these same courts did not merely resolve disputes, but also played an important role in shaping and enforcing norms. Ironically, the aspects of the Athenian legal system that seem to us the most removed from a "rule of law" may actually have been the most effective in fostering order and compliance with norms. The citation of laws other than the specific law under which the case was brought may have helped foster order through the law's expressive function. For example, the frequent references to *hubris* in court cases, including discussion of the protection of slaves under the law, may have had a symbolic effect even though cases under the *hubris* statute were rare, and even though there may have been no *hubris* cases brought on behalf of slaves. We have also seen that the use of character evidence, including descriptions of an opponent's bad behavior in completely unrelated situations, may have helped foster order by boosting deterrence and compensating for underenforcement in a regime that depended on private initiative. Moreover, the lack of strict legal rules and the jurors' ad hoc approach toward decision making made it easier for litigants to advocate for changes in the law and for jurors to accommodate shifting norms, thereby bringing the law into line with current community sentiment. And the loose approach to evidence allowed the Athenians to

[1] Lanni 2006.

accomplish transitional justice goals within the framework of the ordinary popular courts.

In describing each of the non-Austinian mechanisms for maintaining order in Athens, I have drawn insights from modern legal sociology as a jumping-off point, adapted to the Athenian context and complicated through thick historical description. In some respects, the sociological models appear to be more applicable to Athens than to contemporary legal systems: the unusual publicity surrounding and frequency of Athenian trials make it much more plausible that discussion of unrelated norms in court served a disciplinary role, that statutes would have an expressive effect, and that court arguments and verdicts would play a strong role in shaping norms.

But the application of sociological theories to a concrete historical context also highlights the limitations of relying purely on abstract models. The case study of Athenian prostitution laws, for example, demonstrates how the expressive meaning of a statute may elicit a variety of reactions, all of which appear to have been unintended, and some of which were clearly counterproductive. These reactions are understandable enough through an expressive theory of law in retrospect, but one would have been hard-pressed to predict the effects the law would have had on Athenian culture ex ante. Perhaps most important, because law is part of culture and the relationship between law and society is recursive, it is impossible in practice to neatly separate out the effects of individual features of the legal system, such as laws, internalized norms, social sanctions, and so forth, in the way that an incentive model can. The goal of this study has not been to delineate with precision the relative contribution of the various elements that fostered order in Athens. Rather, I have tried to trace the counterintuitive ways in which formal legal institutions encouraged compliance with norms, using a combination of plausible inferences based on the incentives created by these institutions, bolstered and refined by traditional historical evidence.

My hope is that this study not only draws fruitfully on the field of modern legal sociology, but can also contribute to it. The Athenian case offers an example of how legal institutions can foster order and compliance with norms in the absence of strong coercive force. More particularly, this study has focused on the complex interaction of formal and informal institutions in maintaining order. While a major strand in the modern literature examines the dichotomy between informal or formal mechanisms of control,[2] the Athenian case suggests that any model should consider not only how formal and informal institutions operate individually or collectively, but also how the interaction between the two enhances or detracts from the maintenance of order. Finally, we have seen that the publicity generated by the Athenian courts played a critical role in translating the informal mechanisms of control usually seen in smaller, face-to-face settings to a large, complex society. As such, it offers some insight into how social norms and informal sanctions can operate in situations beyond close-knit groups or interactions marked by repeat play.

The picture of Athenian society that emerges from this study suggests that formal legal institutions were much more involved in ordinary Athenians' lives than is readily apparent. Despite the relatively weak coercive force of the Athenian "state," and despite the ideology of freedom from state interference in private lives, in subtle and not so subtle ways the legal apparatus played a disciplinary role. Even as the Athenian jury narrowly resisted Lycurgus' attempt to formally expand the reach of the state to include prosecution of ordinary citizens for lapses of patriotism,[3] Athenian jurors routinely indirectly punished litigants for their moral failings unrelated to the case.

This approach had its advantages, even beyond its efficacy in maintaining order. As I discussed in *Law and Justice in the Courts of Classical Athens*,[4] the Athenian courts produced individualized and contextualized justice, democratically determined. Athenian verdicts did not skirt justice in the name of technicalities. And the norms reinforced through the courts were not imposed from above but were collectively and deliberatively debated and defined in Athens' legislative and judicial institutions. Many norms were far from static or universally held. Litigants had the opportunity to argue against the wisdom of the prevailing norms in a relatively receptive forum: a litigant did not need to convince the jury that a wholesale and permanent revision of the law was necessary, but merely that the law should be adjusted for the purpose of application in the instant case.

Of course, democratic justice came at a cost. In the absence of a developed notion of legality, it was impossible for a citizen to be confident that

---

[2] E.g., Ellickson 1991; Bernstein 1992, 2001. To be sure, legal sociology has not ignored the interaction between formal and informal institutions.

[3] For discussion of Lycurgus' prosecution of Leocrates, see Chapter 5.

[4] Lanni 2006.

his conduct conformed to the law and would not be found wanting by a jury. For prominent citizens with political or personal rivals, the possibility of a lawsuit must have posed a constant threat. Once in court, any prior misdeed (even a nominally legal one) could come back to haunt a litigant. The Athenian court system vastly magnified the power of gossip — of the juicy anecdote, of the raised eyebrow — that operates only informally in smaller societies, or that does not operate much at all for people in impersonal societies like our own. The Athenians were free: free from almost all the rules and regulations that govern modern lives. But they were always being watched by another — watched and judged, and very often judged in court.

Bibliography

Adkins, A.W.H. (1975) *Merit and Responsibility: A Study in Greek Values*, Chicago, Ill.

(1976) "Polupragmosune and 'Minding One's Own Business': A Study in Greek Social and Political Values" *Classical Philology* 71: 301–327.

Allen, D.S. (2000a) *The World of Prometheus: The Politics of Punishing in Democratic Athens*, Princeton, NJ.

(2000b) "Changing the Authoritative Voice: Lycurgus' 'Against Leocrates'" *Classical Quarterly* 19.1: 5–33.

Arnaoutoglou, I. (1998) *Ancient Greek Laws*, London.

Austin, J.L. (1995) *The Province of Jurisprudence Determined*, Cambridge.

Azoulay, V. (2011) "Les métamorphoses du *koinon* athénien: autour du *Contre Léocrate* de Lycurgue" in V. Azoulay and P. Ismard, eds., *Clisthène et Lycurgue d'Athènes: autour du politique dans la cité classique*, 191–218, Paris.

Babbitt, E.F. (2003) "Evaluating Coexistence: Insights and Challenges" in A. Chayes and M. Minow, eds., *Imagine Coexistence: Restoring Humanity after Violent Ethnic Conflict*, 102–127, Malden, Mass.

Balot, R.K. (2014) *Courage in the Democratic Polis: Ideology and Critique in Classical Athens*, Oxford.

Berent, M. (2000) "Anthropology and the Classics: War, Violence, and the Stateless Polis" *Classical Quarterly* 50.1: 257–289.

Bernstein, L. (1992) "Opting Out of the Legal System: Extralegal Contractual Relations in the Diamond Industry" *Journal of Legal Studies* 21:115–157.

(1996) "Merchant Law in a Merchant Court: Rethinking the Code's Search for Immanent Business Norms" *University of Pennsylvania Law Review* 144: 1765–1821.

(2001) "Private Commercial Law in the Cotton Industry: Creating Cooperation through Rules, Norms, and Institutions" *Michigan Law Review* 99: 1724–1788.

Bers, V. (1985) "Dikastic Thorubos" in P.A. Cartledge and F.D. Harvey, eds., *Crux: Essays Presented to G.E.M. de Ste. Croix on His 75th Birthday*, 1–15, London.

(2002) "What to Believe in Demosthenes 57, *Against Eubulides*" *Hyperboreus* 8: 232–239.

(2003) *The Oratory of Classical Greece Vol. 6: Demosthenes, Speeches 50–59*, Austin, Tex.

(2009) *Genos Dikanikon: Amateur and Professional Speech in the Courtrooms of Classical Athens*, Cambridge, Mass.

Boegehold, A.L. (1996) "Resistance to Change in the Law at Athens" in J. Ober and C. Hedrick, eds., *Demokratia: A Conversation on Democracies, Ancient and Modern*, 203–214, Princeton, NJ.

Borah, W. (1983) *Justice by Insurance: The General Indian Court of Colonial Mexico and the Legal Aides of the Half-Real*, Berkeley, Calif.

Bourdieu, P. (1977) *Outline of a Theory of Practice*, Cambridge.

Bresson, A. (2000) *La cité marchande*, Bordeaux.

Burns, R.P. (1999) *A Theory of the Trial*, Princeton, NJ.

Cairns, D.L. (1993) *Aidos: The Psychology and Ethics of Honour and Shame in Ancient Greek Literature*, Oxford.

(1996) "Hybris, Dishonour, and Thinking Big" *Journal of Hellenic Studies* 116: 1–32.

Calfee, J.E. and R. Craswell (1984) "Some Effects of Uncertainty in Compliance with Legal Standards" *Virginia Law Review* 70: 965–974.

Canevaro, M. (2013) *The Documents in the Attic Orators: Laws and Decrees of the Demosthenic Corpus*, Oxford.

Cantarella, E. (1989) "L'omosessualitá nel diritto ateniese" in G. Thür, ed., *Symposion 1985: Vorträge zur griechischen und hellenistischen Rechtsgeschichte*, 153–175, Cologne.

(1991) "*Moicheia*. Reconsidering a Problem" in M. Gagarin, ed., *Symposion 1990: Vorträge zur griechischen und hellenistischen Rechtsgeschichte*, 289–296, Cologne.

(1992) *Bisexuality in the Ancient World*, New Haven, Conn.

(2005) "Gender, Sexuality, and Law" in M. Gagarin and D. Cohen, eds., *The Cambridge Companion to Ancient Greek Law*, 236–253, Cambridge.

Carawan, E.M. (1984) "*Akriton apokteinai*. Execution without Trial in Fourth-Century Athens" *Greek, Roman, and Byzantine Studies* 25: 111–121.

(1985) "*Apophasis* and *Eisangelia*: The Role of the Areopagus in Athenian Political Trials" *Greek, Roman, and Byzantine Studies* 28: 167–208.

(1998) *Rhetoric and the Law of Draco*, Oxford.

(2002) "The Athenian Amnesty and the 'Scrutiny of Laws'" *Journal of Hellenic Studies* 122: 1–23.

(2006) "Amnesty and Accounting for the Thirty" *Classical Quarterly* 56: 57–76.

(2013) *The Athenian Amnesty and Reconstructing the Law*, Oxford.

Carey, C. (1993) "Return of the Radish or Just When You Thought It Was Safe to Go Back in the Kitchen" *Liverpool Classical Monthly* 18: 53–55.

(1994) "Rhetorical Means of Persuasion" in I. Worthington, ed., *Persuasion: Greek Rhetoric in Action*, 26–45, London.

(1995) "Rape and Adultery in Athenian Law" *Classical Quarterly* 45: 407–417.

(1996) "*Nomos* in Attic Rhetoric and Oratory" *Journal of Hellenic Studies* 116: 33–46.

(1998) "The Shape of Athenian Laws" *Classical Quarterly* 48: 93–109.

(2000) *The Oratory of Classical Greece Vol. 3: Aeschines*, Austin, Tex.

(2004) "Offence and Procedure in Athenian Law" in E.M. Harris and L. Rubinstein, eds., *The Law and the Courts in Ancient Greece*, 111–136, London.

Carter, L.B. (1986) *The Quiet Athenian*, Oxford.

Cartledge, P.A. (1993) "Like a Worm i'the Bud? A Heterology of Classical Greek Slavery" *Greece and Rome* 40: 163–180.

(2009a) "'Rights,' Individuals, and Communities in Ancient Greece" in R.K. Balot, ed., *Greek and Roman Political Thought*, 149–163, Oxford.

(2009b) *Ancient Greek Political Thought in Practice*, Cambridge.

Carugati, F., G. Hadfield, and B.R. Weingast (2015) "Building Legal Order in Ancient Athens" *Journal of Legal Analysis* 7.2: 291–324.

Chayes, A. and M. Minow, eds. (2003) *Imagine Coexistence: Restoring Humanity after Violent Ethnic Conflict*, Malden, Mass.

Chigas, D. and B. Ganson (2003) "Coexistence Efforts in Southeast Europe" in A. Chayes and M. Minow, eds., *Imagine Coexistence: Restoring Humanity after Violent Ethnic Conflict*, 59–84, Malden, Mass.

Christ, M.R. (1998a) *The Litigious Athenian*, Baltimore, MD.

(1998b) "Legal Self-Help on Private Property in Classical Athens" *American Journal of Philology* 119: 521–545.

(2006) *The Bad Citizen in Classical Athens*, Cambridge.

(2007) "Review of Gabriel Herman, *Morality and Behaviour in Democratic Athens*" *Bryn Mawr Classical Review* 7: 37.

(2010a) "Helping and Community in the Athenian Lawcourts" in R. Rosen and I. Sluiter, eds., *Valuing Others in Classical Antiquity*, 205–232, Leiden.

(2010b) "Helping Behavior in Classical Athens" *Phoenix* 64: 254–290.

(2012) *The Limits of Altruism in Democratic Athens*, Cambridge.

Cohen, D. (1983) *Theft in Athenian Law*, Munich.

(1985) "A Note on Aristophanes and the Punishment of Adultery in Athenian Law" *Zeitschrift der Savigny-Stiftung* 102: 385–387.

(1991a) *Law, Sexuality and Society: The Enforcement of Morals in Classical Athens*, Cambridge.

(1991b) "Sexuality, Violence, and the Athenian Law of 'Hubris'" *Greece and Rome* 38.2: 171–188.

(1995) *Law, Violence, and Community in Classical Athens*, Cambridge.

(2001) "The Rhetoric of Justice: Strategies of Reconciliation and Revenge in the Restoration of Athenian Democracy in 403 B.C." *European Journal of Society* 42: 335–356.

(2005a) "Crime, Punishment, and the Rule of Law in Classical Athens" in M. Gagarin and D. Cohen, eds., *The Cambridge Companion to Ancient Greek Law*, 211–235, Cambridge.

(2005b) "Theories of Punishment" in M. Gagarin and D. Cohen, eds., *The Cambridge Companion to Ancient Greek Law*, 170–182, Cambridge.

Cohen, E.E. (1973) *Ancient Athenian Maritime Courts*, Princeton, NJ.

(1992) *Athenian Economy and Society: A Banking Perspective*, Princeton, NJ.

(1998) "Wealthy Slaves of Athens: Legal Rights, Economic Obligations" in H. Jones, ed., *Le monde antique et les droits de l'homme*, 105–129, Brussels.

(2000a) *The Athenian Nation*, Princeton, NJ.

(2000b) "Whoring under Contract: The Legal Context of Prostitution in Fourth-Century Athens" in V. Hunter and J. Edmondson, eds., *Law and Social Status in Classical Athens*, 113–148, Oxford.

(2003) "Athenian Prostitution as a Liberal Profession" in G.W. Bakewell and J.H. Sickinger, eds., *Gestures: Essays in Ancient History, Literature, and Philosophy Presented to Alan L. Boegehold*, 214–236, Oxford.

Bibliography

(2005) "Commercial Law" in M. Gagarin and D. Cohen, eds., *The Cambridge Companion to Ancient Greek Law*, 290–304, Cambridge.

(2007a) "Laws Affecting Prostitution at Athens" in E. Cantarella, ed., *Symposion 2005: Vorträge zur griechischen und hellenistischen Rechtsgeschichte*, 201–224, Vienna.

(2007b) "Slave Power at Athens: Juridical Theory and Economic Reality" in E. Perrin-Saminadayar, P. Ismard, and V. Azoulay, eds., *Individus, Groupes, et Politique à Athènes de Solon à Mithradate*, 155–170, Paris.

Comaroff, J.L. and S. Roberts (1981) *Rules and Processes: The Cultural Logic of Dispute in an African Context*, Chicago, Ill.

Connor, W.R. (1971) *The New Politicians of Fifth-Century Athens*, Princeton, NJ.

(1985) "The Razing of the House in Greek Society" *Transactions of the American Philological Association* 115: 79–102.

Conover, K. (2010) *Bribery in Classical Athens* (PhD diss., Princeton University).

Cooter, R. (1996) "Decentralized Law for a Complex Economy: A Structural Approach to Adjudicating the New Law Merchant" *University of Pennsylvania Law Review* 144: 1643–1696.

(1998) "Expressive Law and Economics" *Journal of Legal Studies* 27: 585–608.

(2000) "Three Effects of Social Norms on Law: Expression, Deterrence, and Internalization" *Oregon Law Review* 79: 1–22.

Couvenhes, J.-C. (2012) "L'introduction des archers scythes, esclaves publics, à Athènes: la date et l'agent d'un transfert culturel" in B. Legras, ed., *Transferts culturels et droits dans la monde grec et hellénistique*, 99–118, Paris.

Cox, C. (2002) "Assuming the Master's Values: The Slaves' Response to Punishment and Neglect in Menander" *Mouseion* 3.2: 23–38.

(2007) "The *Astynomoi*, Private Wills, and Street Activity" *Classical Quarterly* 57: 769–775.

Craswell, R. and J.E. Calfee (1986) "Deterrence and Uncertain Legal Standards" *Journal of Law, Economics, and Organization* 2: 279–303.

Davidson, J.N. (1998) *Courtesans and Fishcakes: The Consuming Passions of Classical Athens*, New York.

(2007) *The Greeks and Greek Love*, London.

Davies, J.K. (1981) *Wealth and the Power of Wealth in Classical Athens*, New York.

De Brauw, M. (2001–2002) "'Listen to the Law Themselves': Citations of Laws and Portrayal of Character in Attic Oratory" *Classical Journal* 97: 161–176.

Debrunner Hall, M. (1996) "Even Dogs Have Erinyes: Sanctions in Athenian Practice and Thinking" in L. Foxhall and D.E. Lewis, eds., *Greek Law in Its Political Setting: Justifications, Not Justice*, 73–89, Oxford.

De Ste. Croix, G.E.M. (1981) *The Class Struggle in the Ancient Greek World from the Archaic Age to the Arab Conquests*, Ithaca, NY.

(2005) "The Date of Solon's *Nomothesia*" in D. Harvey and R. Parker, eds., *G.E.M. de Ste. Croix: Athenian Democratic Origins and Other Essays*, Oxford.

Dickenson, L. (2003) "The Promise of Hybrid Courts" *American Journal of International Law* 97: 295–310.

Dodds, E.R. (1951) *The Greeks and the Irrational*, Berkeley, Calif.

Donnelly, C. and J. Hughes (2009) "Contact and Culture: Mechanisms of Reconciliation in Schools in Northern Ireland and Israel" in A. Quinn, ed., *Reconciliation(s): Transitional Justice in Postconflict Societies*, 147–173, Montreal.

Bibliography

Dorjahn, A.P. (1946) *Political Forgiveness in Old Athens: The Amnesty of 403 B.C.* (PhD diss., Northwestern).

Dougherty, C. and L. Kurke, eds. (2000) *The Cultures within Greek Culture*, Cambridge.

Dover, K.J. (1989) *Greek Homosexuality*, Cambridge, Mass.

(1994) *Greek Popular Morality in the Time of Plato and Aristotle*, Indianapolis, Ind. [Reprint from 1974].

Edwards, M. (2007) *The Oratory of Classical Greece, Vol.11: Isaeus*, Austin, Tex.

Ellickson, R.C. (1991) *Order without Law: How Neighbors Settle Disputes*, Cambridge, Mass.

Elster, J. (2004) *Closing the Books: Transitional Justice in Historical Perspective*, Cambridge.

Faraguna, M. (1992) *Atene nell'eta di Alessandro*, Rome.

Feldman, E.A. (2006) "The Tuna Court: Law and Norms in the World's Premier Fish Market" *California Law Review* 94: 313–369.

Figueira, T. (1986) "'Sitopolai' and 'Sitophylakes' in Lysias' *Against the Graindealers*': Governmental Intervention in the Athenian Economy" *Phoenix* 40.2: 149–171.

Finley, M.I. (1983) *Politics in the Ancient World*, Cambridge.

(1985a) *Democracy Ancient and Modern*, London.

(1985b) *Ancient History: Evidence and Models*, London.

Fisher, N.R.E. (1990) "The Law of *hubris* in Athens" in P. Cartledge, P. Millett, and S. Todd, eds., *Nomos: Essays in Athenian Law, Politics, and Society*, 123–139, Cambridge.

(1992) *Hybris: A Study in the Values of Honour and Shame in Ancient Greece*, Warminster.

(1993) *Slavery in Classical Greece*, Bristol.

(1995) "*Hybris*, Status and Slavery" in A. Powell, ed., *The Greek World*, 44–84, New York.

(1998) "Violence, Masculinity, and the Law in Classical Athens" in L. Foxhall and J. Salmon, eds., *When Men Were Men: Masculinity, Power, and Identity in Classical Antiquity*, 68–97, London.

(1999) "Workshop of Villains: Was There Much Organized Crime in Classical Athens?" in K. Hopwood, ed., *Organised Crime in Antiquity*, 53–96, London.

(2001) *Aeschines Against Timarchos*, Oxford.

Ford, A. (1999) "Reading Homer from the Rostrum: Poems and Laws in Aechines' *Against Timachus*" in S. Goldhill and R. G. Osborne, eds., *Performance Culture and Athenian Democracy*, 231–256, Cambridge.

Forsdyke, S. (2005a) *Exile, Ostracism, and Democracy: The Politics of Expulsion in Ancient Greece*, Princeton, NJ.

(2005b) "Riot and Revelry in Archaic Megara: Democratic Disorder or Ritual Reversal?" *Journal of Hellenic Studies* 125: 73–92.

(2012) *Slaves Tell Tales and Other Episodes in the Politics of Popular Culture in Ancient Greece*, Princeton, NJ.

(Forthcoming a) "Rule of Law, Popular Justice, and the Politics of Interpreting the Past."

(Forthcoming b) "Les valuers démocratique et l'esclavage en Grèce ancienne."

(Forthcoming c) "Greek Conceptions of the Rule of Law."

Foxhall, L. (1998) "The Politics of Affection: Emotional Attachments in Athenian Society" in P. Cartledge, P. Millett, and S. von Reden, eds., *Kosmos: Essays in Order, Conflict, and Community in Classical Athens*, 52–67, Cambridge.

Frug, J. (1988) "Argument as Character" *Stanford Law Review* 40: 869–927.

Bibliography

Gabrielsen, V. (1994) *Financing the Athenian Fleet: Public Taxation and Social Relations*, Baltimore, MD.

Gagarin, M. (1978) "Self-Defense in Athenian Homicide Law" *Greek Roman and Byzantine Studies* 19: 111–120.

(1979) "The Athenian Law against *hubris*" in G.W. Bowersock, W. Burkert, and M. Putnam, eds., *Arktouros: Hellenic Studies Presented to Bernard M. W. Knox on the Occasion of His 65th Birthday*, 229–236, Berlin and New York.

(1996) "Torture of Slaves in Athenian Law" *Classical Philology* 91: 1–18.

(2003) "Who Were the *kakourgoi*? Career Criminals in Athenian Law" in G. Thür and F.J. Fernandez Nieto, eds., *Symposion 1999: Vorträge zur griechischen und hellenistischen Rechtsgeschichte*, 183–192, Cologne.

(2005) "La violence dans les plaidoyers attiques" in J.-M. Bertrand, ed., *La violence dans les mondes grec et romain*, 365–376, Paris.

(2008) *Writing Greek Law*, Cambridge.

(2012) "Law, Politics, and the Question of Relevance in the Case on the Crown" *Classical Antiquity* 31.2: 23–314.

Gagarin, M. and D. Cohen, eds. (2005) *The Cambridge Companion to Ancient Greek Law*, Cambridge.

Gagarin, M. and MacDowell, D. M (1998) *The Oratory of Classical Greece Vol. 1: Antiphon and Andocides*, Austin, Tex.

Gallant, T.W. (1991) *Risk and Survival in Ancient Greece: Reconstructing the Rural Domestic Economy*, Stanford, Calif.

Garlan, Yvon (1982) *Slavery in Ancient Greece*, Ithaca, NY.

Garland, D. (1990) *Punishment and Modern Society*, Chicago, Ill.

Garland, R. (1990) *The Greek Way of Life*, London.

Gauthier, P. (1971) "Les xenoi dans les texts athéniens de la seconde moitié du Ve siècle av. J.C." *Revue des études grecques* 84: 44–79.

(1981) "De Lysias à Aristote (Ath. Pol. 51,4): Le commerce du grain à Athènes et les fonctions des sitophylakes" *Revue historique de droit français et étranger* 59:5–28.

Geertz, C. (1983) *Local Knowledge*, New York.

Gernet, L. (1955) "Le droit de la vente et la notion du contrat en Grèce d'après M. Pringsheim" in L. Gernet, *Droit et société dans la Grèce ancienne*, 201–224, Paris.

Gneezy, U. and A. Rustichini (2000) "A Fine Is a Price" *Journal of Legal Studies* 29: 1–77.

Golden, M. (1984) "Slavery and Homosexuality at Athens" *Phoenix* 38: 308–324.

(2003) "Childhood in Ancient Greece" in J. Niels and J. Oakley, eds., *Coming of Age in Ancient Greece*, 12–29, New Haven, Conn.

Goodman, R. (2001) "Beyond the Enforcement Principle: Sodomy Laws, Social Norms, and Social Panoptics" *California Law Review* 89: 643–740.

Goodman, R. and D. Jinks (2004) "How to Influence States: Socialization and International Human Rights Law" *Duke Law Journal* 54: 621–703.

Gordon, R. (1984) "Critical Legal Histories" *Stanford Law Review* 36: 57–125.

Gowder, P. (2014) "Democracy, Solidarity, and the Rule of Law" *Buffalo Law Review* 62: 1–67.

(2015) "Trust and Commitment: How Athens Rebuilt the Rule of Law" in C. Corradetti, N. Eisikovits, and J.V. Rotundi, eds., *Theorizing Transitional Justice*, 225–236, Burlington, Vt.

Bibliography

Green, T.A. (1985) *Verdict According to Conscience: Perspectives on the English Criminal Trial Jury, 1200–1800*, Chicago, Ill.

Grief, A. (1993) "Contract Enforceability and Economic Institutions in Early Trade: The Maghribi Traders' Coalition" *American Economic Review* 83: 525–548.

Gwatkin, W.E. (1957) "The Legal Arguments in Aischines' *Against Ktesiphon* and Demosthenes' *On the Crown*" *Hesperia* 26: 129–141.

Hadfield, G. (1994) "Weighing the Value of Vagueness: An Economic Perspective on Precision in the Law" *California Law Review* 82: 541–554.

Halperin, D.M. (1990) *One Hundred Years of Homosexuality and Other Essays on Greek Love*, New York.

Hamel, D. (1998) "Coming to Terms with *Lipotaxion*" *Greek, Roman, and Byzantine Studies* 39: 361–405.

Hansen, M.H. (1974) *The Sovereignty of the People's Court in Athens in Fourth Century B.C. and the Public Action against Unconstitutional Proposals*, Odense.

    (1975) *Eisangelia: The Sovereignty of the People's Court in Athens in the Fourth Century B.C. and the Impeachment of the Generals and Politicians*, Odense.

    (1976) *Apagoge, Endeixis, and Ephegesis against Kakourgoi, Atimoi, and Pheugontes: A Study in the Administration of Justice in the Fourth Century B.C.*, Odense.

    (1979) "Misthos for Magistrates in Classical Athens" *Symbolae Osloenses* 54: 5–22.

    (1980) "Seven Hundred *archai* in Classical Athens" *Greek, Roman, and Byzantine Studies* 21: 315–330.

    (1985) "Athenian *nomothesia*" *Greek, Roman, and Byzantine Studies* 26: 345–371.

    (1999) *The Athenian Democracy in the Age of Demosthenes*, London [Reprint 1991].

    (2002) "Was the *Polis* a State or Stateless Society?" in T.H. Nielson, ed., *Even More Studies in the Ancient Greek Polis*, 17–48, Stuttgart.

    (2010) "Democratic Freedom and the Concept of Freedom in Plato and Aristotle" *Greek, Roman, and Byzantine Studies* 50: 1–27.

Harcourt, B.E. (2000) "After the 'Social Meaning Turn': Implications for Research Design and Methods of Proof in Contemporary Criminal Law Policy Analysis" *Law and Society Review* 34: 179–211.

Harrell, H.C. (1936) *Public Arbitration in Athenian Law*, Columbia, Mo.

Harris, E.M. (1992) "Review of MacDowell, *Demosthenes: Against Meidias (Or. 21)*" *Classical Philology* 87: 71–80.

    (1994a) "Law and Oratory in Persuasion: Greek Rhetoric in Action" in I. Worthington, ed., *Persuasion: Greek Rhetoric in Action*, 130–150, London.

    (1994b) "'In the Act' or 'Red-Handed'? *Furtum Manifestum* and *Apagoge* to the Eleven" in G. Thür, ed., *Symposion 1993: Vorträge zur griechischen und hellenistischen Rechtsgeschichte*, 169–184, Cologne, Weimar, and Vienna.

    (1999) "The Penalty for Frivolous Prosecutions in Athenian Law" *Dike* 2: 123–142.

    (2000) "Open Texture in Athenian Law" *Dike* 3: 27–79.

    (2001) "Introduction to Lycurgus" in I. Worthington, C.R. Cooper, and E.M. Harris, *The Oratory of Classical Greece Vol. 5: Dinarchus, Hyperides, and Lycurgus*, 155–159, Austin, Tex.

    (2002) "Workshop, Marketplace, and Household: The Nature of Technical Specialization in Classical Athens and Its Influence on Economy and Society" in P. Cartledge, E.E. Cohen, and L. Foxhall, eds., *Money, Labour, and Land: Approaches to the Economies of Ancient Greece*, 67–99, London.

(2006) *Democracy and the Rule of Law in Classical Athens*, Cambridge.

(2007) "Who Enforced the Law in Classical Athens?" in E. Cantarella, ed., *Symposion 2005: Vorträge zur griechischen und hellenistischen Rechtsgeschichte*, 159–176, Vienna.

(2008) *The Oratory of Classical Greece: Vol. 12: Demosthenes, Speeches 20–22*, Austin, Tex.

(2013) *The Rule of Law in Action in Democratic Athens*, Oxford.

Harris, W.V. (1991) *Ancient Literacy*, Cambridge, Mass.

Harrison, A.R.W. (1998) *The Law of Athens. Vol. II: Procedure*, London [Reprint from 1971].

Hay, D. (1975) "Property, Authority, and the Criminal Law" in D. Hay, P. Linebaugh, J.G. Rule, E.P. Thompson, and C. Winslow, *Albion's Fatal Tree: Crime and Society in Eighteenth-Century England*, 17–63, London.

Herman, G. (1993) "Tribal and Civic Codes of Behaviour in Lysias 1" *Classical Quarterly* 43: 406–419.

(1994) "How Violent Was Athenian Society?" in R. Osborne and S. Hornblower, eds., *Ritual, Finance, Politics: Athenian Democratic Accounts Presented to David Lewis*, 99–107, Oxford.

(2006) *Morality and Behaviour in Democratic Athens: A Social History*, Cambridge.

Hindley, C. (1991) "Law, Society and Homosexuality in Classical Athens" *Past and Present* 133: 167–183.

Holmes, O.W. (1997) "The Path of the Law" *Harvard Law Review* 110: 991–1009 (Reprint of 10:457–478 [1897]).

Hubbard, T.K. (1998) "Popular Perceptions of Elite Homosexuality in Classical Athens" *Arion* 6: 48–78.

(2000) "Pederasty and Democracy: The Marginalization of a Social Practice" in T.K. Hubbard, ed., *Greek Love Reconsidered*, 1–11, New York.

(2003) *Homosexuality in Greece and Rome: A Sourcebook of Basic Documents*, Berkeley, Calif.

Humphreys, S.C. (1983) "The Evolution of Legal Process in Attica" in E. Gabba, ed. *Tria Corda. Scritti in onore di Arnaldo Momigliano*, 229–256, Como.

(1985) "Lycurgus of Butadae: An Athenian Aristocrat" in J.W. Eadie and J. Ober, eds., *The Craft of the Ancient Historian: Essays in Honor of Chester G. Starr*, 199–252, Lanham, MD.

Hunt, P. (Forthcoming) "Violence against Slaves in classical Greece" in G. Fagan and W. Riess, eds., *The Topography of Ancient Greek and Roman Violence*, Cambridge.

Hunter, V.J. (1994) *Policing Athens: Social Control in the Attic Lawsuits, 420–320 B.C.*, Princeton, NJ.

(1997) "The Prison of Athens: A Comparative Perspective" *Phoenix* 51: 296–326.

(2000a) "Introduction: Status Distinctions in Athenian Law" in V.J. Hunter and J. Edmonson, eds., *Law and Social Status in Classical Athens*, 1–30, Oxford.

(2000b) "Policing Public Debtors in Classical Athens" *Phoenix* 54: 21–38.

(2007) "Did the Athenians Have a Word for Crime?" *Dike* 10: 5–18.

Hunter, V.J. and J. Edmondson, eds. (2000) *Law and Social Status in Classical Athens*, Oxford.

Isaacs, A. (2009) "Truth and the Challenge of Reconciliation in Guatemala" in A. Quinn, ed., *Reconciliation(s): Transitional Justice in Postconflict Societies*, 136–139, Montreal.

Johnstone, S. (1999) *Disputes and Democracy: The Consequences of Litigation in Ancient Athens*, Austin, Tex.

Bibliography

(2003) "Women, Property, and Surveillance in Classical Athens" *Classical Antiquity* 22: 248–274.

(2011) *A History of Trust in Ancient Greece*, Chicago, Ill.

Jones, N.F. (1999) *The Associations of Classical Athens: The Response to Democracy*, Oxford.

Jordan, D. (2000) "A Personal Letter Found in the Athenian Agora" *Hesperia* 69: 91–103.

Kahan, D.M. (2000) "Gentle Nudges vs. Hard Shoves: Solving the Sticky Norms Problem" *University of Chicago Law Review* 67: 607–645.

Kamen, D. (2013) *Status in Classical Athens*, Princeton, NJ.

Kapparis, K. (1995) "When Were the Athenian Adultery Laws Introduced?" *Revue internationale des droits de l'antiquité* 42: 97–122.

(1996) "Humiliating the Adulterer: The Law and the Practice in Classical Athens" *Revue internationale des droits de l'antiquité* 43: 63–77.

(2014) "Assessors of Magistrates (*Paredroi*) in Classical Athens" *Historia* 47.4: 383–393.

Karekezi, U., A. Nshimiyimana, and B. Mtamba (2004) "Localizing Justice: Gacaca Courts in Post-genocide Rwanda" in E. Stover and H. Weinstein, eds., *My Neighbor, My Enemy: Justice and Community in the Aftermath of Mass Atrocity*, 69–84, Cambridge.

Karayiannis, A.D. and A.N. Hatzis. (2010) "Morality, Social Norms, and the Rule of Law as Transaction Cost-Saving Devices: The Case of Ancient Athens" *European Journal of Law and Economy* 33: 621–643.

Katyal, N.K. (1997) "Deterrence's Difficulty" *Michigan Law Review* 95: 2385–2476.

Kennedy, D. (1993) *Sexy Dressing, Etc.*, Cambridge, Mass.

Kessler, A. (2004) "Enforcing Virtue: Social Norms and Self-Interest in an Eighteenth-Century Merchant Court" *Law and History Review* 22: 71–118.

Klees, H. (1975) *Herren und Sklaven*, Wiesbaden.

(1998) *Sklavenleben im klassischen Griechenland*, Stuttgart.

Konstan, D. (1997) *Friendship in the Classical World*, Cambridge.

Koskenniemi, M. (2002) "Between Impunity and Show Trials" *Max Planck Yearbook of United Nations Law* 6: 1–32.

Krentz, P. (1982) *The Thirty at Athens*, Ithaca, NY.

Kucharski, J. (2012) "Vindictive Prosecution in Classical Athens: On Some Recent Theories" *Greek, Roman, and Byzantine Studies* 52: 167–197.

Kurihara, A. (2003) "Personal Enmity as a Motivation in Forensic Speeches" *Classical Quarterly* 53.2: 464–477.

LaCroix, A.L. (2004) "To Gain the Whole World and Lose His Own Soul: Nineteenth Century American Dueling as Public Law and Private Code" *Hofstra Law Review* 33: 501–568.

Lambert, S.D. (2011) "What Was the Point of Inscribed Honorific Decrees in Classical Athens?" in S.D. Lambert, ed., *Sociable Man: Studies in Ancient Greek Social Behaviour in Honour of Nick Fisher*, 193–214, Swansea.

Lang, M. and M. Crosby (1964) *The Athenian Agora Vol. X*. Princeton, NJ.

Lanni, A. (1997) "Spectator Sports or Serious Politics? *Hoi periestekotes* and the Athenian Lawcourts" *Journal of Hellenic Studies* 117: 183–189.

(2004) "Arguing from 'Precedent': Modern Perspectives Athenian Practice" in E.M. Harris and L. Rubinstein, eds., *The Law and the Courts in Ancient Greece*, 159–171, London.

Bibliography

(2005) "Relevance in Athenian Courts" in M. Gagarin and D. Cohen, eds., *The Cambridge Companion to Ancient Greek Law*, 112–128, Cambridge.

(2006) *Law and Justice in the Courts of Classical Athens*, Cambridge.

(2008) "The Laws of War in Ancient Greece" *Law and History Review* 26: 469–489.

(2009) "Social Norms in the Ancient Athenian Courts" *Journal of Legal Analysis* 1.2: 691–736.

(2010a) "The Expressive Effect of the Athenian Prostitution Laws" *Classical Antiquity* 29.1: 45–67.

(2010b) "Transitional Justice in Ancient Athens: A Case Study" *University of Pennsylvania Journal of International Law* 32.2: 551–594.

(2010c) "Judicial Review and the Athenian Constitution" in M.H. Hansen, ed., *Démocratie athénienne-démocratie moderne: tradition et influences*, 235–263, Geneva.

(2012) "Publicity and the Courts of Classical Athens" *Yale Journal of Law and Humanities* 24.1: 119–135.

(Forthcoming) "Collective Sanctions" in D. Kehoe and T.A. McGinn, eds., *Ancient Law, Ancient Society*, Ann Arbor, Mich.

Lape, S. (2006) "The Psychology of Prostitution in Aeschines' Speech *Against Timarchus*" in C. Faraone and L.K. McClure, *Prostitutes and Courtesans in the Ancient World*, 139–160, Madison, Wis.

Lear, A. and E. Cantarella (2008) *Images of Ancient Greek Pederasty: Boys Were Their Gods*, New York.

Lessig, L. (1995) "The Regulation of Social Meaning" *University of Chicago Law Review* 61: 943–1045.

(1996) "Social Meaning and Social Norms" *University of Pennsylvania Law Review* 144: 2181–2189.

(1998) "The New Chicago School" *Journal of Legal Studies* 27: 661–691.

Lewin, U.M. (2008) "Internet File-Sharing: Swedish Pirates Challenge the U.S." *Cardozo Journal of International and Comparative Law* 16: 173–206.

Lewis, D.M. (1966) "After the Profanation of the Mysteries" in E. Badian, ed., *Ancient Society and Institutions: Studies Presented to Victor Ehrenberg*, 177–191, Oxford.

Lewis, S. (1995) "Barbershops and Perfume Shops: 'Symposia without wine'" in A. Powell, ed., *The Greek World*, London.

(1996) *News and Society in the Ancient Greek Polis*, Chapel Hill, NC.

Lintott, A. (1982) *Violence, Civil Strife, and Revolution in the Classical City 750–330 B.C.*, London.

Llewellyn-Jones, L. (2011) "Domestic Abuse and Violence against Women in Ancient Greece" in S.D. Lambert, ed., *Sociable Man: Essays on Ancient Greek Social Behaviour*, Swansea.

Loening, T.C. (1987) *The Reconciliation Agreement 403/402 B.C. in Athens*, Wiesbaden.

Loraux, N. (1986) *The Invention of Athens: The Funeral Oration in the Classical City*, trans. A. Sheridan, Cambridge, Mass.

(2002) *The Divided City: On Memory and Forgetting in Ancient Athens*, trans. C. Pache and J. Fort, New York.

MacDowell, D.M. (1963) *Athenian Homicide Law in the Age of the Orators*, Manchester.

(1971) "The Chronology of Athenian Speeches and Legal Innovations in 401–398 B.C." *Revue internationale des droits de l'antiquité* 18: 267–273.

Bibliography

(1976) *"Hybris* in Athens" *Greece and Rome* 23: 14–31.

(1990) *Demosthenes. Against Meidias* (Oration 21), Oxford.

(1991) "The Athenian Procedure of *Phasis"* in M. Gagarin, ed., *Symposion 1990: Vorträge zur griechischen und hellenistischen Rechtsgeschichte,* 187–198, Cologne.

(1993) *The Law in Classical Athens,* Ithaca, NY [Reprint from 1978].

(2000) "Athenian Laws about Homosexuality" *Revue internationale des droits de l'antiquité* 42: 13–27.

(2004) *The Oratory of Classical Greece Vol. 8: Demosthenes Speeches 27–28,* Austin, Tex.

Mann, B.H. (1987) *Neighbors and Strangers: Law and Community in Early Connecticut,* Chapel Hill, NC.

Mayer-Rieckh, A. and P. de Greiff, eds. (2007) *Justice as Prevention: Vetting Public Employees in Transitional Societies,* New York.

McAdams, R.H. (1997) "The Origin, Development, and Regulation of Norms" *Michigan Law Review* 96: 338–433.

McGinn, T.A.J. (2003) *Prostitution, Sexuality, and the Law in Ancient Rome,* Oxford.

(Forthcoming) "The Expressive Function of Law and the *Lex Imperfecta."*

Meares, T.L. 1997. "Charting Race and Class Differences in Attitudes toward Drug Legalization and Law Enforcement Lessons from Federal Criminal Law" *Buffalo Criminal Law Review* 1: 137–174.

Meares, T.L. and D. Kahan (1998) "Law and (Norms of) Order in the Inner City" *Law and Society Review* 32: 805–838.

Meineke, J. (1971) "Gesetzinterpretation und Gesetzasanwendung im attischen Zivilprozess" *Revue internationale des droits de l'antiquité* 18: 275–360.

Merry, S. (1988) "Legal Pluralism" *Law and Society Review* 22: 869–896.

Meyer-Laurin, H. (1965) *Gesetz und Billigkeit im attischen Prozess,* Weimar.

Millett, P.C. (1991) *Lending and Borrowing in Ancient Athens,* Cambridge.

(2005) "The Trial of Socrates Revisited" *European Review of History* 12.1: 23–62.

Milgrom, P.R., D. North, and B. Weingast (1990) "The Role of Institutions in the Revival of Trade: The Medieval Law Merchant, Private Judges, and the Champagne Fairs" *Economics and Politics* 2: 1–23.

Minow, M. (1998) *Between Vengeance and Forgiveness,* Boston, Mass.

Mirhady, D.C. (1996) "Torture and Rhetoric in Athens" *Journal of Hellenic Studies* 116: 119–131.

(2000) "The Athenian Rationale for Torture" in V. Hunter and J. Edmondson, eds., *Law and Social Status in Classical Athens,* 53–74, Oxford.

Mirhady, D.C. and C. Schwarz (2011) "Dikastic Participation" *Classical Quarterly* 61.2: 744–767.

Mirhady, D.C. and Y.L. Too (2000) *The Oratory of Classical Greece, Vol. 4: Isocrates I,* Austin, Tex.

Missiou, A. (2011) *Literacy and Democracy in Fifth-Century Athens,* Cambridge.

Monoson, S.S. (2000) "The Allure of Harmodius and Aristogeiton" in T.K. Hubbard, ed., *Greek Love Reconsidered,* 42–51, New York.

Moore, S. Falk (1978) *Law as Process: An Anthropological Approach,* London.

Morris, I. (2002) "Hard Surfaces" in P. Cartledge, E.E. Cohen, and L. Foxhall, *Money, Labour, and Land: Approaches to the Economies of Ancient Greece,* 8–43, London.

Morris, S.P and J.K. Papadopoulos (2005) "Greek Towers and Slaves: An Archaeology of Exploitation" *American Journal of Archaeology* 109.2: 155–225.

Bibliography

Morrow, G.R. (1937) "The Murder of Slaves in Attic Law" *Classical Philology* 32.3: 210–227.

Murray, O. (1990) "The Solonian Law of *Hubris*" in P. Cartledge, P. Millett, and S. Todd, eds., *Nomos: Essays in Athenian Law, Politics, and Society*, 139–147, Cambridge.

Nelson, W.E. (1975) *Americanization of the Common Law: The Impact of Legal Change on Massachusetts Society, 1760–1830*, Cambridge, Mass.

Ober, J. (1989) *Mass and Elite in Democratic Athens*, Princeton, NJ.

    (1994) "Power and Oratory in Democratic Athens: Demosthenes 21, *against Meidias*" in I. Worthington, ed., *Persuasion: Greek Rhetoric in Action*, 85–108, London.

    (2000) "Quasi-rights: Participatory Citizenship and Negative Liberties in Democratic Athens" *Social Philosophy and Policy* 17: 27–61.

    (2001) "The Debate over Civic Education in Classical Athens" in Y. Lee Too, ed., *Education in Greek and Roman Antiquity*, 273–305, Leiden.

    (2007) *Athenian Legacies: Essays on the Politics of Going on Together*, Princeton, NJ.

    (2008a) *Democracy and Knowledge: Innovation and Learning in Classical Athens*, Princeton, NJ.

    (2008b) "What the Greeks Can Tell Us About Democracy" *Annual Review of Political Science* 11: 67–91.

Omitowoju, R. (Forthcoming) "The Crime That Dare Not Speak Its Name: Violence against Women in Athenian Courts" in G. Fagan and W. Riess, eds., *The Topography of Ancient Greek and Roman Violence*, Cambridge.

Osborne, R.G. (1985a) "Law in Action in Classical Athens" *Journal of Hellenic Studies* 105: 40–58.

    (1985b) *Demos: The Discovery of Classical Attika*, Cambridge.

    (1988) "Social and Economic Implications of Leasing Land and Property in Classical and Hellenistic Greece" *Chiron* 18: 279–323.

    (1997) "Law, the Democratic Citizen, and the Representation of Women in Classical Athens" *Past and Present* 155: 3–33.

    (2000) "Religion, Imperial Politics, and the Offering of Freedom to Slaves" in Virginia Hunter and Jonathan Edmondson, eds., *Law and Social Status in Classical Athens*, 75–92, Oxford.

Osiel, M. (1997) *Mass Atrocity, Collective Memory, and the Law*, New Brunswick, NJ.

Ostwald, M. (1986) *From Popular Sovereignty to the Sovereignty of Law: Law, Society, and Politics in Fifth-Century Athens*, Berkeley, Calif.

Parker, R.C.T. (1996) *Athenian Religion: A History*, Oxford.

Patterson, C. (2000) "The Hospitality of Athenian Justice: The Metic in Court" in V. Hunter and J. Edmondson, eds., *Law and Social Status in Classical Athens*, 93–112, Oxford.

Pellizer, E. (1990) "Outlines of a Morphology of Sympotic Entertainment" in O. Murray, ed., *Sympotica: A Symposium on the Symposium*, 177–184, Oxford.

Phillips, D.D. (2006) "Why Was Lycophron Prosecuted by *Eisangelia*?" *Greek, Roman, and Byzantine Studies* 46: 375–394.

    (2008) *Avengers of Blood: Homicide in Athenian Law and Custom from Draco to Demosthenes*, Stuttgart.

    (2009) "Hypereides 3 and the Athenian Law of Contracts" *Transactions of the American Philological Association* 139.1: 89–122.

    (2013) *The Law of Ancient Athens*, Ann Arbor, Mich.

Piddocke, S. (1968) "Social Sanctions" *Anthropologica* 10.2: 261–285.

Bibliography

Polinsky, A.M. and S. Shavell (2009) "Public Enforcement of Law" in N. Garoupa, ed., *Criminal Law and Economics*, 1–59, Northampton, Mass.

Posner, Eric A. (1996) "Law, Economics, and Inefficient Norms" *University of Pennsylvania Law Review* 144: 1697–1744.

(2002) *Law and Social Norms*, Cambridge, Mass.

(2007) *Social Norms, Non-Legal Sanctions, and the Law*, Northampton, Mass.

Posner, E. and Vermeule, A. (2004) "Transitional Justice as Ordinary Justice" *Harvard Law Review* 117: 761–825.

Quillin, J.M. (2002) "Achieving Amnesty: The Role of Events, Institutions, and Ideas" *Transactions of the American Philological Association* 132: 71–107.

Quinn, A., ed. (2009) *Reconciliation(s): Transitional Justice in Postconflict Societies*, Montreal.

Raaflaub, K. (2001) "Father of All, Destroyer of All: War in the Late Fifth-Century Athenian Discourse and Ideology" in D. McCann and B.S. Strauss, *War and Democracy: A Comparative Study of the Korean War and the Peloponnesian War*, 307–356, London.

Reiss, A.J. and J.A. Roth, eds. (1993) *Understanding and Preventing Violence: Report of the National Research Panel on the Understanding and Control of Violence*, Washington, DC.

Rhodes, P.J. (1972) *The Athenian Boule*, Oxford.

(1979) "*Eisangelia* at Athens" *Journal of Hellenic Studies* 99: 103–114.

(1993) *A Commentary on the Aristotelian* Athenaion Politeia, Oxford [Reprint from 1981].

(1998) "Enmity in Fourth-Century Athens" in P. Cartledge, P. Millett, and S. von Reden, *Kosmos: Essays in Order, Conflict and Community in Classical Athens*, 144–161, Cambridge.

(2004) "Keeping to the Point" in E.M. Harris and L. Rubinstein, eds., *The Law and the Courts in Ancient Greece*, 137–158, London.

Rhodes, P.J. and R. Osborne (2007) *Greek Historical Inscriptions, 403–323 B.C.*, Oxford.

Riess, W. (2008) "Private Violence and State Control – The Prosecution of Homicide and Its Symbolic Meanings in Fourth-Century BC Athens" in C. Brélaz and P. Ducrey, eds., *Sécurité collective et ordre public dans les sociétés anciennes*, 49–101, Geneva.

(2012) *Performing Interpersonal Violence: Court, Curse, and Comedy in Fourth-Century BCE Athens*, Berlin.

Roberts, S. (1976) "Law and the Study of Social Control in Small Scale Societies" *Modern Law Review* 39: 663–679.

Robinson, P.H. and J.M. Darley, "The Utility of Desert" *Northwestern University Law Review* 91: 453–499.

Roebuck, D. (2001) *Ancient Greek Arbitration*, Oxford.

Roisman, J. (2005) *The Rhetoric of Manhood: Masculinity in the Attic Orators*, Berkeley, Calif.

(2006) *The Rhetoric of Conspiracy in Ancient Athens*, Berkeley, Calif.

Rosenberg, T. (1996) *The Haunted Land: Facing Europe's Ghosts after Communism*, New York.

Roth, M.T. (2000) "The Law Collection of King Hammurabi: Toward an Understanding of Codification and Text" in E. Lévy, ed., *La codification des lois dans l'antiquité*, 9–31, Strasburg.

Roy, J. (1991) "Traditional Jokes about the Punishment of Adulterers in Ancient Greek Literature" *Liverpool Classical Monthly* 16: 73–76.

Rubinstein, L. (2000) *Litigation and Cooperation: Supporting Speakers in the Courts of Classical Athens*, Stuttgart.

Bibliography

(2003) "Volunteer Prosecutors in the Greek World" *Dike* 6: 87–114.

(2007) "Arguments from Precedent in the Attic Orators" in E. Carawan, ed., *The Attic Orators*, 359–371, Oxford.

(2012) "Individual and Collective Liabilities of Boards of Officials in the Late Classical and Early Hellenistic Period" in B. Legras and G. Thür, eds., *Symposion 2011: Vorträge zur griechischen und hellenistischen Rechtsgeschichte*, 329–354, Vienna.

(Forthcoming) "Summary Fines in Greek Inscriptions and the Question of 'Greek Law'" in P. Perlman, ed., *Greek Law in the Twenty-First Century*, Austin, Tex.

Ruiz, F. (1994) *Use and Control of Violence in Classical Athens* (PhD diss., Johns Hopkins University).

Scafuro, A.C. (1994) "Witnessing and False Witnessing: Proving Citizenship and Kin Identity in Fourth-Century Athens" in A.L. Boegehold and A.C. Scafuro, eds., *Athenian Identity and Civic Ideology*, 156–198, Baltimore, MD.

(1997) *The Forensic Stage: Settling Disputes in Graeco-Roman New Comedy*, Cambridge.

(2006) "Magistrates with Hegemony in the Courts of Classical Athens" in H-A. Rupprecht, ed., *Symposion 2003: Vorträge zur griechischen und hellenistischen Rechtsgeschichte*, 27–51, Vienna.

(2011) *The Oratory of Classical Greece Vol.13: Demosthenes, Speeches 39–49*, Austin, Tex.

(2014) "Patterns of Penalty in Fifth Century Attic Decrees" in A.P. Matthaiou and R.K. Pitt, eds., *Athenaion episkopos: Studies in Honour of Harold B. Mattingly*, 299–326, Athens.

Schaps, D. (1998) "What Was Free about a Free Athenian Woman?" *Transactions of the American Philological Association* 128: 161–188.

Schmitz, W. (2004) *Nachbarschaft und Dorfgemeinschaft im archaischen und klassichen Griechenland*, Berlin.

Schwartz, W.F., K. Baxter, and D. Ryan (1984) "The Duel: Can These Gentlemen Be Acting Efficiently?" *Journal of Legal Studies* 13: 321–353.

Schwartzberg, M. (2004) "Athenian Democracy and Legal Change" *American Political Science Review* 98.2: 311–325.

(2010) "Shouts, Murmurs, and Votes: Acclamation and Aggregation in Ancient Greece" *Journal of Political Philosophy* 18.4: 448–468.

Sealey, R. (1987) *The Athenian Republic: Democracy or Rule of Law?*, University Park, Pa.

Shapiro, H.A. (1981) "Courtship Scenes in Attic Vase-Painting" *American Journal of Archaeology* 85: 133–143.

Sinclair, R.K. (1988) *Democracy and Participation in Athens*, Cambridge.

Sissa, G. (2002) "Sexual Bodybuilding: Aeschines, *Against Timarchus*" in J.I. Porter, ed., *Constructions of the Classical Body*, 147–168, Ann Arbor, Mich.

Sotiropoulos, D.A. (2007) "Swift Gradualism and Variable Outcomes: Vetting in Post-Authoritarian Greece" in A. Mayer-Rieckh and P. de Greiff, eds., *Justice as Prevention: Vetting Public Employees in Transitional Societies*, 120–145, New York.

Stanley, P.V. (1979) "*Agoranomoi* and *Metronomoi*: Athenian Market Officials and Regulations" *Ancient World* 2.1: 13–19.

Steinbock, B. (2011) "A Lesson in Patriotism: Lycurgus' *Against Leocrates*, the Ideology of the Ephebeia, and Athenian Social Memory" *Classical Antiquity* 30.2: 27–317.

Stern, S.J. (1993) *Peru's Indian Peoples and the Challenge of Spanish Conquest: Huamanga to 1640*, Madison, Wis.

Bibliography

Stilt, K. (2011) *Islamic Law in Action: Authority, Discretion, and Experiences in Mamluk Egypt*, Oxford.

Stover, E. (2004) "Witnesses and the Promise of Justice in the Hague" in E. Stover and H. Weinstein, eds., *My Neighbor, My Enemy: Justice and Community in the Aftermath of Mass Atrocity*, 104–120, Cambridge.

Stover, E. and H. Weinstein, eds. (2004) *My Neighbor, My Enemy: Justice and Community in the Aftermath of Mass Atrocity*, Cambridge.

Strauss, B.S. (1986) *Athens after the Peloponnesian War*, New York.

Stroud, R.S. (1974) "An Athenian Law on Silver Coinage" *Hesperia* 43: 157–188.

Sunstein, C.R. (1996a) "On the Expressive Function of Law" *University of Pennsylvania Law Review* 144: 2021–2053.

(1996b) "Social Norms and Social Roles" *Columbia Law Review* 96: 903–968.

Taylor, W.B. (1979) *Drinking, Homicide, and Rebellion in Colonial Mexican Villages*, Stanford, Calif.

Teegarden, D.A. (2014) *Death to Tyrants! Ancient Greek Democracy and the Struggle Against Tyranny*, Princeton, NJ.

Teitel, R.G. (2000) *Transitional Justice*, Oxford.

Thomas, R. (1996) "Written in Stone? Liberty, Equality, Orality and the Codification of Law" in L. Foxhall and A.D.E. Lewis, eds., *Greek Law in Its Political Setting: Justifications, Not Justice*, 9–31, Oxford.

Thür, G. (1977) *Beweisführung vor den Schwurgerichtshöfen Athens. die Proklesis zur Basanos*, Vienna.

(1996) "Reply to D.C. Mirhady: Torture and Rhetoric in Athens" *Journal of Hellenic Studies* 116: 132–134.

(2008) "The Principle of Fairness in Athenian Legal Procedure" *Dike* 11: 51–73.

Todd, S.C. (1993) *The Shape of Athenian Law*, Oxford.

(1998a) "Lysias against Nikhomakhos: The Fate of the Expert in Fourth-Century Athens" in L. Foxhall and A.D.E. Lewis, eds., *Greek Law in Its Political Setting: Justifications, Not Justice*, 31–51, Oxford.

(1998b) "The Rhetoric of Enmity in the Attic Orators" in P. Cartledge, P. Millett, and S. von Reden, eds., *Kosmos: Essays in Order, Conflict, and Community in Classical Athens*, 144–161, Cambridge.

(2000a) "How to Execute People in Fourth-Century Athens" in V.J. Hunter and J. Edmondson, eds., *Law and Social Status in Classical Athens*, 31–52, Oxford.

(2000b) *The Oratory of Classical Greece Vol. 2: Lysias*, Austin, Tex.

(2007) *A Commentary on Lysias, Speeches 1–11*, Oxford.

(2010) "The Athenian Procedure(s) of *Dokimasia*" in G. Thür, ed., *Symposion 2009: Vorträge zur griechischen und hellenistischen Rechtsgeschichte*, 73–97, Vienna.

Tushnet, M. (1998) "'Everything Old Is New Again': Early Reflections on the 'New Chicago School'" *Wisconsin Law Review* 1998: 579–590.

Tyler, T.R. (1990) *Why People Obey the Law*, Princeton, NJ.

Usher, S. (1999) *Greek Oratory: Tradition and Originality*, Oxford.

van Effenterre H. (1990) "Le contrôle des étrangers dans la cité grecque" in G. Nenci and G. Thür, eds., *Symposion 1988: Vorträge zur griechischen und hellenistischen Rechtsgeschichte*, 251–259, Cologne.

Vélissaropoulos-Karakos, J. (2002) "Merchants, Prostitutes, and the 'New Poor': Forms of Contract and Social Status" in P. Cartledge, E.E. Cohen, and L. Foxhall, eds., *Money, Labour, and Land: Approaches to the Economies of Ancient Greece*, 130–139, New York.

Bibliography

Vlassopoulos, Kostas (2007) "Free Spaces: Identity, Experience, and Democracy in Classical Athens" *Classical Quarterly* 57.1: 33–52.

Wallace, R.W. (1989) *The Areopagos Council to 307 B.C.*, Baltimore, MD.

(1993) "Personal Conduct and Legal Sanction in the Democracy of Classical Athens" in J. Zlinsky, ed., *Questions de responsabilité*, 397–413, Miskolc-Eger.

(1997) "On Not Legislating Sexual Conduct in Fourth-Century Athens" in G. Thür and J. Vélissaropoulous-Karakostas, eds., *Symposion 1995: Vorträge zur griechischen und hellenistischen Rechtsgeschichte*, 151–166, Cologne.

(1998) "Unconvicted or Potential *atimoi* in Ancient Athens" *Dike* 1: 63–78.

(2005) "'Listening to' the Archai in Democratic Athens" in R.W. Wallace and M. Gagarin, eds., *Symposion 2001: Vorträge zur griechischen und hellenistischen Rechtsgeschichte*, 147–158, Vienna.

(2006) "Withdrawing Graphai in Ancient Athens" in H.-A. Rupprecht, ed., *Symposion 2003: Vorträge zur griechischen und hellenistischen Rechtsgeschichte*, 57–66, Vienna.

(2007) "The Legal Regulation of Conduct at Athens: Two Controversies on Freedom" *Dike* 9: 107–128.

(2012) "When the Athenians Did Not Enforce Their Laws" in B. Legras and G. Thür, eds., *Symposion 2011: Vorträge zur griechischen und hellenistischen Rechtsgeschichte*, 115–125, Vienna.

Weisberg, R. (2003) "Norms and Criminal Law, and the Norms of Criminal Law Scholarship" *Journal of Criminal Law and Criminology* 93: 467–592.

West, M.D. (1997) "Legal Rules and Social Norms in Japan's Secret World of Sumo" *Journal of Legal Studies* 26: 165–201.

Westbrook, R. (1989) "Cuneiform Law Codes and the Origins of Legislation" *Zeitschrift für Assyriologie und vordasiatische Archäologie* 79: 201–222.

Whitehead, D. (1977) *The Ideology of the Athenian Metic*, Cambridge.

(1983) "Competitive Outlay and Community Profit: *Philotimia* in Democratic Athens" *Classica et Medievalia* 34: 55–74.

(1982–83) "Sparta and the Thirty Tyrants" *Ancient Society* 13/14: 106–130.

(1984) "Immigrant Communities in the Classical Polis: Some Principles for a Synoptic Treatment" *L'Antiquité classique* 53: 47–59.

(1986) *The Demes of Attica 508/7-ca. 250 B.C.: A Political and Social Study*, Princeton, NJ.

(1993) "Cardinal Virtues: The Language of Public Appropriation in Democratic Athens" *Classica et Mediaevalia* 44: 37–75.

(2000) *Hypereides. The Forensic Speeches*, Oxford.

(2006) "Absentee Athenians: Lysias against Philon and Lycurgus against Leocrates" *Museum Helveticum* 63: 132–151.

Wilke, C. (2007) "The Shield, the Sword and the Party: Vetting the East German Public Sector" in A. Mayer-Rieckh and P. de Greiff, eds., *Justice as Prevention: Vetting Public Employees in Transitional Societies*, 348–401, New York.

Willrich, M. (2003) *City of Courts: Socializing Justice in Progressive Era Chicago*, Cambridge.

Winkler, J.J. (1990) *The Constraints of Desire*, New York.

Wohl, V. (2010) *Law's Cosmos: Juridical Discourse in Athenian Forensic Oratory*, Cambridge.

Wolpert, A. (2002) *Remembering Defeat: Civil War and Civic Memory in Ancient Athens*, Baltimore, MD.

Bibliography

Worthington, I. (1994) *"The Canon of the Ten Attic Orators"* in I. Worthington, ed., *Persuasion: Greek Rhetoric in Action*, 244–263, London.

Worthington, I., C.R. Cooper, and E.M. Harris (2001) *The Oratory of Classical Greece Vol. 5: Dinarchus, Hyperides, and Lycurgus*, Austin, Tex.

Yakobson, A. (2011) "Political Stability and Public Order – Athens vs. Rome" in G. Herman, ed., *Stability and Crisis in the Athenian Democracy*, 139–156, Stuttgart.

Youni, M.S. (2001) "The Different Categories of Unpunished Killing and the Term *atimos* in Ancient Greek Law" in G. Thür and E. Cantarella, eds., *Symposion 1997: Vorträge zur griechischen und hellenistischen Rechtsgeschichte*, 117–137, Cologne.

Yunis, H. (1996) *Taming Democracy: Models of Political Rhetoric in Classical Athens*, Ithaca, NY. (2001) *Demosthenes: On the Crown*, Cambridge. (2005) *The Oratory of Classical Greece, Vol. 9: Demosthenes Speeches 18 and 19*, Austin, Tex.

Zasu, Y. (2007) "Sanctions by Social Norms and the Law: Substitutes or Complements?" *Journal of Legal Studies* 36.2: 379–396.

Zuckerman, M. (1970) *Peaceable Kingdoms: New England Towns in the Eighteenth Century*, New York.

Index